AWSNA PUBLICATIONS

TABLE OF CONTENTS

DEVELOPMENTAL INSIGHTS
Discussions Between Doctors and Teachers

ii

/ELOPMENTAL
INSIGHTS

DISCUSSIONS BETWEEN
DOCTORS AND TEACHERS

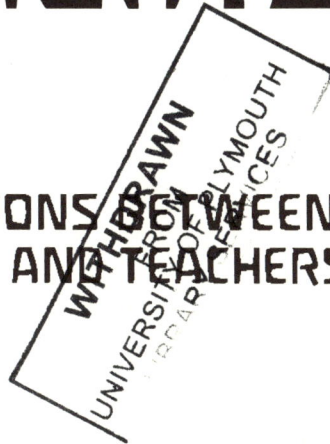

Edited By

David S. Mitchell

Published by:
The Association of Waldorf Schools of North America
3911 Bannister Road
Fair Oaks, CA 95628

DEVELOPMENTAL INSIGHTS
Discussions Between Doctors And Teachers

ISBN # 1-888365-03-X

Editor and designer: David Mitchell

Proofreader: Nancy Jane

Cover Photograph by Robert Schiappacasse (Shining Mountain Waldorf School) of David Mitchell (Life Science teacher), Dr. Phillip Incao, and Vicki Kirsch (remedial teacher).

Curriculum Series

The Publications Committee of AWSNA is pleased to bring forward this publication as part of its *Curriculum Series*. The thoughts and ideas represented herein are solely those of the authors and do not necessarily represent any implied criteria set by A.W.S.N.A. It is our intention to stimulate as much writing and thinking as possible about our curriculum, including diverse views. Please contact us with feedback on this publication as well as requests for future work.

David S. Mitchell
For The Publications Committee
A.W.S.N.A.

DEVELOPMENTAL INSIGHTS
Discussions Between Doctors and Teachers

INTRODUCTION

by

David S. Mitchell

The articles included in this book were lectures given at the first International Kolisko Conference, a meeting between Waldorf teachers and anthroposophic physicians, held in Stuttgart, Germany, in the spring of 1989. The Conference was named in honor of Dr. Eugen Kolisko, MD.

Eugen Kolisko was the doctor of the first Waldorf School and was one of Rudolf Steiner's most distinguished pupils. He was educated at Vienna University as a doctor of medicine. He was an authority on the natural sciences and history. As a lecturer in medicine, zoology, chemistry, and history, he was in demand, both in Europe and America. He died in London in 1939, at the age of 46.

The editor is grateful to the following individuals who have read parts of the manuscript: Joan Almon, Susan Howard, Dr. Gary Hubiak, DDS, and Dr. Philip Incao, MD. Their suggestions have been appreciated.

AWSNA Publications would like to express its thanks to Dr. Michaela Glöckler and the Verlag am Goetheanum for allowing us to translate and publish this edition.

Eugen Kolisko

CHAPTER 1

EUGEN KOLISKO AND THE ROLE OF THE SCHOOL PHYSICIAN[1]

by

Gisbert Husemann

The heart is the key to the world and to life.

– Novalis

On January 16, 1921, when the Waldorf School in Stuttgart had been in existence for almost two-and-a-half years, Rudolf Steiner had the following to say at a teachers' meeting about the role of the school doctor: "As I see it, there ought to be a school doctor who knows and keeps an eye on every single pupil. It is not his job to teach any particular subject, but he ought to have opportunities to work with the children in each class in whatever way can be managed. He ought to be aware of the health of all the children."

For a doctor to be aware of the health of five to nine hundred children and to follow their progress for many years is the exact equivalent of the task faced by a teacher who gets to know the pupils of a number of classes and follows their progress. The doctor's job is a full-time one, but if he is prepared to do any teaching, the most obvious subject is the study of the human being in the widest sense. More important, though, would be for him or her to give courses on this subject for the teachers who are members of the college of teachers. By working on the mysteries of the human being, teachers gain educational insights and ideas with regard to children in general, the pupils in the school, and above all the children in their own class if they are class teachers. [2]

To illustrate this, an example is given below which clearly shows how important it is for teachers to develop an idea of the function of the human heart that is based on Anthroposophy. The image given to students in the upper classes may be said to be equally important. In our technological age both the scientific and the popular image of the heart is that it is a pump. The logical conclusion must be that organs can be repaired or exchanged like spare parts. This attitude is the beginning of people going seriously astray and becoming ever more detached from themselves and also from their fellow human beings.

THE HEART

In the first address Rudolf Steiner gave at the founding of the Stuttgart Waldorf School on September 9, 1919, he said that the education to be practiced at this school would not be based on a view of the human being in which the heart was regarded as a pump.[3] The first and most profound task of the school doctor, who is a product of modern scientific training, is therefore to gain a different view of cardiac physiology. Eugen Kolisko's book on the search for new truths contains two essays (in German) entitled "Saint Thomas Aquinas on the movements of the heart" and "It is not the heart which drives the blood, but the blood which drives the heart", in which the author discusses the movement of the blood and cardiac function. These two essays provided a starting point for the approach to cardiac function presented below.

Kolisko was essentially concerned with the functional and emotional aspects of the circulation. Going one step lower initially and considering the physical aspect, we find that in the world of physics the hydraulic ram is analogous to the human blood circulation (see Appendix). A natural brook or stream flows into a pipe; the resulting pressure closes the outlet valve and flow ceases. The pressure of water piling up causes a reversal now. The water then rises in a pipe with narrower bore (it is pushed up - hence the term "ram"), the valve opens under its own weight, closes again, reversing flow, and a hydrodynamic period has been set in motion. The heart is positioned in the living blood stream, with flow stopped and reversed in the apex. Myocardial organs capable of sensing pressure serve to perceive flow and pressure conditions.

The waters and rivers of the earth are part of a system which also includes the atmosphere. If a hydraulic ram is positioned in a natural system of flowing water, conditions are created where flow is stopped and falling water is made to rise. The flow, fall and rise of the earth's waters is recapitulated in condensed form in the apparatus. It should be evident from the above that it is meaningless to say that the apparatus makes the water move.

An even simpler analogy is provided by an elastic ball, the form of which is quickly restored when an indentation has been made. We do not have a valve to interrupt flow in this case, but the ball permits comparison with a mirror reflecting a ray of light. The eye is such a mirror. An image of the environment is produced at the site where the light is reflected in the retina. The sites where interruption occurs are actually in the retinal nerves. In the ram, the site corresponding to the "image" created in the eye would be the point where the valve interrupts flow and reverses it.

These analogies taken from the field of physics immediately make us see the heart in a new way: as a sense organ for the blood stream. This does, of course, only relate to the superficial, physical aspect of its function, but it brings to mind the sensitive valvular functions of the heart and especially also the reversal of flow at the apex, both of which may be seen as organic ram functions.

In the human blood circulation, which we can experience in heart beat and peripheral pulse, the rate of flow is approximately 5 liters a minute. A much larger volume exists in the tissues, in organs and muscles, and in the nervous system. Between this tissue fluid, which also includes the lymphatic system and the pulsating vascular system, lies the capillary system. Blood passes from one leg of the capillary system into the tissue fluid and is absorbed back into the capillary system by the other leg. This is where the living (intermediary) exchange processes of metabolism, internal respiration, and anabolism take place in the human organism. Recent researches have shown that the volume passing between tissue fluid and capillaries is 100 liters a minute.[5] This makes it practically impossible to go on thinking of a pump, since a pump with 5-liter capacity cannot possibly move 100 liters in the periphery. Scientists who established earlier theories of the circulation identified the same problem, though in a different way. Their solution was to include additional, smaller "extracardial pumps" in organs and vessels between the periphery and the heart. Kolisko drew attention to the issue.

If one thinks in terms of living, moving peripheral waves of fluid, the heart, being part of the blood stream, becomes the mirroring apparatus, rather like a hydraulic ram. M. Mendelsohn, a Berlin cardiologist, was fully in accord with this when he wrote in 1928: ". . . the heart must inevitably be a secondary organ inserted into the circulation of fluids in a living organism; it cannot be the primary, dominant organ."[6] Rudolf Steiner was thinking along the same lines when he said in 1921: "This human heart evolves entirely from the... interaction between nutrition and tissue fluid [with protein synthesis], and its function can be none other but to reflect the inner activity of the tissue fluid."[7] Thus, the 100 liters a minute are like living, flowing waves, with the heart placed among them. The heart beat then reflects the waves, so that the periphery is mirrored at the center. When physicians feel a patient's pulse (or listen to the heart), they are using touch to perceive a thermometer which indicates the internal conditions of life. Kolisko made reference to pathology at this point: "The heart can only be understood in terms of the periphery, and we shall never understand the circulation if we start from the center, the heart. We know that hearts get enlarged when an organ such as the musculature demands too much blood during intense physical effort. The normal, and not only the enlarged heart, is created from the periphery in the same way."[8]

A common objection is that we are simply replacing the pump with another apparatus. But this merely shows that the issue has not been thought through. Comparison with a physical apparatus is not condemned on principle, but methodologically, it is of the utmost importance to find the right comparisons and understand them.[9] Many other elements based on principles in the science of physics are to be found in the organism, like the eye, for example, and the buoyancy of the brain floating in fluid.

Moreover, inorganic substances are metamorphosed into organs, with all the major metals represented by organs, having become organic metal nature. The hydraulic ram presents the basic phenomena which in the human organism embody periodicity, or the cosmic rhythm.

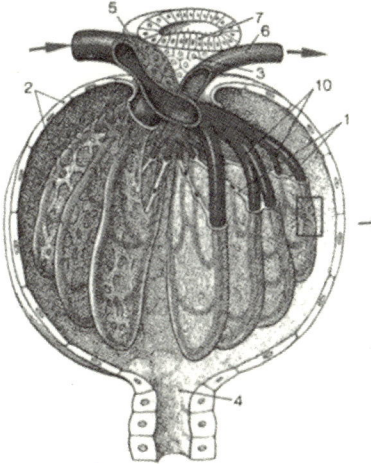

Figure 1
Kidney corpuscles at 7: the sense
of branching organ – macula densa
interlobularis.
(after H. Leonhardt 1986)

Figure 2
Overview of the manner of Vera
(after Otrfried Müller, 1932)

With regard to the function of the heart as well as other organs, it is of considerable interest that in 1911 the anatomist Jacoby Sr. compared the lumina of the afferent and efferent vessels in the renal glomerulus with those "of a hydraulic ram", where the bore of the feed pipe is larger than that of the outlet pipe. Quoting Jacoby, Otfried Mueller showed that the same applied to the hepatic veins. He provided an illustration of an intralobular vein and the sinusoids arising from it which are like capillary vessels. "One immediately thinks of a fruit tree."[10] See Figure 1. The rhythm of fluid dammed up in organs and then released would thus be the common element, like tree trunk and branches, which has become a hydraulic ram in the physical world outside the human organism and is particularly well developed in the periodicity of the heart.

Observations like those of Jacoby Sr. and O. Mueller help us to see the functions of organs such as the kidney and liver in a new way: as modified cardiac functions. A system of vessels comparable to the pipes of a ram thus exists in numerous variations in the vascular system, and the concept of extracardial circulation appears in a new light. The wave of peripheral tissue fluid, the lumen of which may be said to be infinitely large, is brought to a halt and reversed in organ functions and in the heart beat, where the lumina of the vessels are much smaller.

The arrangement of the myocardial fibers is like a "frozen image" of falling, stopped, and rising flow. Descending spirals (muscle fibers), moving in opposite directions, surround the two ventricles, with the point of reversal slightly above the apex. The ascending fibers in the myocardium of the left ventricle terminate in the papillary muscles which project into the lumen. The arrangement of the muscle fibers is a physical and etheric image of the circulation from periphery to cardiac apex, reversal of flow, and the blood rising above the papillary muscles into aorta and lung. It also is an image of the hydrodynamics of the ram (Fig. 2).[11]

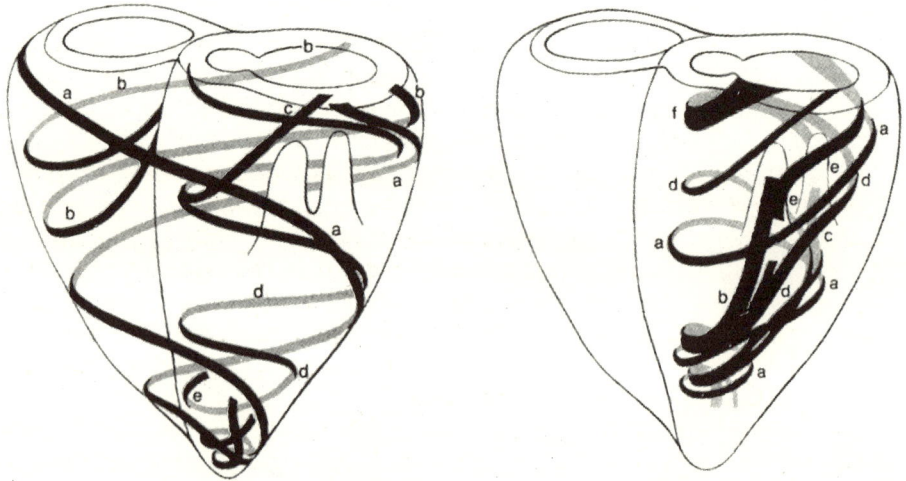

Fig. 2 Ascending and descending spirals in myocardium

Left: Schematic representation of arrangement of fibers in outer and middle muscle layers of left ventricle. a) external fibers running obliquely, b) deeper layer of oblique external fibers, c) ventral cross-over of subbasal loop fibers in middle layer, d) descending fibers in middle layer, which rise again at e) above the apex (H. Leonhardt, 1988).

Right: Schematic representation of arrangement of fibers in inner layer of ventricular myocardium. a) external spiral fibers of inner layer, branching to ventral papillary muscle, b) deep fibers of inner layer radiating to c) dorsal papillary muscle, d) steeply ascending interpapillary spirals of deep inner layer, e) fibers descending from left fibrous ring, with fibrous roots going to papillary muscles at the turn (from Puff, 1960); (H. Leonhardt, 1988).

We can now consider the issue in relation to the genesis of the eye. The eye evolved out of the light to perceive the light. In the same way the heart evolved out of the circulation for the circulation. In this sense, the heart of the teacher is the central organ for perceiving the periphery, i.e. the children.

This is the point where a first conclusion may be drawn, both educationally and medically, as to the relationship between teacher and pupils. Teachers quite rightly have a sense of being a spiritual and psychological center towards which the waves of expectation and hope, of sympathy and awareness of self, of hunger for learning and the satisfaction of that hunger, of a troubled mind and delight may flow. In the encounter with the teacher, the pupils grow increasingly aware of themselves. Each child in the periphery becomes an individual as it meets the heartbeat of the center. Altogether a living organism has come into being, and the question to be asked concerns the extent to which teachers can become properly conscious of their position and of being part of the karmic stream. The image of the pump blinds us to all the potential which the situation holds.

The rhythmic system as a whole is the bearer of the soul element, for, as Kolisko said, "in addition to the purely physiological aspect described by science today, organs also have a psychological aspect." Once the organs have developed, mental and psychological powers are released which form the soul element of the human being. While the organs are growing, the soul is tied up in the process of growth and is in a kind of pre-psychological state.

The psyche is released from the organs in the same way as memory becomes free. "The circulation is the link, the rhythmic balancing principle between organs of the metabolic and nervous systems and, therefore, also between the polar aspects of the inner life - thinking and will activity. The movements of the blood in fear, joy, and all other stirrings of the ego in the human soul show that the ego experiences itself in the circulation of the blood."[12]

So far we have described a physical, a vital, and a psychological level. Blushing in shame and turning pale with fright reveal the effect of the ego and emotions on the circulation. This level also has its anatomical equivalent. In Figure 3, the upper loop is a schematic representation of the pulmonary circulation going from the heart to the lung and back to the heart. The lower loop represents the systemic circulation from the heart to the body and back to the right heart. Two distinct states of life combine to form a lemniscate with its cross-over point in the heart. When the heart first begins to develop in the embryo, the two "halves" show lateral symmetry. They later combine in an asymmetric organ positioned more to the left. The left heart is filled with living, oxygenated arterial blood coming from the lung. The blood stream in the right heart holds the "inoculation of death" (Novalis), for it is charged with carbon dioxide coming from all the organs.

The cross-over phenomenon is quite common. When the eyes focus on an object, the visual axes cross at the focal point. The visual nerves cross backwards and inwards in the optic chiasma. Almost all cerebral and cerebellar tracts from the central nervous system to the extremities also cross. In this case the optic principle has become inward and therefore less conscious. When we fold our hands or put one arm across the other, gaining experience of self in the process, this is essentially how crossovers achieve different levels of feeling the ego, responding to the ego, and ego awareness. The seeing ego lives in the maya of sensory images, but where the blood stream crosses in the heart, this is accompanied, rhythmically, by a feeling ego experience as part of physical existence. Heart and respiration make things merely learned in the head into stirrings of the soul. This comes fully to expression in the action of shaking hands, where we add something that is our own. Our words or the way we look at someone or something may come from the head or from the heart. The human heart can shine out through the eyes.

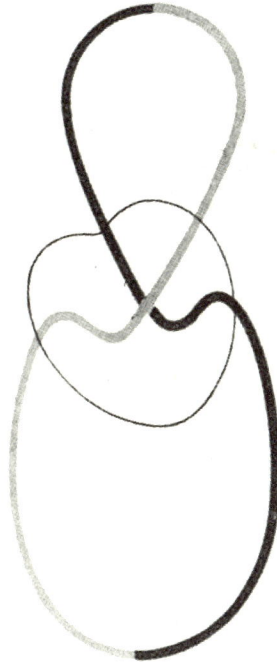

*Fig. 3. Blood circulates, with outline of heart. Dark line arterial blood; gray line: venous blood (from H. Leonhardt, **Taschenatlas der Anatomie**, 1986).*

In the alveoli, which are the smallest anatomical units of the lung, the organism discharges its carbon dioxide, for otherwise it would be poisoned by the inner life. Our organism needs the cosmic environment and its atmospheric oxygen. Being oneself changes to an experience of the environment; carbon dioxide is exchanged for oxygen. The chemical changes in the blood thus have parallels at the higher levels of soul and spirit.

Goethe had a feeling for the moral rhythm of the self coming into existence and passing out of it again in inhalation and exhalation. The soul moves in rhythm with the archetypal principles of death and life.

FOUR DEVELOPMENTAL STAGES OF CARDIAC FUNCTION

Taking an overall view, we can discern four stages of development:

Earth - hydraulic ram

• **physical body;** arrangement of myocardial fibers

Water - atmosphere: clouds, rain and rivers on earth

• **ether body;** peripheral waves of proteinaceous tissue fluid

Surrounding **Air**

• **astral body**; respiration, emotional ups and downs, blush of shame, pallor of fear

Warmth

• **ego organization;** blood temperature, blood stream crossing in the heart

Every stage reveals something of the character and essential nature of the heart. At the physical level we noted periodic congestion causing a simple vessel to be enlarged into the myocardium. At the next stage we became aware of the waves of tissue fluid and their reflection in the heart beat. At the psychic and astral level these elements are raised to a new plane and related to conscious and semi-conscious inner activities and the ego. Emotions such as wonder and delight are based on the rhythmic system just as much as are the facts that we are born to suffer and to overcome in the process of our life destiny.

The insights gained in this field can become a key element in our approach to the natural elements of earth, water, air (which unites with the human psyche in respiration) and heat (in the blood temperature an expression of the ego organization). Out of warmth, the heart and the blood have been created to give expression to the ego organization. The positive and negative pressures created by warmth allow the ego's activity in this element to shine through in the pulsating movement of the blood.[13] Thus, looking at the world of nature in the mirror of our image of the human being, we can see why the heart may be called the key to the world, seeing that it holds the whole world in itself.

WARMTH OF HEART IN EDUCATION AND FOR TEACHING METHODS

On September 7, 1919, Rudolf Steiner spoke of seeing the heart in a living way in the new approach to education. Four weeks after the opening of the Stuttgart Waldorf School, on October 4, 1919, he discussed the warmth needed in teaching and the consequences this would have for the children in later life. It goes without saying that the usual subjects have to be taught and learned, but over and above this there are other aspects that vibrate in the relationship between the souls of pupils and teacher. "The warm enthusiasm of the teacher is transmitted to the child and the child absorbs what is taught because the teacher gets it across by means of enthusiastic teaching."[14] From the anthroposophic point of view, this means that teaching from the head is not sufficient; in a way, the teacher's heartbeat must be echoed by the heartbeat of the child. The social implications of this are profound. Knowledge transmitted via the head disappears from memory as life goes on ". . . what matters for subsequent development is what is absorbed purely out of the warmth of the teacher. It is this which comes alive again in the mind and gives strength for life."[15]

Just as doctors know what medicines to prescribe for their patients, so do teachers know what educational measures to use for the whole class or for an individual pupil. There are many ways of thus giving a therapeutic aspect to teaching. Vitality, which normally decreases as the middle of life approaches, receives a boost for later life with this kind of teaching. It is no exaggeration to speak of education as preventive treatment.

If we know how to read in a way that bears fruit, we discover that the statements made by Steiner on September 7 and October 4, 1919, belong together. They complement each other and enable us to look more closely at the heart as an organ for medical and educational work.

Warmth is created in the heart. Teachers can sense this if they leave everyday life behind on entering the classroom, as a snake sheds its skin. They can achieve this if they manage to reject the idea of the heart as a hydrodynamic apparatus and rediscover its true nature. To let the heart come truly into its own in education could provide a key to solving the growing problems of today's younger generation.

The different approaches to understanding the heart may be summarized by saying that for teachers, the heart must be seen as a symbol that can give support in the "renewal of the art of education and teaching."[16] This is not a question of maxims and dogmas. Someone who is aware of being part of the destiny of a group of children brings a true teacher to birth within him or herself – a teacher whose heart comes alive. You become a teacher when you understand "that the heart is not a pump to move the blood around the body. Human beings are inwardly alive in such a way that the movements of the body fluids and of the heart are the outcome of being thus alive."[17] If the inner eye is aware of this, the teacher develops an eye for the development of the child. "With our eyes thus opened, significant insights may be gained with regard to one particular child in a large class which one has only known for a few months. Training mind and spirit in this way, which makes contact powerful, it is possible to have an almost clairvoyant view of the child's individual nature." It is not merely a matter of intellectual understanding, for those who learn to train mind and spirit out of a heart with living inner vision, "will come alive in a new way to the development of one child or even a whole group of children. This will also enable us to evolve the curriculum out of the very nature of the developing child."[18] It is now also possible to see what Steiner meant in that address on September 7,1919: The curriculum for the new education was developed not from the head but from the heart; it arose from a heart that spans the world, the hearts of teachers and children.

Rudolf Steiner wanted to know if the children's hearts went out to their teachers. This is why he would always ask the children about their feelings towards their teachers at the monthly school festivals. Their replies created a living threefold chord combining his own heart with the hearts of the teachers and those of all the children present in the great hall of the Waldorf School on these occasions. Gaining insight and understanding of Anthroposophy feeds the living capabilities of teachers. The heart occupies a central, indeed the central position in the training of teachers. In the following quotation from Novalis, the ideal of education and medicine is seen as the same as the ideal of the human being:

"The heart is the key to the world and to life. We are in this helpless state in order to love and be beholden to others. Being imperfect we are open to others, and it is openness to the influence of others which is the purpose. In sickness, help can, and indeed should, only come from others. Seen from this angle, it is Christ who is the key to the world."[19]

Novalis was able to sense that human beings express themselves with their destiny in their heart. Having perceived the role of the imperfect, ego bearing creature, he considered the extreme case when sickness makes human beings dependent on others. Novalis saw love as a goal of humanity; out of the powers of the heart, a vessel can be created in which human ego and universal ego unite.[20]

MEDICAL ASPECTS OF TEACHING

Functionally, heart and lung are one organ – the rhythmic system which extends through the whole organism in the pulsating vessels. Respiration becomes going to steep and waking up at another level. The hydraulic ram could be the subject of technology or physics lessons, and above all lessons on the nature of the human being.

Many medical problems were discussed with Eugen Kolisko, the school doctor. Here we can only refer to one example, which is how to help school-age children develop regular sleeping habits. No other field shows so clearly the profound insight into children and their health which a school doctor must seek to gain. Regular sleeping habits were discussed at a teachers' meeting on May 25, 1923.[21] Too much sleep during the growing period leads to weakness in the power to envisage forms, for example, in geometry; the state of sleep continues on into the daytime ability to shape ideas. It is not too difficult for us to understand this. Too little sleep leads to weakness in the capacity for profound feeling in connection with music and history. The intellectual understanding of children who are awake for too long influences the respiratory system, so that their breathing becomes too shallow. As a result, the movements of the soul in the breathing rhythm become superficial and cannot enter into full experience. History easily remains mere factual knowledge if the soul cannot fully enter into its heights and depths. Notes are heard in the head, but when we have a feeling for the music we hear, this enters into the rhythm of our breathing and is carried by it. You often see concertgoers taking a deep breath. From the medical point of view, educating a child into good sleeping habits is a matter of taking serious responsibility for the growth metamorphosis in later life. More deeply experienced vibrant sounds enter into the breathing movements of the diaphragm, which penetrate into the sphere of metabolism and growth, loosening it up from inside, so that growth can become as entirely spiritual as memory. Residual growth principles that have not been released to become powers of memory and that remain active at the cellular level create the preconditions for neoplastic tumor development, and this happens at a time of life when the warmth of enthusiasm for the lessons taught should renew the powers of life. This is how the pathological processes underlying tumors and inflammation at the physical level relate to the metamorphosis achieved by education. Learning with brain and heart thus becomes preventive treatment if the teacher is truly skilled in the art of education.

SUMMARY

The physical equivalent of heart and blood circulation is the hydraulic ram. The flowing blood moves the heart, just as the ram is set in motion by running water. In embryonic development blood flow is uninterrupted until the heart begins to beat. Vascular muscle becomes enlarged to form the myocardium, because the flow is stopped, just as flow is periodically stopped by the valve in the ram. Flow is then reversed in both the ram and the heart. The eye is positioned in the skull and the lens in the eye. In the eye, incoming light is reflected to become image.

Images have been considered of organs which are part of the human organism. In respiration, inspiration is reversed to become expiration, showing the process of reflection we also see in the blood stream when it reaches the heart. The sense organ comes to realization in the blood stream.

Since dreams are a phenomenon of the inner life, and the rhythmic system is the bearer of the soul, let us conclude with an example of how great truths can be revealed in dreams.

K. F. Burdach (1776-1847), an anatomist at Dorpat and Koenigsberg Universities, was amazed when he had the following dream:

"In 1811, for instance, I took the generally accepted view of the circulation, having never been exposed to any views to the contrary. Anyway, I had quite other matters on my mind when I dreamt that the blood flowed by its own power and set the heart in motion. If one considered the heart to be the driving force in the circulation, this would be tantamount to saying that water driving a mill was actually being driven by the mill."[22]

Burdach was unable to believe the truth he had seen in his dream. It is our task to bring the truth which dreams in us out into the bright light of the wide awake mind.

Paraphrasing Novalis we might say:

"The heart is the key to the art of education."

APPENDIX

Less well-known statements by Rudolf Steiner on the heart:

"Twenty-five years ago at most, the criminal anthropologist Moritz Benedikt, an eminent scientist in this field, with the necessary training in mathematics, first drew attention to the extremely important fact, frequently ignored again nowadays, that the pulses of the radial arteries on the left and right sides of the body are not identical. This is most important for insight into the relationship between different aspects of the human being. Another significant fact was discovered by someone who was not the least bit famous in this field, but a very ordinary person, Dr. Karl Schmidt. He published his findings in the medical journal *Wiener medizinische Wochenschrift* in 1882 in a paper entitled (in translation): *Heart beat and sphygmogram*s. He made some very important observations. These things are still in their beginnings, but with more detailed study a start will have been made in discovering the connection between a self-conscious ego and the blood circulation on the one hand and between the animal spirit active in animals and the blood circulation of animals on the other." (***Antworten der Geisteswissenschaft auf die grossen Fragen des Daseins*** [GA 601]. Lecture given in Berlin on November 17, 1910.)

Elsewhere the spiritual consequences of the physical pump theory are discussed in detail. Rudolf Steiner also referred to Dr. K. Schmidt and to Moritz Benedikt's mention of Schmidt's work when speaking to the teachers, though no direct mention is made of the apparatus:

". . . But none of this goes far enough; it is quite elementary. Only a few people have noticed that the movements of the heart result from the movement of the blood, and that it is the movement of the blood which is the elemental living principle. . . the movement of the heart, the whole activity of this organ, is really merely the consequence of the blood circulation; the heart merely positions itself in the living blood circulation . . ." (See Note 17, below; lecture given in Basel on April 22, 1920).

In the last of the above sentences, the hydraulic ram is clearly there in the background to the phrase: "merely positions itself". (See also ibid., lecture given in Basel on April 23, 1920). As the lecture proceeds, a description is given of the functions of the heart in the life of the psyche and what it means when teachers are able to gain a spiritual view of the heart:

"The way of thinking we are concerned with here is intended to enable teachers to manage even very large classes, where social conditions make this necessary. Understanding the human being in living motion leads to the realization 'that the heart is not a pump to move the blood around the body. Human beings are inwardly alive in such a way that the movements of the body fluids and of the heart are the outcome of being thus alive.' If a configuration of mind and spirit is created that enables a teacher to think like this, certain powers in the teacher become visionary with regard to the child's development. With our eyes thus opened, significant insights may be gained with regard to one particular child in a large class which one has only known for a few months. Training mind and spirit in this way, which makes contact powerful, it is possible to have an almost clairvoyant view of the child's individual nature."

This is the crucial element. It is not so much a matter of knowing that the heart is not the cause of the blood circulation but its result. The point is that those who develop the ability to visualize this, in contrast to today's materialistic way of looking at things, those who learn to train mind and spirit out of a heart with living inner vision, "will come alive in a new way to the development of one child or even a whole group of children. This will also enable us to evolve the curriculum out of the very nature of the developing child ." (See Note 18, below).

All this goes to show that our civilization, especially with regard to education, is a civilization of the heavy heart. A pumping heart has taken the place of a living, spiritual center of life. This is yet another tangible consequence of the Council of 869. Heart research must thus be taken up equally by the medical and the teaching professions. Twelve Model III apparatuses have been offered and bought for use in Waldorf schools (biology and physics teachers). The hydraulic ram has become the object of scientific research in both medicine and education.

BIBLIOGRAPHY AND NOTES

GA = Collected works of Rudolf Steiner, German edition, Dornach.

l. Steiner, R., *Conferences with Waldorf Teachers, Part I* (GA 300a).
2. Developing the collaboration between the medical and teaching professions so that it will be a source of educational impulses is one of the central functions of the teachers' colleges at Waldorf schools.
3. Steiner, R., *Rudolf Steiner in der Waldorfschule* (GA 298). Kolisko, E. Auf der Suche nach neuen Wahrheiten. Dornach, 1989.
4. Kolisko, E., *Auf der Suche nach neuen Wahrheiten*. Dornach, 1989.
5. Lauboeck K.H., "Beziehungen zwischen Blutkreislauf und Herzbewegung," *Merkurstab* Nr. 3, 1989.

6. Mendelsohn, M., Das Herz ein sekundaeres Organ. ***Zschr. Kreisfauf,*** 1928, 20:19. The author does not refer to the hydraulic ram as such, but what matters is the idea of 'insertion'. The vital fluids have inherent mobility. I assume Mendelsohn was thinking of the ram but did not explicitly refer to it. It is evident from his discussion of the subject that the pump concept had become suspect in his eyes.

7. Steiner, R., ***The Spiritual-Scientific Aspect of Therapy*** (GA 313). Lecture on April 16, 1921.

8. See Note 5.

9. Goethe, J.W., ***Naturulissenschaftliche Schriften,*** with introduction, footnotes and commentary by Rudolf Steiner (GA 1 e). p. 363.

10. Mueller, 0., ***Die feinsten Blutgefaesse des Menschen***. Band 1. Enke 1937.

11. In Figure 1, 7 indicates the macula densa, an organ with closely packed epithelial cells. This is a chemical sense organ located in the angle between the two vessels with their different lumina. It has developed from the median layer in the wall of the afferent vessel. Every kidney contains 1-16 million of these sense organs. Depending on the sodium chloride concentration of the urine, they control blood pressure and blood volume in a process which also includes the efferent vessel. Thus, a sense organ is found at the point where blood flow is reversed. The functions of a sodium peptide hormone found in the atria of the heart with its synthesis triggered by atrial dilatation include control of blood volume, elimination of sodium, and urinary excretion (cardiac hormone). Kidney and heart are part of the sensitive silicic acid organism, which permits them to perceive each other. See also Steiner, R. & Wegman, ***Fundamentals of Therapy*** (CA 27) Ch. 14, and Husemann, F. "Das Herz als endokrines Organ" ***Merkurstab*** Nr. 4, 1991.

12. See Note 5. above.

13. Steiner, R., ***Heat. Second Scientific Lecture Course*** (GA 321).

14. Steiner R. ***Soziales Verstaendnis aus geisteswissenschaftlicher Erkenntnis*** (GA 191), Lecture of October 4, 1919.

15. Ibid.

16. Steiner, R. *The Renewal of Education through the Science of the Spirit* (GA 301).
17. Ibid. Lecture given in Basel on 26 April 1920.
18. Ibid.
19. Novalis, *Fragmente,* Dresden, 1929.
20. See also Steiner, R., *Knowledge of the Higher Worlds* (GA 10), Ch. "Stages of Initiation, Preparation", and Steiner, R. *Wahrspruchworte* (GA 40). *Die geistige Grundsteinlegung.*
21. Steiner, R., *Conferences with Waldorf Teachers* Part 2, sections A and B (CA 300b).
22. Jezower, (ed). *Buch der Träumer,* Reinbek 1927.

Additional Literature on Medical and Educational Heart Research (1892-1995)

See literature quoted in Notes 6 and 7 above, and in the Appendix.

Schmidt, K., Ueber Herzstoss und Pulskurven. *Wiener Medizinische Wochenschrift,* 1892; lS ff. Reprinted in *Beitr. Er w. Heilkunst,* 1973; Nr.3.

Benedikt, M., *Das biosmechanischce Denken in der Medizin.* Jena 1903. Only brief, affirmative reference to above. See *Beitr. Er w. Heilkunst,* 1982; Nr.1.

Steiner, R., *Spiritual Science and Medicine* (GA 312), lecture of 2 March 1920.

Havlicek, H., Arbeitet das Hers wie eine Druckpumpe oder wie ein Stossheber. Eine neue Herztheorie. *Archiv für Kreislaufforschung:* 1937; 1: l88. A compromise between pump and hydraulic ram.
Husemann, G., Husemann F., Der hydraulische Widder und die Herzbewegung. *Beitr. Erw. Heilkunst,* 1974; Nr. 4.

Manteuffel-Szoege, L., On the movement of the blood. *Br. Homeopathic Journal,* 1969; 58: 196-211, 218-223, and 1970; 59: 35-4 1.

Basfeld, M., *Experimentelle Untersuchungen an einem Modell eines hydraulischen Widders,* Dissertation at the Max-Planck-Institut, Goettingen, 1980.

Basfeld, M., Der hydraulische Widder als reales Symbol der menschlichen Herztätigkeit. *Beitr. Erw. Heilkunst,* 1982; Nr. 1.

Husemann, G., Demonstrations given for Upper Schools, teachers and physicians in German speaking countries, 1946-1949 with the first model (W. Wolf), 1964-1965 with the second model (Gebr. Braun), 1970-1973 with the third model (Gebr. Braun).

Basfeld, M., Demonstrations 1982 (internal teachers conference in Germany) physics and biology teachers.

Husemann, A. J., Demonstrations for Upper Schools from 1988.

Marinelli, R., "The Heart Is Not a Pump: A Refutation of the Pressure Propulsion Premise of Heart Function", *Frontier Perspectives*, Volume 5, Number 1, Fall/Winter 1995, The Center for Frontier Sciences at Temple University.

CHAPTER 2

CONSTITUTIONAL TYPES
IN SCHOOL-AGE CHILDREN

by

Michaela Glöckler, M.D.
Translated by Linda Maloney

1. The large-headed and the small-headed child

When we look at what Rudolf Steiner has to say with regard to difficult children, we will not find diagnoses such as "minimal brain dysfunction", "aggressive behavior", "hyperactivity", or "change brought on by the child's environment." So, as contemporaries now dealing with this terminology, we have to first try to come to an understanding of the way Steiner describes children, a way which can help us draw nearer to the true nature of the child. In this lecture of February 6, 1923[1], as well as in the lecture series *"Menschenerkenntnis und Unterrichtsgestaltung" (Knowledge of Man and the Form of the Lesson)*[2], he describes children in terms of six constitutional types: large-headed and small-headed, earthly and cosmic, fantasy-rich and fantasy-poor. Together with the four temperaments this typology connects the fundamental constitutional characteristics with the help of which a child learns to express himself in the most varied ways to reveal his inner being. It is the common task of pedagogy and medicine to assist the child during his school years with the full individualization of his constitution necessary for this expression. As work with these six types is not so widespread as is that with the four temperaments, it is my hope that this contribution will help to stimulate further interest.

Steiner bases his description of large-headed and small-headed children on the threefold nature of the human being. In the presence of school physician Eugen Kolisko, he made the fundamental statement that viewing the nature of the human being as threefold must become second nature to the teacher and the physician. For not until we have inwardly experienced the reality of these three systems – until we have arrived at our own intuition of the forces and functions connected with them – can these insights guide us and awaken our understanding for what children suffer and experience – but also for what they need in the classroom.

Let's examine then the threefold nature of the human being and its connections to the surrounding world more closely. There are three ways for the human being to be connected with the world in body, soul, and spirit. First, we have the connection through the senses of hearing, taste, smell, touch, and sight. Bound up with the senses is our thinking, which brings sense experience to consciousness. This nerve sense connection to the world is such that our nerve and sense organs work better, more successfully when we are in actually immersing ourselves in the qualities of the world – in perceiving and picturing in our minds the true reality of what is. In the acts of perception and thinking, we make ourselves similar to the world, we carefully adapt ourselves to what is there, and we try to understand its true nature. We search for concordance with our surroundings through observation and thought. If, for example, someone I am talking to has seen a particular flower, and I decide to go look at it as well, then we have both seen the same thing. We meet in viewing an objective truth. In the upper sphere of our nerve sense system, we have the capacity to take in the world – to let it impress itself upon us – as it is. The richness of our soul life is formed from these impressions.

Our relationship to the world through our metabolic system – especially through the mouth, intestinal tract, and anus – is quite different. Think of your weekend shopping cart, filled with all the good things you picked out, right down to the ice cream and the frozen fish and spinach for the freezer.

During the course of the week, all this makes its way through you. Here we have exactly the opposite of what happens in the nerve/sense system. When the digestive process proceeds normally, nothing remains the way it was. We immediately begin to "impress" ourselves upon "the world" with our teeth . When we press down and bite into something, it changes as it receives our imprint. In the further course of digestion we dissolve, analyze, and mineralize these substances. The world dies in terms of its own existence and is born anew in us through metabolic activity, becoming human substance. A dying and a being born take place, but what is typical for the metabolism is this building up of the substance of the human body from plant and animal substances which have died, as well as from dissolved mineral substances. This new creation, totally individual and formed only once in material existence, is created through the metabolism, through the building up of the individualized protein of the body. Just as we become world in the process of perception, so the world becomes human being through the work of the digestive organs.

The third connection and opening to the world is through respiration. Here we are not dealing with solid and liquid substances as with food, or with light, air, sound, and warmth as with sense impressions, but with an opening to the surrounding air. Here in the middle sphere of the body a very peculiar process takes place. Something of the world is taken in - as in metabolism - and is then exchanged (i.e. oxygen and carbon dioxide). We extract from the air we breathe in about 4% of the oxygen, then breathe out the carbon dioxide which has been formed in us and which is no longer needed. But the peculiar thing is that the major portion of the air we breathe in is exhaled unchanged. With respect to this portion of the air that remains unchanged, we discover a similarity with the activity of our nerve/sense system, where we take in the world as it is and allow it to remain unchanged. The strange thing is that quantitatively speaking, it is not the individual element which predominates in this middle sphere, but the part which we allow to remain unchanged as "world", due to the fact that in inhaling and exhaling the major portion of the air we breathe goes in and out "unused." All this is also indicated by the fact that there is still enough oxygen (about 17%) in the air we exhale to be able to resuscitate someone who has stopped breathing. He or she can also extract 4% of the oxygen for his or her own respiration or "exchange of gases." So it is in the middle sphere of the body that the concerns of the world and personal need are harmonized in a wonderful way to the advantage of the world. In our bodily nature, we have at our disposal a surplus which allows us to give ourselves over to the world to an extent which is greater than any demand we need to place upon it.

In our middle sphere we also breathe between the "heavy" and the "light" spheres of the body. Related to this, we have two peculiar features of the opposite poles of the nervous and the digestive systems. The nervous system, with its center in the brain, floats in the cerebrospinal fluid, which gives it buoyancy and partially frees it from the effects of gravity. But when we examine the intestinal cavity below the diaphragm, we see how the organs hang down very much subject to gravity. In the case of a slim person, for example, the stomach really hangs down; in the case of a heavy person, where the inner walls are cushioned with fat, it is pushed up somewhat. So it is clearly visible that below the diaphragm, the influences of gravity are at work on the metabolic system, whereas the nervous system is largely free of these influences, buoyed up according to Archimedes' Law. We experience the faculty of soul connected with each of these three systems in a corresponding way.

We experience the content of our conscious thought life as being light and bright, not material or heavy. Even when we have "heavy" thoughts, they are light in this respect. In this middle sphere - in the lungs located in the chest cavity – there is a constant negative pressure, which increases during inhalation and continues as we exhale, so that the lungs do not collapse. Thus, in the process of breathing in and out – of sucking in and pressing out – a balance of upper and lower, of lightness and heaviness is created, which is also characterized by lightness. We experience our feelings as being correspondingly light and flexible, even though certainly more clearly bound up with our bodies than our thinking is. By contrast, we feel that our willing is completely bound up with our body and its heaviness. It is as if we had to wrest each movement from the force of gravity moving our limbs in opposition to it.

Through our bodies we are connected with the world in a threefold way. We relate to the world through our soul life in a threefold way as well, for we live in willing, thinking, and in the middle, feeling – searching for the balance between ourselves and the world. The rhythm of our breathing is in harmonious accord with the rhythms of the cosmos. At rest we breathe 18 times per minute – that means 1080 times per hour, and 25,920 times per 24 hour period. This is the same as the number of years it takes the sun's point of sunrise at the vernal equinox to pass through the entire zodiac. 25,920 years are a so-called "Platonic world-yea.r." Time and again Rudolf Steiner referred to this special connection of human life with the course of the world. What is contained in the sun cycle through the year – winter and summer (cold and heat) with the transitional periods of spring and autumn – is comparable to one 24-hour period experienced on earth, with night and day (also cold and heat) and the wonderful mood of transition at dawn and dusk in between.

In the case of the infant and of the small child, the nerve/sense system and the metabolic system are connected, but without the benefit of a vigorous, autonomous middle sphere as yet. When children start school, it is the principal task of teacher and physician to support the formation of this middle sphere both pedagogically and medically. For it is in this sphere where personal needs and the concerns of the world should be harmonized – that we feel ourselves to be truly human. If someone speaks to us in an unfriendly way, we feel touched by inhumanity, whereas an understanding look or an appropriate gesture comfort us and are experienced as an expression of our common humanity. It is in this sphere of accord with the world – where knowledge and experience of oneself and of the world can meet in harmony – that our humanity lives. Our task is to help strengthen and encourage this humanity through education.

There are children in whom the nerve/sense system and the metabolic system are out of balance right from the start. Steiner speaks about these children in the above mentioned lecture of February 6, 1923, in which he also makes the comforting statement that in reality there is no one in whom the two systems interact in total harmony. The scales are always tipped a little more to one side or the other. For this reason it is important to look at every child with the silent question – how are these three systems interrelated in your case? How can I help you to strengthen your middle sphere?

In the course of the lecture referred to, Steiner describes the characteristic features of the two types of children that we can readily grasp in connection with this threefold division, namely the small-headed and the large-headed child: "We have the nerve/sense system. But we only understand it rightly if we are aware that the nerve/sense system is actually governed by laws which are not the physical-chemical laws of earthly materiality. Through the nerve/sense system the human being is raised above the laws of earthly materiality. For in its formation, the nerve/ sense system is entirely the product of pre-earthly existence. The human being has the nerve/sense system that he has received in accordance with his pre-earthly existence so that – because in reality all the material laws of the nerve/sense system have been raised above earthly materiality – his nerve/sense system is also capable of the parallel development of all the functions related to the soul and spirit."[4]

Now in the case of a child in whom the head is overdeveloped by comparison with the torso and limbs, this is an indication that the nerve/sense system is not harmoniously integrated into the other members. Referring to this constitutional type, Steiner noted that the child's astral body and ego do not really want to take hold of the nerve/sense system. For this reason, such children have a tendency to daydream – removed from the earthly activities around them – rather than taking an alert and active part in them through open sense-organs. Just as the brain floats in the cerebrospinal fluid, for the most part unaffected by gravity, and is protected within the skull, so these children are in danger of giving themselves up too much to the particular dynamics of the nerve/sense system. The phenomenon of "large-headedness" connected with this is not only a question of external measurement (it can be more or less clearly recognized by the circumference of the head). Most importantly, it is a question of the thought function outweighing an alert grasping of one's surroundings through the senses due to faulty integration of the nerve/sense processes into the rest of the organism.

Let's try to picture such a large-headed child. He walks somewhat unconsciously, moving dreamily around the classroom, lost in thought. He seems not to take in his surroundings very actively, and shows correspondingly no spirited reactions. He can often be observed standing somewhere and looking dreamily around. You don't get the impression that he is observing things very carefully; he seems to have more of a general impression of what is going on. When you arrive at school, you usually find such a child already at his desk, or else by the window, and in the winter, over by the heating. He finds it somewhat difficult to concentrate and to differentiate precisely, and tends to listen and grasp things in a superficial way. He cannot hold things he encounters clearly in his thoughts so as to have them at his disposal. On the other hand, he is full of images and dreams, has a rich soul-life and is endowed with a certain cheerfulness. In terms of his temperament, he is predominantly sanguine/phlegmatic.

The question now is what can be done to help balance things out. What feelings and sensations have to be awakened in order to stimulate the child to differentiate, to make things clear to himself – to bring them "down to earth?" Figuratively speaking, he must learn to feel the difference between cold and heat – particularly the delimitation and contraction which takes place in the presence of hazy, shimmering heat – as opposed to the way we experience cold, which we brace ourselves against, which wakes us up. We use the term "biting cold", not "biting heat." And each of us can experience the way that being cool-headed helps us to reach a clear, rational view of things. For this reason, Steiner recommended creating sensations of cold, especially in the area of the head, to help these "large-headed" children. For some children, wiping the head with cool water in the morning is sufficient; others need to be wiped down to the waist. What happens when this is done? Through the sensations that are thus awakened - sensations of differentiation between hot and cold – the child's thought life is connected to the functions of the sense-organs. For the imbalance between the systems has come about because the child's ego and astral body are only willing to connect with the bodily instrument of the nervous system in tentative fashion. If, however, strong stimuli are given which encourage a differentiation in perception and shake the child out of his hazy dreaming, then the astral body and the ego are stimulated to a stronger connection with nerve/sense activity. The child would really prefer to just dream and let things pass before him rather than go into something that hurts, bites, is cold, that engenders consciousness and self-awareness. By wiping the child gently with cool water in the morning, we are helping him into the world of the senses - the world of differentiation, of coldness, of hardness, of clarity. This is one aspect of the therapy. We create a bit of winter, so to speak, so that alertness and clarity may develop.

DEVELOPMENTAL INSIGHTS
Discussions Between Doctors and Teachers

As a second aspect, Steiner recommended supporting this process of awakening to the sense world through the metabolism, in order to promote a balance in the systems from this point of view as well. We can understand why when we ask how the ability to differentiate – the elements of the analytical, the hard, the unrelenting – live in the metabolism. They live in our capacity to disintegrate substances, to separate them out of their compounds. This is one aspect of metabolic activity. Its other task is the diametric opposite: after the substances taken in have been broken down and isolated, then the metabolic system performs the creative task of building up the body's own substance. The more we are truly ourselves in healthy metabolic activity, the better we are able to give ourselves over to the world via our nervous system. Here Steiner calls our attention to a law of effects on opposites: if the child's head has been wiped with cool water, and he is more aware, then in his metabolism the breakdown and processing of foodstuffs will be correspondingly supported. If, on the other hand, the organism is stimulated to separate substances out and to take them into the life of the body – working in synthesizing fashion – then the ability to synthesize and connect in thinking will be correspondingly strengthened. Steiner recommended that physicians get detailed information on family eating habits. A child may, for example, be getting too little salt if a low-salt diet is being followed in the home because a parent has heart problems. And as a crystalline compound formed from the diametric opposites of acid and base, salt has a special significance. For if the organism doesn't learn to dissolve salt, to take it into its total context and to process it, then the functioning of the nervous system and metabolic activity cannot be kept in proper balance. Sufficient salt in the diet, or medication in the form of lead compounds - (certain lead salts which can be administered) – support the organism in the analysis of solid substances, of pure salt substances. In this way, the conscious capacity for clear differentiation, separating and connecting, is stimulated via the metabolism. All these things are aids for the large-headed child.

Now let's turn to the small-headed child, who does not tend to give himself over to the dynamics of the nerve/sense system. In his case, the dynamics of metabolic activity are not sufficiently under control, because the child's astral body and ego do not take hold of the metabolism properly; they are not willing to connect themselves in sufficiently close fashion with this

28

death and resurrection of substance. What happens when this connection is not close enough, when the child's individuality does not sufficiently penetrate his metabolism? We then have a child who is always somewhat tense, having to hold his own against the particular dynamics and forces of the substances he eats. These children are to some extent driven, so to speak, by the nutritional and digestive processes. They often eat greedily, hastily, in fits and starts, depending on what they have in front of them. Their bowel movements are often irregular as well. Occasionally they may have a very solid, incompletely digested stool. Sometimes they may have no bowel movement for two days, and then everything "moves along" again. When we investigate more closely, we find that the rest of the child's behavior also has something impulsive, something driven about it. If a child is at the mercy of the warmth generated by metabolic activity – but also of the forces and the particular dynamics of various substances, because these have not been sufficiently controlled and processed – then he may become excitable, bad-tempered, choleric, driven due to the after-effects of the substances. When these forces have spent themselves, he may brood, be pale and exhausted, in a corner, burdened by melancholy and by substances. On this point Steiner noted the following: "Of the human being's three systems, it is the metabolic/limb system which is the most dependent on continuing external material processes within itself. So when we become familiar with the processes that take place on the earth through physics and chemistry, it is these processes that have their continuation within the human being insofar as the metabolic/limb system is concerned. But we learn nothing about the laws which govern his nerve/sense system."[5]   He continues: "If a child's ability to synthesize, to be constructive in his imagination is too limited, if he cannot make things clear to himself in pictures, if in art he is a little primitive and unformed, as is often the case with children today – this is a symptom that the metabolic/limb system is not in order. . ."[6] In this case the astral body is not willing to take hold of the metabolic/limb system properly, and so it requires some support. How can we help such a child to deal with the particular tendencies of the metabolism? How can the child's astral body and ego be supported through the metabolism with respect to their integration into the total organism? A marvelous way is through warmth in the form of a warm tummy wrap after the noon-day meal or in the evening before bedtime.

DEVELOPMENTAL INSIGHTS
Discussions Between Doctors and Teachers

Modern medicine would say: warmth relaxes the autonomic nervous system and stimulates the digestive nerves in harmonious fashion. It thus stimulates, relieves tension, and promotes digestion. Rudolf Steiner brings this to us in the form of a picture: "The divine spiritual powers cause it to be warm in summer and cold in winter; these are spiritual effects which are achieved by the divine spiritual powers through material means.[7] The application of warmth is external summer therapy, which supports the transformation of matter into human substance. From the point of view of diet, these children can also be helped by the use of a key substance – sugar – to stimulate the metabolism. Their diet should be richly varied and easily digestible, and always include something sweet for dessert. Nowadays the indication that these children need a good helping of something sweet sounds rather strange. We should keep in mind, however, that Steiner was speaking at a time – three years after the end of the First World War – when sugar was still in very short supply, and there were many undernourished children in the schools. For the children we have been talking about, the important thing is the invigorating effect which sugar originating in the blossom and fruit warmth of plants has on the metabolism. Nowadays we have to add that the sugar should, of course, be part of a healthy meal and not enjoyed in the form of sweets between meals.

These aids can be complemented medicinally by giving homeopathic doses of silver (argentum). Silver is a substance that completely conforms to this will to synthesize the metabolism, giving the child's astral body and ego the opportunity to find a connection to the digestive processes. With regard to medication, however, it is important to call in the school physician or the child's family doctor. Parents react somewhat negatively – and rightly so – when they get advice on medication from the teacher. However, if the teacher recommends that they speak to the school physician about the possibility of medication, because experience has shown that this often has a positive effect on the child's behavior in school, then they are more likely to follow up on the suggestion.

From the case history of a little boy – a typical small-headed child – whom I was introduced to when he was in the first grade, I learned that this therapy can only really be completely successful when it is carried out over the course of a year, or at least over a longer period of time, especially the tummy wrap. There will be periods when no medication is given, so that the child can be reassessed on an on-going basis. But the metabolism needs the summer warmth of this wrap over a longer period of time like a kind of education for the body corresponding to the cold wiping for the large-headed child. Sometimes children become so accustomed to their warm tummy wrap that they continue to ask for it in the evening for a second and third year - something we should let them enjoy. In such a case, a pedagogical problem is often involved as well – and here is where the teachers can help the physician. For the latter may prescribe the warm tummy wraps, but then not have the time to follow-up by telling the parents that it's not enough to apply something warm to their child's stomach and then rush off again. They need to take the time to sit awhile by the child – creating a cozy, summery feeling of inner warmth, to tell him a nice story, so that this little driven bundle of energy can really relax, and his imagination is stimulated to personal, living images and ideas. In this way the teachers can help the child to love this therapy, because suddenly mother or father, a favorite aunt or a big sister has some time. It is these children in particular who are in need of this.

In the above-mentioned lecture, Steiner followed these two guidelines for therapy with several fundamental instructions for teachers and school physicians with respect to pedagogy. Many school physicians teach nowadays as well, and thus find it easy to speak with the teachers about pedagogical problems. Permit me to make a comment here. I continually experience the difficulty that many school physicians have in communicating with teachers on these issues when they themselves have little or no teaching experience. Yet, in the course of sitting in on classes, they observe many things that could be very useful, even if they themselves don't know how to translate them into pedagogical terms. So it is important to take these observations into consideration, but the school physician must also learn to state his pedagogical ideas only when he is actually asked. One of my most painful first experiences as a school physician came the third time I sat in on a certain second-grade class. I was full of ideas about what the teacher could do better, so I simply mentioned everything I had noticed. The upshot was that it was two years before I was invited back into this class, because the teacher couldn't handle the revelations and suggestions in this form. Knowledge is only beneficial when it is sought after. Only then does it leave the other free.

DEVELOPMENTAL INSIGHTS
Discussions Between Doctors and Teachers

Only then can it truly be of help. This is something that we school physicians have to practice: viewing things with a loving eye such that images of the situation arise, not judgments. When we are asked, we can then safely speak from our view of these images, advising, trying to characterize things, to depict processes, and to answer in such a way that the teacher can accept what we have said and find the proper pedagogical application.

So what can be done from the pedagogical point of view to help large-headed and small headed children? What can be done every day in the classroom to help strengthen the middle sphere in these children? What could we term the "winter" and "summer" qualities of the middle sphere? The answer is that they correspond to the coldness and warmth of the feelings of antipathy and sympathy. Antipathy: drawing boundaries, meeting things head-on, closing oneself off. Sympathy: opening oneself up. And in between, to be at rest, as in breathing. Opening, closing, rest – always threefold, with the turning point, where breathing in becomes breathing out, in rest. Correspondingly, inner peace and quiet is the middle-point in our feeling life.

In every lesson there is an opportunity to allow the children to experience the full range of emotions. Antipathy, terror, and crying all obviously increase the strength with which we breathe in, holding ourselves back. When we sob, we draw in our breath spasmodically, irregularly, until our limit is reached. On the other hand, laughing is exhalation, opening up, sharing – it is a long breathing out. We pour out our feelings, so to speak, in laughter, until we are red in the face and completely "laughed out." So we have opposite processes: antipathy, in which we step back behind a limit (crying as a process of in-breathing); sympathy, in which we open ourselves up (laughter as a process of out-breathing). Steiner encourages us to bring the children to the point of laughter and then – now serious again and full of compassion – to bring them almost to the point of tears in every lesson, so that through their living experience of the content of the lesson, the children can experience and build up this middle ground between the two extremes.

They may be angry, irritated, or indignant, this is, followed by complete sympathetic participation in what is being said. Regardless of whether the subject is English or arithmetic, if the teacher wants to bring the children to an experience of these feelings of warmth and coldness in every lesson, he will scarcely have time or an opportunity to look at his notes, as this would interrupt the flow of the lesson while he considered what he still wanted to do. For this reason, Steiner stated that teaching from memory is a pedagogical and therapeutic necessity. If the teacher doesn't have a clear picture of what he wants to teach, then he is not sufficiently "into" what he wants to say to be able to create the mood the child needs in order to enter into what is being said with interest. For what the teacher wants to say should not be mere book knowledge which lives only in his thinking. It must also have penetrated his feelings and his will if it is to move the child and be of significance and of interest to him. The child's inner being must meet the inner essence of the content that speaks through the teacher. This high standard has an astonishing effect on the teacher as well, who is strengthened and centered by this identification with the content of his lessons. It works wonders when one feels that one is totally exhausted, for if I am able to do what I do with all the love and strength in me, then I am strengthened in return. I must not divide myself by doing what I don't really want to do, for this would mean tearing my inner being in two, and that depletes strength. The therapeutic aspect underlying this identification with the content of the lessons was formulated by Steiner as follows: "The teacher should really try not to bring himself, i.e., who he is as a private person, into the classroom. Instead, he should have a picture of what he will become through the materials he is dealing with in a specific lesson. Then he will become something through the material. And what he himself becomes in this way will have an extraordinarily enlivening effect on the whole class. The teacher should have the feeling that when he is indisposed, he can overcome the indisposition – at least to a certain extent – through his teaching; then he will have the most favorable effect possible on the children. He should teach out of the mood that teaching is beneficial to himself as well, for if he has a morose disposition, for example, he can become cheerful while teaching."[8] The effect of such an attitude toward teaching can be directly experienced. However, the identification with the content must be so strong that, for example, a particular song you want to sing with the children fills every pore of your being; so to speak, you are completely caught up in your enjoyment of it. Even if you're not quite sure of the words yet, don't search desperately through your songbook: instead, just hum the song at first, but really "get into it" and enjoy the tones. This gives the children the opportunity to enter in soul – that is in the middle sphere, with their feelings – into what you're talking about or presenting.

In terms of this therapeutic aspect, artistic activity in the lesson has a special effect, for in artistic activity we have this complete identification in its purest form. Let's take eurythmy as an example. This art form can only be created if we enter into the sounds and processes without reservation. This identification is expressed in a threefold way: in the movement, in the feeling of the movement, and in the character, the personal note that each person gives to his movements. We practice the arts for a great variety of reasons, but in the final analysis they are the high path to schooling ourselves in identification.

Such teaching is based on the teacher's presence of mind. Anyone can, of course, suddenly forget what he wanted to say. But it is in just such a desperate situation that he may then begin talking about something that is of far greater importance for the children than what he originally intended to say. This also involves a certain amount of risk, but it is this element of risk that makes us interesting to the children. A teacher who is a model of self-confidence and mastery can, of course, teach well and perhaps also maintain good discipline. But he produces a different effect on the children from the teacher about whom the pupil senses, "He still has to work and learn like I do – I can really learn something from him. He doesn't have everything yet, but is still working on things." And this is exactly what pupils should be learning in school: *how to work* – for what we teach them in terms of content will be forgotten again. However, the way in which we guide them to inner and outer work – that ability will remain with them for the rest of their lives. The way we have exerted ourselves is the most essential thing for our pupils and the way that we succeed in making them part of this process, this struggle. It may become so quiet you could hear a pin drop as the teacher recounts a personal experience where he is totally wrapped up in feelings of fear, concern, or joy. The more his individuality is revealed and the more the pupils really experience their teacher as a human being, the easier it is for them to come to love him and to learn from him. And love, as we all know, is the best foundation for discipline. Pupils always have a tendency to be cheeky, but they "stifle" it, either because they feel sorry for the teacher, or because they love him.

But in-between times, they're cheeky. Compassion and love are the forces we rely on.

The last means of pedagogically strengthening the middle sphere (spoken of by Steiner in the same lecture as above) is the moral disposition of the educator – the most important means of working hygienically through teaching. What the teacher is in moral terms, what he has made of himself through his own efforts, what he has achieved in overcoming his weaknesses, not putting his personal problems first, but giving himself over to the content of his lessons and to the children – all of these things enable him to have a hygienic effect, making him a healthy role-model for the children that he teaches. For health, both of body and of soul, is the result of work which the Being alive in the body and soul of the child must perform on the way to integrating all the functions and individual activities of the organs in harmonious fashion.

2. The "earthly"and the "cosmic" child

In the language of current conventional medical diagnosis, we regularly find descriptions of final states. Several of these we mentioned in the preceding chapter: minimal brain disfunction, problems of aggressive behavior, various problems brought on by the child's environment, hyperactivity. If we look up the causes of these illnesses in the appropriate books, we find "brain hemorrhage", "neonatal sepsis", "multifactorial causes", "cause unknown", and so on. With this type of diagnosis and research into causes, attention is not focused on the preparation by the organism to receive an illness. A triggering factor in connection with the final state is described, but why this particular organism was predisposed to an infection, for example, is not taken into account. This type of diagnosis does not get to the heart of the matter. Rather, it looks at something external which appears in the end state – and often not even at that, focusing instead on a mental picture, a model, that someone has made of the situation. Because of this, we often have a lot to get past in order to gain a clear perspective on what diagnosis means in the true sense of the word. "Dia" means "through", and "gnosis" is "knowledge", thus, to know through and through the being which is manifesting itself in the symptom.

DEVELOPMENTAL INSIGHTS
Discussions Between Doctors and Teachers

What is the nature of the human being? When someone has died or has not yet been born, we imagine him as pure spirit, cosmic, somewhere far away. But when he has arrived and has started crying, eating and soiling his diapers, we experience him as very much of the earth, physical - often as a burden as well. Not all children are born into situations where they fit smoothly into the daily routine; families often have to make very earthly adjustments. What then is the nature of the child? The human being is connected both to the earth and to the cosmos as a whole. This is why his being can manifest its relationship to the heavens, to the spiritual world, as a characteristic. This same human being, however, also reveals his connectedness with the earthly through what he has received from the earth – his metabolism, his limbs, his ability to be active. On the basis of previous lives, each person brings with him the very individual relationships of his own being with the heavens and the earth, and these live in the varied forms and configurations of his etheric body.

Rudolf Steiner points out to teachers and school physicians that the head, with its spherical curvatures, is an image of the vault of the heavens. It is here that thinking can raise itself to the spirit. You may have been struck by children whose head had a particularly well-formed, sculpted appearance, which contrasted to some extent with the formation of their limbs. In his lectures *"Menschenerkenntnis und Unterrichtsgestaltung"*[9], Steiner speaks of the well-formed plasticity of the head that predominates in these children. Something from the past has been given to them in their etheric body which was able to work particularly on the development of the head system. By contrast, the rest of the body's forms have been developed to varying degrees. We seldom find a person, in whom as a child, the head and the rest of the body are equally well formed such that we have the impression of already encountering the individuality of the child as a unity. Some children have faces which we could call "typical" children's faces, where it is difficult to experience in the facial expression or in the formation of the head a finished form penetrated by the personality of the child. Conversely, there are children who have hands with soft, rounded fingers and a weak handshake. Here we ask ourselves whether the individual is already fully present or whether that is yet to come. Then suddenly, in the fifth grade, we get a real handshake from such a child and realize – now you've arrived!

But we can also get a handshake from a three-year-old which gives us a very different impression. During the examinations to determine school readiness, we sometimes come across children with dirt on their hands and under their nails. Their parents did wash their hands at home, but on the way to school all kinds of things happened. Here we see the connection to the earth, the relationship to it – I'd like to say the gift of interest at first sight in everything earthly. An airplane, a car, the earth in all its detail, and especially the colorful, noisy television set, so enormously stimulating to the senses – all this is fascinating. These children love the earth, love all its details; they are totally caught up in the world, and are endowed with a gift for facing earthly existence. I have one particular child in mind who was introduced to me as being hyperactive. It was not immediately clear that this was an "earthly" child – a sweet little up-turned nose, cute round eyes, small pouting lips, tousled hair – a lovely child's face. It wasn't until I saw the hands that I knew whom I had before me. He couldn't be recognized by his face or his head because he wasn't really "there" yet as a person. His actions were often correspondingly impetuous, "headless." He was not a heavenly gifted child, one who simply brings with him a rich thought-life, and qualities of inwardness and calmness. Conversely, there are children one can hardly get an alert, sensible answer out of in response to a question, but where one has the feeling that this is an enchanted prince or princess with inner treasures, but with clumsy limbs not yet endowed for earthly life – a cosmic child.

Rudolf Steiner's description of a child's nature is not an analysis of defects indicating what the child lacks or what is not in order. It is a description of the gifts, characteristics, and relationships within the child's own being. We have children who are gifted in dealing with the earth and their surroundings, who have a very practical orientation, but who are not quiet and thoughtful enough, and so are not really able to put their gift to good use. This is why they need our help. We also have heavenly gifted children who bear inner riches somewhere within themselves, riches which they cannot yet really express, really make fruitful for the earth, because they are not yet sufficiently gifted in dealing with the earthly. Since these aspects primarily involve the functioning of the etheric body and the way in which qualities of the child's being are brought from the past and expressed in the plasticity of his form, Steiner gives no specific medical indications here. Of course, in treating these children, the physician may still use an appropriate constitutional remedy depending on the needs of the child.

What treatment did Steiner recommend for earthly children? Independent of their temperament – they can be sanguine, choleric, melancholic, or phlegmatic – these children have a slight, melancholic overtone in their nature, a certain predisposition to be out of sorts. This can, of course, be the source of a host of so called behavioral problems. If someone is already out of sorts, and then something unpleasant happens to him, it's obviously easier to upset him than someone who has a cheerful disposition and can take more as a result. The melancholy overtone is the result of the fact that this gift for dealing with the earthly also means being burdened by the earth. The hereditary factors – what grows towards the child from the earth – predominate in these children when they incarnate. The heavenly is not strong enough to balance out the earthly, and so they tend to be overwhelmed and defined by what comes from the stream of heredity. The recommendation here in terms of therapy is that the children's needs be met at the point where they are. This is a kind of axiom which teachers and physicians should continually bear in mind, especially in child psychiatry, in psychology and in teaching children with special needs – *to meet the child's needs with the appropriate measures at the point where he is.* If a melancholic overtone is present, meet the child with a melody in a minor key and then guide him into a major key; the mood should only be changed after you have struck the child's own tone. As a rule, earthly children have a real gift for movement, so it is easy to meet them there. Inner movement is music, singing; outer movement is of course bodily movement. Thus, music and eurythmy are the key elements in therapy for earthly children. This can present a real challenge to the teachers, since these are precisely the children who throw themselves on the floor during eurythmy and don't want to participate. And yet it is eurythmy which has the greatest therapeutic value for them. To be able to help here requires the strongest identification on the part of the teacher, of course, for what is the crucial factor? These children have a gift for movement; they also tend to be musical, and often enjoy listening to music. (Rudolf Steiner has indicated, however, that this musical ability may be a latent one which first needs to be awakened.) What is it that these children have to learn through movement and music? They have to learn to be involved with their feelings in what they are doing, and they can only do this if the teacher himself feels a strong sense of identification with the task at hand. Let's look at an example of this in eurythmy.

If you have a class of these little rascals, you could begin with something which allows the children to move quite freely. Their needs are being met at the point where they are. Some of them will be really happy to be able to "let off steam", especially if the previous lesson was one where they had to sit still. From such free movement you can then turn to practicing a movement whereby, for example, you have the earthly children watch the rest of the class, with the task of observing where a movement or form is being well done. Then these children should be allowed to do the same thing in front of the rest of the class. The children's attention is called to the beauty of a movement. What happens through this? A feeling is aroused for their own gift. The children learn to develop a feeling for the particular gift that they have been given in their own nature – namely, the ability to move and to relate to all that is earthly. Through the frequent repetition of such experiences, the individuality of the child learns to recognize his gift more and more and thus to deal with it.

Thus, feelings should be awakened for music and movement, and for the elements of the beautiful, of light and dark, of tense and relaxed. Through this the child becomes aware of what his abilities and interests are. And these feelings, once awakened, in turn help to wake up the still sleeping head, for if we feel like learning something, thoughts come to us far more easily than if the feeling life is a gray area. It is the feelings which can awaken the sleeping thoughts, so that the heavens can also begin to speak to this child. Thus, it is crucial that the feeling life be awakened first, and that the child learn to have a sense of the gift of his own nature.

In the case of the "cosmic" child, who brings with him a certain mobility in his thinking, Steiner calls our attention to all the subjects which require observation and reflection: history, geography, natural history, literature, poetry. Here, too, the teacher is challenged to meet the child's needs at the point where he is. But now it is a question of presenting every thing to be observed in such a way that strong feelings are aroused *in* the child. After a parents' evening once I was told how one mother reported that her son, who was in the fifth grade, would come home every afternoon during the history block and tell her the latest news from Rome. But one day he came home silent from school, walked past the open kitchen door, threw his backpack in the corner, and only called out into the kitchen as he passed, "Mom, Caesar's dead!" With that he ran to his room and didn't reappear for quite a while. The teacher had aroused feelings which were still reverberating at home. This is ideal for cosmic children. In this process it is not so important to know precisely when Caesar lived, and whether all the details were exactly as the teacher described them in the feeling of the moment, what kind of clothing Caesar wore, how he smiled, how he walked. These things are certainly depicted somewhat differently in different schools – this is not the crucial part. What is crucial, however, are the elements of Caesar's being that live in the teacher and speak through him to the child, so that the child, in taking this into his feelings, develops a personal relationship to Caesar. The most important thing is first to create the basis in feeling and the motivation for the later acquisition of knowledge, which will come much more easily if it is founded on such a basis.

Both the earthly and the cosmic child are in special need of artistic treatment of the content of their lessons, for art is always concerned with feelings and experience. To characterize a true artist, we could take the example of an opera singer who, after singing a magnificent aria that was so enthusiastically received that bouquets of roses covered the stage at her feet, now sits dejected in a corner because she didn't sing one particular passage quite cleanly. Now she knows exactly how she will sing the role of Santa in "The Flying Dutchman" for the hundred and seventy-third time, and the next time she will again see how to improve still more. And we might think that when we've practiced a poem for four weeks, we can give a good recitation. This indicates that we are not yet on the path of true art, where perfection is never reached, but where one learns to set to work to arrive at the experience of beauty that can only be achieved through artistic practice. "The teacher needs to be an artist who can present the stories he tells the class in dramatic fashion. For example, in stirring words and with personal sympathy and interest he can describe granite – what it experiences in the evolution of the world, in the northern mountains, along the fjords, what weighs it down, why it exists. He needs to do this in such a way that sympathy, a connection to the feelings and to reality, and an interest in the world are engendered."[10] Such teaching brings the cosmic child down to earth, because he also senses and feels through the teacher's portrayal what he experiences in thought. In the process, interest in the world, in his surroundings, is awakened, and his own being is able to find a connection with the metabolic limb system – his tool on earth – via the feelings thus awakened. Conversely, the "headless" child with the gift for movement, the gift for dealing with the earth, comes into his own through experiencing the power and beauty of a form and the ability to master a movement, slowly finding the connection to the capacity for thought, the spiritual capacity, that he has brought with him from pre-earthly existence. The sum and substance of Steiner's indications for the treatment of earthly and cosmic children is the development of "feeling for the world." The world is not made up solely of light, color, and stories; it also consists of musical movement – of sounding earthiness. To strive to experience all this in the depth of one's feelings – that is the task. Some teachers may think to themselves, "I can't do something special for each child during the lesson – that's impossible." But if the teacher takes this key thought as his guideline – *to develop a feeling for the world* – and works on his gestures, his expression, and his intonation, because he knows that for the earthly children each timbre, each modulation of the voice signifies a feeling, then he is educating them in the middle sphere which mediates between heaven and earth, between thought and action – the sphere of the feelings. When, on the other hand, he makes manifest and embodies the feelings within what is being observed, he then pulls the cosmic children into the realm of feeling for the world. In both cases it is the strengthening of the middle system that is essential; thus, the former type of child can participate with no problem in exercises intended for the latter and vice versa.

In closing, a final word on eurythmy. This artistic form of teaching eurythmy is the most important means of self-education, the most important training ground, for the teacher himself. Today it is more and more difficult for children to really hold themselves erect, to be present in their gestures and in their movements. The attractions of the outer world make many children more earthly than they otherwise would be. When the teacher works especially hard on his posture, on his gestures, on the way his ego manifests itself through his body, this has a great effect on the children. It is important, however, that eurythmy be studied and practiced with the three aspects of each sound as they are represented on the eurythmy figures. We shouldn't learn only the form of the movement – how to form a "B", for example – but also the quality which is hinted at in the color of the veil, and which Rudolf Steiner terms feeling. So we should feel the quality of "B" – as in the blue cloak of Mary, for example. Even more importantly, we should become acquainted with the character of the sounds, which is indicated by brush-strokes in a third color on specific areas of the human figure or of the garment. That is where the will impulse for the form of the movement imbued with feeling manifests itself. If we enter into the three aspects – first, on the level of thought as to the meaning of the form and how it is made; second, on the level of feeling as to what it expresses and whether I truly live in it with my feelings; and third, in terms of its character – then through this threefold effort we are schooling our own threefold human nature such that our ego is then truly present within it.

People often ask whether the earthly aspect isn't always associated with the small-headed child and the cosmic with the large-headed child. Observation has confirmed that this is not the case. There are both large-headed and small-headed children with the earthly or the cosmic aspect. Having a large or a small head is the expression of the physical condition and of the interaction of the nerve/sense and the metabolic systems. Accordingly, treatment aims at supporting the physical functions, such as nutrition and sense perception. In the case of the earthly and the cosmic child, things are different, for here the child's being is addressed on the etheric level. Here everything depends on whether the child's "I" can individualize the head or the limbs in a suitable way. Only an etheric body which has been penetrated by the "I" is capable of completely adapting to what comes from heredity and of transforming it adequately. Where this does not take place to a sufficient extent, one of the two opposing spheres will predominate. In this case, therapy focuses primarily on the feeling life, because feelings can mediate between the etheric and astral bodies. The activity of the etheric body is stimulated by feelings. "To experience" means, in fact, to be able to immerse oneself – one's attention, i.e., activity of the "I" – in the etheric body through the medium of the feelings. The basic concepts on the nature of the human being which Steiner introduces into pedagogy are like letters that, read in connected form, for the first time make the nature of the child so clear that we also know how we can help through a particular treatment. However, we must first approach the individual child with each of these basic concepts and see for ourselves how they aid us in recognition in our observations. A consideration of the temperaments, for example, helps us to recognize different qualities in the child than a consideration of whether the child is large-headed or small-headed, earthly or cosmic.

3. The "fantasy-rich" and the "fantasy-poor" child

In "*Menschenerkenntnis und Unterrichtsgestaltung*" Rudolf Steiner follows his depiction of earthly and cosmic children by a description of fantasy-rich and fantasy-poor children. What is meant by these terms? "Fantasy-poor" children are those who have difficulty calling images and ideas to mind, whereas "fantasy-rich" children have the problem of not being able to let go of something once it has entered their consciousness. "Richness of fantasy" should be understood here in the broadest sense as the thought content of consciousness, also as recall and memory. In his book *Occult Science*[12] Steiner calls our attention to the fact that the human "I" lives in remembering and forgetting, just as the astral body lives in waking and sleeping – in the lighting up and extinguishing of consciousness. There are people who are tormented by the fact that they can't forget, and others who suffer because they can't remember. In both cases they are touched in the central core of their being, in their "I". Self-awareness depends to a great extent on whether experiences and memories can be consciously dealt with in such a way that they neither intrude nor are inaccessible. The child's emotional health for the remainder of his life depends on whether we succeed in creating the basis for a healthy experience of the "I" and self-awareness. This is the task we are faced with in the treatment of these two types of children.

Let's first ask ourselves where thoughts come from in the first place. Isn't the etheric body also the bearer of the thought life? "Knowing that the human being's ordinary powers of thought are refined formative and growth forces is of the greatest importance. Something spiritual reveals itself in the formation and growth of the human organism. For this spiritual element then appears during the course of life as the spiritual form of thinking."[13] This is the way Rudolf Steiner describes the origin of thought; it is this description we must understand and keep in the back of our minds when we approach the treatment of fantasy-rich and fantasy-poor children. Just think how in the course of three times seven years the human body grows from 50 centimeters to one meter eighty. The growth forces which bring this about, which differentiate the organs right down to the elaboration of the central nervous system, become available step-by-step for human thinking. Characteristic steps in the development of the power of thinking take place which correspond to the body's growth.

In the second half of life, a gradual process of involution begins. The forces of regeneration now become increasingly weaker. The nervous system loses some of its water; all the organs gradually begin to atrophy, and regeneration becomes more and more difficult. When the body can no longer be used, death occurs. In the case of the person who is growing old in healthy fashion, the development of his powers of thought is miraculously able to continue even though his body has entered the involution of old age. This is possible because the etheric body's powers of regeneration have now been freed up and are available to the activity of thinking as new, creative possibilities. They make possible the new qualities of thought in old age.

A person in the first half of life, who thinks with the growth forces that have been freed up, thinks in a more personal way, looking at things in relation to himself. He goes to school, then on to higher education, striving to find his place in the world: for him, his own plans are his central concern. The leitmotif here is "self-realization." This corresponds completely to the dynamics of the growth forces, which are focused on building up one's own body. This tendency is then still connected with thinking. In the second half of life, on the contrary – from approximately the age of 40 to 50 onwards, when we are in a position to really become conscious of the quality of these powers of regeneration – the disposition becomes increasingly apparent to think in a way that is no longer so strongly bound up with one's own body and own self-preservation .

It suddenly becomes easier to think of others in a more selfless way, to make the concerns of the world central, and to strive for "world-realization" rather than "self-realization." The body becomes heavier, burdened by this or that limitation; thinking becomes healthier, more selfless, more self-sacrificing. The wisdom of old age arises, for these new possibilities in thinking are the result of a renunciation of the regeneration and youthful freshness of one's own body.

It is important to prepare young people for a developmental process which will enable growth forces, as they are released from the body, to be released in such a way that they can be taken up by the "I", and remembering and forgetting can be dealt with in as conscious a manner as possible. This capacity cannot develop if we merely let ourselves be carried along by the daily flow of events. We have to regularly take a few minutes in which to think about what has happened, to practice gaining an overview of what we have experienced, then consciously forgetting it again. This is an exercise of the will.

Rudolf Steiner wants to draw our attention to the preparation for such possibilities when he describes fantasy-rich and fantasy-poor children. He indicates that in children who have an imbalance in either direction, we are dealing with a disturbance in the metamorphosis of the growth forces.

Let's turn once more to the process of the freeing up of the growth forces from the body. Initially, we have unconscious life forces bound up with the body; when these forces are freed up from the body, we then have unconscious thought life. This thought life – which is initially available for getting to know the world only at an unconscious level – is made conscious through the transmission of impressions either in school or by life in general. We all know much more at an unconscious level than we do consciously. It then depends on the strength of our will to learn whether we become clear on how much latent knowledge we have. On becoming acquainted with Anthroposophy, some people say that what they read in Steiner's works is as if spoken from their own heart. They had actually already thought that many things were so – they just hadn't known it clearly. Thoughts are there, but we are often not clearly enough aware of them.

This whole question is closely connected to health and illness. Do the forces which are freed up from the body and are to become conscious thought forces spring from a body that is ready, and are they really "in excess" – are they free to be taken up by the "I" in thinking – or have they been freed up prematurely from the body, so that the particular dynamics of the growth forces from the organs are still present, connected with the body? In this case they may suddenly manifest themselves as involuntary inner soul-content of a compulsive or hallucinatory nature.

Steiner states that mental illness comes about when a premature or untimely metamorphosis of growth forces takes place. A fantasy-rich child, one who cannot let go of ideas and images, is not mentally ill in the true sense of the word. However, he is in a situation in which more growth forces have been freed up than the "I" can freely cope with. His thoughts have retained their own dynamics which bind them up with the body and which cannot be sufficiently controlled by the "I". You can actually see this in the children. If the teacher has said something that is important to him, it may be taken in by a fantasy-rich child, who then continues to think about it till the end of the lesson and is thus no longer open to anything else during that time. In a manifestation such as this there is already a tendency to illness, for illness is, in the final analysis, always connected to the phenomenon whereby the integration of the many possible functions and activities of body and soul can no longer be managed by the "I". Instead of this integration, we have manifestations of isolation and fixation.

Or we have the opposite situation, where the teacher says something, and it goes in one ear and out the other. The "I" is powerless to hold the thoughts. We are often glad if the children have learned anything at all, so we don't pay much attention to whether their knowledge is of a fixed nature or whether it has been taken in in a living way. We must learn, however, to pay attention to this. At various stages in the lesson, are the children able to grasp things and then let them go? Or do they get stuck on certain things? A breathing process must be introduced here as well: taking in, holding, and releasing, so that one is free again for something new. In the case of the opposite extreme, a teacher may teach a whole main lesson, and what he presents does indeed reach the child, but lands deep in his body – his consciousness remains open and clear, without the slightest memory of what has gone on. In terms of the treatment indicated by Steiner, we again have the fundamental rule of therapy mentioned previously: Meet the children's need at the point where they are.

At what point is a fantasy-rich child, who has a tendency to have compulsive thoughts, who is unable to forget, to let go of ideas and images? When we adults have too many problems on our mind and don't know how to deal with them any more, or how to come up with some fresh ideas, we start running, moving, in the hope that through the movement and the fresh air, something will also start moving in our minds. Movement is also the remedy for the children we have described. The main point is to take subjects where this "getting in motion" can be consciously practiced – for example, in writing, where the teacher should make sure that the children don't get stuck on individual letters, but really write in a flowing hand.

Singing is also a "moving" subject. When you are afraid, you are also troubled by ideas and images you cannot shake off. In this situation, some people start singing, and then actually feel freer. Singing can be of real help to the fantasy-rich child, for his whole body is permeated with the vibrations of his own activity, allowing the images and ideas in his mind to flow freely again, without obstruction.

In the case of the fantasy-poor child, the teacher should concentrate all his love and attention on helping the child to learn to make use of his senses. For through this activity of the senses, his thought life can be firmed up into ideas and images which can be recalled. Having the children watch while someone is painting, or observe carefully or listen attentively – these are the means. Instrumental music, where precise listening is required, is also useful. Steiner encourages having the children sing and play instrumental music in the same lesson, so that making music oneself and listening to music can alternate. In this way, the children have a hygienic effect on each other, even though the fantasy-rich children are supposed to make music and the fantasy-poor to listen.

Eurythmy plays a special role in the treatment of these two types of children. This seems obvious in the case of fantasy-rich children who cannot let go of ideas and images. For them it is of tremendous help to be able to move with the whole body – in threefold walking, in skipping, and in running. The vowel sounds have a special effect on these children, for the vowels live in the bloodstream and form the organs. When the children practice them while doing threefold walking - in movement – they have a calming effect on the ideas and images arising too intrusively from the organism. They stimulate the growth forces to develop the organs, and anchor the forces there, so that they cannot so easily be freed up. In his curative eurythmy course[15], Steiner describes how the vowels stimulate "self-becoming", the consolidation of the development of forms. Fantasy-poor children, who have difficulty bringing ideas and images to consciousness, can also be helped through eurythmy. "They can benefit by practicing the consonant sounds, mostly while standing in place (i.e. only with the arms). Consonants help to dissolve fixed forms, to counteract deformations – they "de-self".

A eurythmy teacher once told me how she had put this indication of Steiner's into practice. The problem was with a high school student who, according to his mother, sat for hours on end every afternoon trying to do his homework, because he had such difficulty remembering what had been done in school. In good-natured fashion, this student was willing to participate, together with some fellow classmates, in a fairy-tale play that was being planned by a local group of eurythmists. The high-school students were used as a narrative group whose function was to demonstrate mostly consonants while standing in place. This involved practicing for an hour twice a week. As performance time neared, it also meant extra rehearsals after school, which the student in question took part in without a murmur. When the teacher asked him if this wasn't becoming too much for him, he said, "Oh no, after yesterday's rehearsal I was in top form and even finished my main lesson book." Here we can see that the consonants – especially if they are practiced while standing in place – have the effect of loosening up the spiritual forces somewhat from the metabolic/limb system. They bring the organs into a situation such that rigid forms are loosened up, allowing them to get accustomed to new possibilities of form and to change in a healthier direction, with the growth forces more easily freed up for thinking.

Thus, we see how self-awareness – so important for later life – lives between remembering and forgetting, and how the "I" is really called upon to stand at the threshold of consciousness as master of sleeping and waking, of remembering and forgetting. This picture of the "I" standing at the threshold and watching over its soul-life can accompany us in every eurythmy and music class, and in every lesson in which these elements are dealt with.

When we look at the large-headed or small-headed child's body size and form, we are dealing with the seal of the "I" in the physical body. For this reason, the treatment is also physical. In the case of the earthly and the cosmic child, we are not dealing with the aspect of form, but rather with the process of how this form originated. We get the impression that here the seal of the "I" lies more in the functioning of the etheric body, and so the therapy is also concerned with the functional aspect of the soul forces. Awakening strong feelings stimulates the growth forces to the full development of the forms by enabling the "I" – via the stimulated astral forces – to work its way into the etheric/physical constitution. With the fantasy-rich and fantasy-poor child, our attention is focused on the content of consciousness – how the "I" deals with what the astral body brings to consciousness, what lives in sleeping and waking, and what is present in the "I" as remembering and forgetting. Here, our therapeutic efforts are also aimed at helping the child to develop his middle system so that a true "indwelling", a feeling of his own humanity, is possible. Here we perceive the seal of the "I" in the astral body.

Time and again Steiner calls the attention of teachers to the task of learning how to breathe properly. In the descriptions of children which start from one of two polarities respectively, with therapy leading to a balance in the middle, we have a manifestation of the archetypal principle of respiration as the harmonization of two polarities: movement and rest. Quiet and concentration are the prerequisites for any meaningful sense/nerve activity. On the other hand, willingness to move is the prerequisite for any metabolic/limb activity. Learning to breathe properly means, in terms of the anthroposophical view of the human being, learning to live in our three-fold organism, learning to find the middle sphere.

In terms of the classroom, learning to breathe properly means receiving the subject of the lessons with interest, manipulating it, and making it one's own with joy. Of course, where there is love, there is always pain. Receiving something with interest or love does not necessarily mean that it is always easy; it may also involve an effort. But if the teacher is imbued with his subject matter and presents it in the way described in connection with the large headed and the small-headed child, then even a child with great learning difficulties can be touched by it in such a way that his sympathies for it are awakened, enabling him to enter into it step-by-step. Thus, dealing with the treatment of these opposite types of children can also be of assistance to the teacher in coming up with ideas for "learning to breathe properly" in his lessons.

BIBLIOGRAPHY AND NOTES

1. Private publication for teachers: **Rudolf Steiner, Faculty Meetings with the Teachers of the Free Waldorf School Stuttgart**, Faculty Meeting on February 6, 1923.
2. Rudolf Steiner, **Knowledge of Man and the Fom of the Lesson,** Bibliography No. 302, 1978, Lecture on June 13, 1921.
3. See note 1.
4. Ibid.
5. Ibid
6. Ibid.
7. Ibid.
8. Ibid.
9. Rudolf Steiner, **Knowledge of Man and the Form of the Lesson,** Bibliography No. 302, 1978, Lecture on June 13, 1921.
10. Ibid.
11. Ibid.
12. Rudolf Steiner, **An Outline of Occult Science,** Bibliography Nr. 23, 1977.
13. Rudolf Steiner/lta Wegmann, **The Foundation for an Extension of the Art of Healing,** Bibliography No. 27, 1991, Chapter 1.
14. Refer to Rudolf Steiner, **Development of Man, World Soul and World Spirit-Part One,** Bibliography, No. 205, 1987, Lectures on July 2 and 15, 1921.
15. Refer to Rudolf Steiner, **Curative Eurythmy,** Bibliography No 315, 1981

CHAPTER 3

DEVELOPMENT, DECAY, CHANGING OF TEETH, AND MALPOSITION OF TEETH AND JAWS

by

Translated by A. R. Meuss FIL, MTA

Phenomena, Problems, Potential for Treatment

"What does it mean in terms of our knowledge of the human being?" is a question I am asked over and over again in my position as dentist and orthodontist when it comes to the many and varied phenomena to be observed on individual teeth, the whole dentition, and the oral cavity. Before we can have a clear answer – and in most cases we are still far from getting it – we need to have thorough knowledge of the facts known to science and the connections between them, and we must also Ptheir ramifications. The same applies to the vast field of malposition affecting both teeth and jaws, which is the field of orthodontics. The whole requires detailed discussion if we are to avoid the danger of adding to the many misconceptions that exist already.

The dental specialist needs to consider the questions that are so often put in a Waldorf school context. The specialist cannot, of course, say he/she will be able to answer them all in terms of our knowledge of the human being, particularly with regard to the transformation of the bodily form through repeated incarnations. Much still remains to be discovered in this area.

DEVELOPMENTAL INSIGHTS
Discussions Between Doctors and Teachers

Below, the subject will be presented above all from the point of view of a dentist who has been working with Waldorf school children for many decades.

Dental Development

Let us first of all consider how a tooth develops. We distinguish between root and crown. This might make us think that – rather as in the case of a tree – there is a seed from which the crown grows upwards and the root downwards. In reality growth begins at the crown, in fact exactly at the border between dental enamel and dentin. The whole occurs in a hollow space within the dental follicle. Enamel develops from the inside towards the periphery. When the crown is fully developed, only a fine cuticle remains of enamel-producing cells which have ceased to produce enamel. This is why a hole in the enamel will never heal – the first non-healing aspect of teeth, which is also due to the fact that finished enamel is about 95% mineral substance, and therefore the hardest but also the deadest tissue in the whole organism. Its mechanical hardness thus means biological weakness.

Dentin on the other hand develops from the outside inwards, starting with the marginal cells of the pulp, which is the live tissue inside the tooth containing afferent and efferent vessels and nerve fibers. It is often just called the "nerve", to simplify matters. As long as the pulp is alive and there is room inside the tooth, additional dentin may form, for instance in response to an external stimulus. This, however, represents the limit of the tooth's self protective potential.

Diseases of Teeth

Caries is the major threat to teeth. To find out about it and about ways of preventing it, please read what I have written under the heading: *"Zahnverfall – kein unabwendbares Schicksal" (Dental Decay – Not an Inevitable Fate)* in **Weleda Nachrichten**. Reprints are available free of charge from Weleda. There I referred to the second non-healing aspect of teeth. People generally only discover they have cavities when a hole has developed, or they experience pain. At that point it is often too late to keep the tooth alive. It is therefore advisable to have regular check-ups at the dentist so that the condition may be detected early, possibly even by means of special X-rays (bite-wing X-rays) and treated.

Let me comment briefly on fillings and the materials generally used today. We have shown that wounds in teeth do not heal naturally. They, therefore, need to be closed up with foreign materials, which cannot be done without some compromise. Plastics can be colored to match teeth very well, but the pulp has to be protected from them by putting in an intermediary filling. They are also not sufficiently resistant to friction and dimensionally stable to be suitable as long-term fillings in the posterior areas. Amalgams, which are also molded, essentially consist of mercury and a silver and tin alloy. Like all metals they need to be isolated from the pulp, because they conduct heat. Their silvery gray color may also be undesirable. A very few individuals do not tolerate them because of their mercury content. The expenditure of time and money in preparing them is reasonable, which is why they are still practically irreplaceable. Inlays, that is, casts made with precious metals, require much time, material, and money, though in the long term they give the best results. One thing to be avoided is to have two metals in the oral cavity, especially if they are close together, as electric currents may develop between them. Unfortunately, there is no ideal material for fillings. Another problem is that they are all sensitive to moisture and have to be protected from saliva whilst working with them. People who feel their fillings are causing harm should try to have a test, using electro-acupuncture, for instance, which can also be a help in detecting hidden foci of infection.

In the first half of life, teeth are usually lost through caries, in later life through periodontopathy, i.e.,. diseases of the tissues investing and supporting the teeth. One hardly ever sees these in school-age children. The most would be inflammation of the gingival margins due to plaque, causing the gingiva to bleed at the slightest touch. If calcium salts have been deposited in plaque, and dental calculus results, a tooth brush alone will no longer suffice, and the teeth have to be cleaned "professionally" by a dentist.

The Change of Teeth

It is a feature of Rudolf Steiner's teaching on the nature of the human being that he repeatedly emphasized this stage of development. The most important references have been compiled by Matthiolius, who for many years was school doctor at the Stuttgart Uhlandshoehe Waldorf School, and published in 1970 under the title *Die Bedeutung des Zahnwechsels in der Entwicklung des Kindes (Significance of the Changing of the Teeth in Childhood Development)*. I had been examining children at this stage at the school and its nurseries from 1965 to 1976, and as a professional was asked to write a postscript to the collection, in which I considered in some detail what Rudolf Steiner meant by "the changing of the teeth." Meanwhile, Wolfgang Schad has written on the subject, and the second edition of the compilation includes the comments of its editor, Helmut von Kuegelgen. He has come to the same conclusion as I, which is that Rudolf Steiner meant the onset of the process, but he also refers to a statement made at a teacher's conference that cannot have been reported correctly; I have discussed this in detail in my postscript. Unfortunately, the postscript written for the second edition was not included, nor was Wolfgang Schad's preface, probably because our views diverge to some extent. What follows is a revised version of that postscript.

Rudolf Steiner generally uses the term "the changing of the teeth" as an expression of time, e g., "from birth to the changing of the teeth." Considering the context, and especially the age he mentions, he can only be referring to the beginning of a process that takes years, the eruption of the first permanent teeth. These are the lower central incisors, which generally erupt at age 6 or 7 when a phenomenon occurs in the lower jaw that is visible to all.

A statement made by Rudolf Steiner on May 11, 1919, in Stuttgart in the first of three lectures published as *A Social Basis for Primary and Secondary Education,* appears to contradict this: "For someone who knows the nature of the human being, it is evident that this education should not intervene in the system of human evolution for any growing child until about the time when the changing of the teeth is complete. That is as scientific a law as any other. If instead of going by rote, we were to take the nature of the human being as our guide, it would become the rule that children start school at the (completion) changing of the teeth."[1] (Words in parentheses not included in the quote given by Lindenberg.[2]) Steiner is therefore using "at completion of the changing of the teeth" in the same sense here as "the changing of the teeth". The only explanation I can think of is that to him, the process is already completed when it becomes visible. In *Boundaries of Natural Science* he also spoke of the "point of the changing of the teeth" on September 29, 1920, in Dornach,[3] comparing it to the melting and boiling points. It is probably right to take his statement that the first epoch of human life extends "to the sixth, seventh, eighth year, until the end of the changing of the teeth" [4] in the same sense.

This interpretation finally becomes the only possible one if we consider that in Oxford, Rudolf Steiner referred to the same period of time like this on August 16, 1922: "Inwardly the child is essentially quite a different creature up to about the 7th or 8th year, when the changing of the teeth begins, than later on in life, from the changing of the teeth until about the 14th, 15th year and puberty", and like this on August 19th: "If one has to educate the child during the time that follows the changing of the teeth, that is, after about the 7th year." [5]

Rudolf Steiner really means the visible phenomenon and not, as Wolfgang Schad suggests, the change from deciduous tooth to permanent enamel which is not immediately apparent, and could in fact only be seen on X-ray pictures, which were after all hardly feasible at the time. We know this from, among other things, the statement made in *The Spiritual-Scientific Aspect of Therapy:* "Now, however, we have an equally significant change, though this time more in an inward direction and not as immediately apparent as, the changing of the teeth, for instance, or learning to speak which anyone can observe; those two come to outward expression.[6]

According to statistics available from Rudolf Steiner's time, the first molars were the first permanent teeth to erupt. Today's latest statistics from Duesseldorf say that sequence occurs in only about half the children, and those from Munich that slightly more than half the children have the lower incisors erupting first. I suspect this indicates a change in the relationship between the different aspects of the human being, probably with the nerves and senses becoming more dominant. This kind of one-sided development is well known in the animal world: rodent incisors that never stop growing (emphasis on nerves and senses); pointed canines of predators (emphasis on rhythmic system); millstone-like molars of ruminants (emphasis on metabolism and limbs). Unfortunately, it has not yet been possible to substantiate this. What I have been able to establish is that the change in sequence has nothing to do with acceleration, i.e. children whose permanent teeth come very early may well have a first molar erupting first. We should really call it a fifth-year rather than sixth-year molar. On examination of school and pre-school children I did not always find it easy to establish if the first tooth to erupt had been a sixth-year molar or a replacement-incisor. It would really have been necessary to observe the developing dentition at intervals shorter than the 6 months that were possible. The earliest permanent teeth I have seen were in children aged $4^{1}/_{2}$, and they certainly were not ready for school. Those were always lower central incisors.

Professor Roland Bay in Basel has established that the sequence of eruptions changed between the period of the great migrations and late medieval times.[7] Before, the second molars would immediately follow the incisors, whereas today, they normally erupt only as twelfth-year teeth, when the changing of the teeth is complete. The old sequence can still be seen today, but only very rarely, though signs of it are still quite common. In some children, the second molars erupt when they still have one or more deciduous teeth. So far, no one has been able to explain this to me.

The terms "sixth-year" and "twelfth-year" molar indicate that on average the changing of the teeth occurs between those ages today. We are, therefore, dealing with a 6-year and not a 7-year period. There are children in whom the change begins at $4^{1}/_{2}$ and ends at about 9 years of age, so that it is highly premature and accelerated. Others start only at about 8 years of age and finish are about 14 or 16, so that the process is late and retarded.

With reference to Waldorf education, we have to ask the following questions. Is a child whose teeth begin to change at age $4^{1}/_{2}$ actually ready to start school? Is another who does not yet have a single permanent tooth at age 8 not ready? For a number of reasons the answer generally has to be in the negative. It is possible that in border-line cases the harmony of development is upset. In less extreme cases children who change early or late may be quite generally early or late developers. Parents frequently report that children who change early also had their deciduous teeth early, and vice versa. We would, of course, never make it a rule that children are ready for school on the basis of just a single developmental criterion such as the changing of the teeth.

When I examined teeth in 26 first-year classes at different Waldorf Schools (1 in Berlin, 1 in Braunschweig, 2 in Bremen, 4 at Engelberg School, 1 in Salzburg, 1 at Uhlandshöhe School, 2 at Wien-Mauer School, 1 in Würzburg), I would on average find one child per class that did not have a new tooth and, as one would expect, more often boys than girls. An experienced class teacher once referred to such a girl(!) as a "typical class 1 child" (6 years 8 months). The examination was mostly done in the first half of the school year and sometimes only in the second half, but never at the beginning of the year. An example of the range seen is Marko H. who was 7 years and 7 months old when first examined and had only deciduous teeth; he had not progressed any further when examined again at the age of 8. In the same class was Katharina who at 7 years and 2 months had all four sixth-year molars and all 8 incisors. At 9 years and 3 months this child showed the extremely rare feature of the upper canines erupting as the first "lateral teeth", with the lower canines erupting only six months later, statistically a highly improbable sequence. Surprisingly, the change was not complete until she was 11 years and 10 months old. That was also the time when the two lower molars appeared. Marko still had two lower deciduous teeth when I last saw him at age 13 years and 9 months.

To get a clearer picture we would need longitudinal as well as transverse studies, so that individual characteristics are not lost by calculating averages. It would be necessary to start at age $4^1/_2$ and continue at least until all second molars have erupted. All major medical, dental and educational development data would have to be collected at intervals of not more than 3 months, and evaluated on each occasion. I have been able to do this for 7 years at the Uhlandshoehe School and its nurseries at Uhlandshoehe and Stuttgart-Sillenbuch, though only at 6month intervals. In the end the problems that arose were such that I had to discontinue the long-term project, one reason being that the Medical Educational Research Department at the German Federation of Independent Waldorf Schools was closed down. In my experience it would be best to limit oneself to a single year at school. It is particularly difficult to obtain data for preschool children, as this requires the cooperation of parents and nursery staff. Ideally, parents would keep detailed records of major steps in development, height, weight, teething, and changing of teeth. Special attention would need to be given to the time interval between losing a deciduous tooth and eruption of its permanent replacement. The differences are enormous, yet to my knowledge nothing is known about it. Specimen record sheets like those in a *Guide to Child Health* [8] or those available from baby food companies are helpful.

The sequence in which teeth appear is easiest to establish and record. The sequences given in tables are based on averages and even so, do not always agree. For our knowledge of the human being, however, data which does not fit in with the statistics, the "runaways", can be extraordinarily important. Examples are unusual and asymmetrical features in space and time, such as first eruption upper, lower, left, right, or crosswise, and unusual sequence, especially if this is not in line with the statistical frequency. It may be possible to gain indications from this on potential connections between individual teeth and specific organs. It is important to realize thatt appallingly widespread caries seriously interferes with all development of dentition (and beyond). Fortunately it does not affect the eruption of deciduous teeth, but it will occasionally interfere with the eruption of permanent teeth and, above all, lateral teeth.

Investigations of this kind offer the additional benefit of early detection of caries. Yet, in my experience indifference to this is sometimes difficult to understand, even in Waldorf schools. It is possible that people do not consider it important to maintain deciduous dentition. Yet with a deciduous molar, loss of substance in the area of contact with a neighboring tooth makes the latter move up, which reduces the space available to the molar's successor, making it difficult, if not impossible, for it to erupt. If such a molar is lost prematurely, two consequences are possible that go in opposite directions. If destruction due to caries causes long-term suppuration, the bone above the successor may be dissolved, causing the permanent tooth to erupt years too early, with root development incomplete. If the deciduous tooth is removed as soon as pain arises because the pulp has become inflamed or decayed, a hard bone layer may develop in the gap and delay eruption of the successor for years, which increases the risk of losing the space. If a deciduous tooth is dead, with or without dental treatment, and remains in situ, it is often not properly resorbed and may cause problems of time or space for eruption of the successor. All it needs sometimes is small remnants of the root, though on the other hand these can also help to preserve space. The deciduous teeth are, therefore, important not only as childhood organs of mastication and speech, but also because they keep the space needed for the permanent teeth.

Anomalies

If the dental arches are already narrow in themselves, it may happen that the permanent lateral incisor is obstructed by the deciduous canine and causes it to be lost, using its space to find its own place in the arch. The permanent canine has then lost most, if not all, of its allotted space. In many of these cases there will later be insufficient space for the permanent teeth, and a balanced dental arch is usually obtained by removing premolars.

Occasionally problems may arise even when the first permanent teeth appear. The upper sixth-year molar may be sharply tilted forward, getting caught up under the deciduous molar anterior to it, undermining it and finally causing both it and the space for its successor to be lost. A less serious situation arises when a permanent incisor erupts behind, or less frequently in front of the deciduous incisor. If the latter is removed and there is sufficient space, the permanent tooth responds to pressure from tongue and lip and assumes its proper place. I have seen this abnormality with remarkable frequency in families where susceptibility to disorders of dental development is hereditary. I was able to prove that the above-mentioned undermining and resorption are part of this hereditary element.

The most common and serious form of hereditary disposition to abnormal development is hypodontia, which affects about 9% of girls and 8% of boys in our population. Hyperdontia is seen in only 2 or 3 per cent. On very rare occasions one also sees hyperdontia and hypodontia in one and the same mouth. Teeth missing from the permanent dentition are usually the upper lateral incisors and/or second premolars, rarely lower middle incisors and first molars, and very rarely canines and second molars. It is highly uncommon for many and different teeth to be missing, and in severe cases this may be linked with other constitutional problems. If there are too few or too many deciduous teeth, or else twin teeth, the total number of teeth in the permanent dentition is usually also incorrect. Hyperdontia is more common than hypodontia in deciduous dentition, both usually occurring in the frontal region. Wisdom teeth are not included in these calculations, and, as already mentioned, hypodontia is common in their case. It is not yet clearly established if this relates to the other anomalies described, but it is probable.

Inherited tendency to anomalies certainly also includes any type and degree of displacement, a condition seen especially with canines and second premolars which then remain partly in the jaw or erupt at an angle, often even in the wrong place. In the case of the upper lateral incisors, the hereditary tendency often also involves a precursor of absence, i.e. a reduction in size that may go so far that only pointed, conical peg teeth remain, which also tend to be late in developing. The upper lateral incisors tend to be the normal shape in this case, but are often rotated in position, as are the premolars. In their case, retarded development is common, another feature of inherited tendency to anomalies.

A particularly strange phenomenon in this context, the origins of which are only partly known, is infraposition, also known as infraocclusion or depression, of deciduous molars. In the upper jaw such a tooth has its occlusal surface above the occlusal plane, in the lower jaw below it, so that it does not reach its opposite, though originally it usually occluded with it. This kind of infraposition develops gradually and gets worse in time. It is an important anomaly, because anyone can observe it without special aids. If it is found, the child in question, its siblings, and cousins should be examined for hypodontia, hyperdontia, and displacement, which will, of course, require X-rays. It is possible to take pan-oral radiographs where the radiation dose is very low.

These, then, are inherited characteristics that may occur in different forms and degrees in both deciduous and permanent dentures but generally appear in the permanent denture only. Rudolf Steiner has frequently stated that deciduous teeth are inherited, but not the permanent teeth. He would sometimes make the statement less decisive, e.g. in the first lecture of *Waldorf Education for Adolescence*[9] where he said: "as we have our first teeth as a kind of inheritance from our parents", and before that, "the first teeth, which are more due to inheritance from our ancestors." Three days later, in *Man, Hieroglyph of the Universe*[10] he said: "Dentition, insofar as the deciduous teeth are concerned, is essentially due to heredity." On November 7, 1910, he put it as follows: "The first teeth are inherited; they come from the organisms of our ancestors and are their fruits, we might say; and only the second teeth develop according to our own physical laws."[11] A little later he said in the same lecture: "On the first occasion the teeth are inherited directly; on the second, the physical organism is inherited and this in turn produces the second teeth."

I have also found it impossible to reconcile the statements made in *Pastoral Medicine,*[12] for instance, with the above phenomena in order to explain these references. I know from the literature and from my own investigations that the inherited tendency to dentition anomalies comes to expression mainly in the permanent dentition. The inherited disposition to certain types of anomaly of the jaws is usually apparent at first dentition but only shows itself fully in the permanent teeth. The greatest German expert in the field, Professor Christian Schulze in Berlin, has the following to say on hereditary factors in lacteal and permanent dentition: "In fact their role is usually crucial."[13] When Rudolf Steiner gave his lectures, no one was able to ask him about these things, as they were still largely unknown. What is more, X-rays are usually needed to show the characteristics of the disposition, and in his day radiology was little used in dentistry.

Some of the things Rudolf Steiner has said about teeth, therefore, continue to puzzle us, especially his comments on the connection between caries and the fluoride or magnesium process.[14] Professor Oskar Roemer, who was an expert and heard the lectures himself, has published *Ueber die Zahnkaries oder Zahnlfaelde mit Beziehung auf die Ergebnisse der Geistesforschung Dr. Rudolf Steiners (Caries in Relation to Dr. Rudolf Steiner's Discoveries in Spiritual Science),* but this did not make the matter clearer to me. Two people who know Rudolf Steiner's works extremely well, the pediatrician Wilhelm zur Linden and Erwin Meyer-Steinbach,[15] have told me that in their opinion the passage has not been correctly recorded. In the final instance it is a matter of what Rudolf Steiner means by "dull" and "clever". Wolfgang Gueldenstern, dentist, suggests that clever means that the individual is not sufficiently earthy and lacks the necessary amount of dumbness to be an earthly human being (that is, a spiritual entity in a physical body). Dull means, in his view, that the individual relates too strongly to the earth and is too intellectual (materialistic). Rudolf Steiner did say: "We develop bad teeth so that we won't get too dull," because this would interfere with the "fluorine-absorbing . . . action of the teeth."[14] Dr. Otto Wolff, on the other hand, considers the phenomenology to be as follows: "It is definitely not the case that fluorine makes us dull in the sense of feeble-minded." For him, it is the "abstract thinker" who is dull, someone divorced from reality who may nevertheless be highly intelligent, like an absent-minded professor. Unfortunately, we can no longer ask Steiner what he really meant.

Another passage that I have always had my doubts about has since been clarified. It is in *Curative Education,* where a "not" has been omitted in the description of the first boy in paragraph 3 of the sixth lecture. The publishers have confirmed this. The correct version would be: "His mouth is slightly open, which is not due to dental development."[16] Considering that this was a course where Rudolf Steiner specially asked for "loving attention to detail even the smallest detail,"[16] one would hope, as a dentist, to find useful statements relating to teeth. But for that, of course, dentists would have had to be present.

In *Pastoral Medicine,*[12] Rudolf Steiner said on September 11, 1924, how important it is for people "that they do not have to get a third set of teeth." Wolfgang Schad made his first attempt at interpreting Rudolf Steiner's concept of "changing of the teeth" in connection with this. He quotes a passage not included in Matthiohius's collection: "until the sixth, seventh, eighth year, until the end of the changing of the teeth."[4] I have already given my own explanation of a similar statement by Rudolf Steiner. Schad also quotes another passage in his *Erziehung ist Kunst (Education is Skilled Work).*[17]

Rudolf Steiner says in this passage that the first three months after birth are really part of the embryonic period. If we add another year, so that the individual would be 15 months old by the usual way of reckoning, "he will be approximately at the stage where he gets his milk teeth." Before that he said, "we have to think in terms of the arithmetic mean, of course, but approximately that is how it is."[18] Schad's comment is that this is about the stage when the enamel crowns "for all the milk teeth are complete." In his illustration, however, the roots are already beginning to develop for all the teeth at age 1 year + 3 months, so that the times are different. However, the arithmetic mean for the period of eruption for all deciduous teeth was between 14.26 and 14.97 months according to 1934 German statistics. H. Ehlers gave 15.63 months as the mean in 1967.[19]

These figures agree very well with Rudolf Steiner's "mean." Thus, there is no reason to take up Wolfgang Schad's suggestion and concentrate instead on the stage of development reached by the enamel crowns of unerupted teeth both at first dentition and at the changing of the teeth, which can be radiologically assessed. He is, of course, right in saying that this is also the time when the first permanent teeth erupt and the enamel crowns of the permanent teeth are complete, except for the wisdom teeth, i.e. the time when the body has managed to create the hardest substance of all, since the enamel of deciduous teeth is somewhat softer. In Schad's opinion, this change in substance is more important to understanding the human being than the change in position, and Rudolf Steiner's references to the changing of the teeth must relate to this. Particularly in passages that seem more contradictory, Schad also assumes, therefore, that X-rays would be helpful if there is doubt about a child being ready for school, with no visible evidence as yet that the change is coming. I am unable to confirm this, particularly as development of the last of the crowns is often greatly delayed by a hereditary disposition to abnormal dental development. I hope to have clearly established that in spite of some passages that appear to be contradictory, Rudolf Steiner meant the beginning of the process when he spoke of the changing of the teeth. It would be helpful if this insight into his teaching and the literature could be unanimously and consistently presented. I do not know any physician or dentist who considers any other explanation either necessary or meaningful.

More than 10 years ago, Armin Johannes Husemann drew attention to an illustration by Stratz first published in 1909. This shows the changes in bodily form by representing total body height in relation to the height of the head at different ages. The figure has also been included in the second edition of Husemann's *Der musikalische Bau des Menschen,* with minor corrections reflecting the current state of knowledge.[20] Ten years ago I immediately realized that human beings are five times the height of the head when five teeth have developed on one side of the jaw, and six, seven or eight times the height of the head when as a rule six, seven or eight teeth are present. This remarkable numerical relationship may have further significance.

The deciduous teeth in each half-jaw are:

2 incisors
1 canine
2 molars

2	1	2	2	1	2	Upper jaw
2	1	2	2	1	2	Lower jaw

The permanent teeth in each half-jaw are:

2 incisors
1 canine
2 premolars
3 molars

3	2	1	2	2	1	2	3	Upper jaw
3	2	1	2	2	1	2	3	Lower jaw

Fig. 2 Regular dentition: lateral and medial view of teeth on the left (from Thiele)

I suspect that relationships exist between dental development and the macro- and microcephaly Rudolf Steiner spoke of. This cannot yet be proved. Perhaps it will be possible after all to evaluate the data from my investigations in this respect. They are lodged with the Medical Educational Research Department in Stuttgart.

On the other hand, I do not expect much to come of further research into the relationship between the shape of the front teeth and Kretschmer's constitutional types. Wolfgang Schad reported on this at the School Doctor's Conference held in Dornach in 1980. This refers to work done by the late K. Hoerauf, dentist.[21] His descriptions are supposed to help us find the right kind of teeth for edentate patients. A major denture producer based their designs for front teeth on those descriptions ("type-related system"). Doing the opposite, which Schad recommended, i.e., drawing conclusions from the shape of a child's teeth as to its future constitution, does not seem justifiable. To my knowledge, Hoerauf's findings have never been confirmed by follow-up. It is, of course, extraordinarily difficult to recognize the defined shapes of teeth in a mouth and fit them into a system. My friend and colleague, Hermann Lauffer and I once made an attempt to establish the effects of polar opposite formative principles, i.e., those due to the magnesium compared to the fluorine processes, in my large collection of plaster casts, but we did not succeed.

The relationship of dental and jaw positions to the essential nature of the human being was extensively investigated by Professor Wilhelm Balters (1893 -1973), who was the most important of my teachers. He also spoke about this to Waldorf school teachers. He would sometimes give amazing details after merely looking at denture casts from individuals who were not known to him personally. On the one hand, he was an extraordinarily careful observer, noting details that others failed to see, and on the other hand, he clearly had intuitive gifts. I will try and include aspects of this in the section on orthodontics but would warn readers not to draw the wrong conclusions. The words the doyen of modem orthodontics wrote beneath a picture of a well developed human denture still apply today: *secretum apertum* – "open secret."

DEVELOPMENTAL INSIGHTS
Discussions Between Doctors and Teachers

Orthodontics

This brings us to the field of orthodontics, the purpose of which is to correct malocclusion and malposition, or rather train the teeth to assume the right position. It is indeed miraculous how the individual teeth growing within the jaws combine to form well-balanced dental arches, providing all goes well. "Normal" does next mean ''according to statistical norms" today, for most dentures are irregular today. Major investigations have shown only about 8% to be normal. If we accept the "minor deviations" seen in about 22% of cases, this gives us about 30% of "proper" dentures. Occlusion and tooth positions are so poor in about 25-30% of children that orthodontic treatment is necessary or desirable. These figures were given by Rudolf Hotz, Professor of Orthodontics in Zurich, a sound man who unfortunately has died since, in the 5th edition of his textbook (1980). In practice the situation is as follows: Parents will almost always only take their children to see an orthodontist because they don't like the look of the teeth. They hardly ever notice, for example, that a tooth may be missing laterally or that the teeth do not occlude properly. The dentist must first of all establish the present situation (diagnosis), the history, and the prospects with treatment given now or later (prognosis). The first impression a child makes, a few words spoken, a look in the mouth, will tell much to the expert. He also needs to know things that are not immediately apparent, especially if the unerupted teeth are all present and pointing in the right direction for successful eruption. This is best established by taking a panoramic X-ray, a tomogram with minimal radiation exposure. Evaluation of about 50,000 such X-rays at the big school dentistry clinic in Zurich, where this picture is taken of every boy and girl in the third grade, showed that on average, two teeth are not preformed in about 8 % of boys and 9% of girls. This does not include the wisdom teeth, which are frequently missing, as their buds are often not visible at this age. By the way, it is quite unknown why the gender difference exists. (See earlier details of hereditary dental development disorders). Recent investigations by Karl Ulrich, orthodontist in Stendal, have shown that some harmless abnormalities in the skin (ectoderm, with the dental enamel also deriving from this) remarkably often go hand in hand with hereditary dental development disorders. Skin abnormalities of this kind include freckles and irregular eyebrows - joined up, sparse, or shortened eyebrows (usually the lateral third missing).

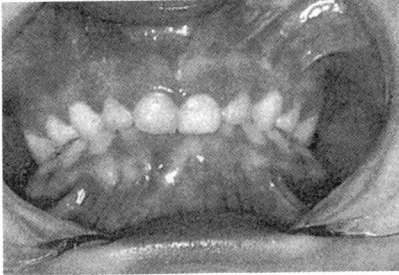

Fig. 3a, 5 years, 5 months. *Overbite with deciduous teeth (close, but balanced)*

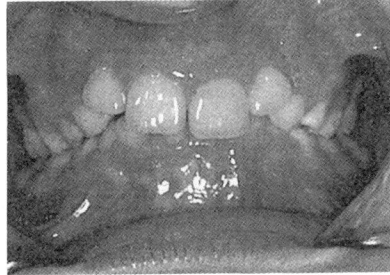

Fig.3b, 9 years, 1 month. *Overbite becoming part of permanent denti tion.. No lateral development, therefore narrow dentition.*

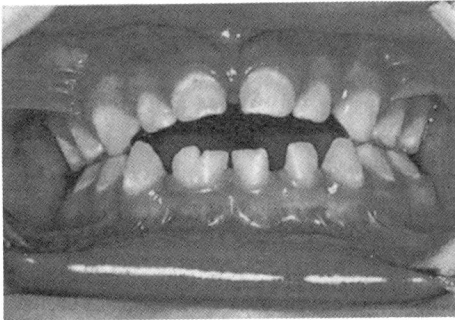

Fig. 4a, 3 years, 5 months.
Deciduous teeth with bite open due to sucking (in addition: the two right lower incisors have grown together).

Anomalies of the jaws may also be hereditary. The most common of these is prognathism, with the lower front teeth projecting well in front of the upper teeth, even in the case of the deciduous teeth. This anomaly may be marked in some, and only minor in other members of the same family. Major regional differences have also been noted, with prognathism about three times as common in Stuttgart as in Hamburg. The condition occurs even in the best families! Well-known individuals with prognathism were Dante, Richard Wagner, Stefan George, and above all the Hapsburg family, where prognathism evidently occurred through many generations.

Overbite, a condition where the upper (middle) incisors extend well below the incisal ridges of the lower incisors, is also hereditary. It causes shortening of the lower face, with distinct dimples in the chin, as in the case of Abraham Lincoln, for instance, and the German actor Hans Albers. Experience has shown that the condition, if severe, cannot be entirely corrected, and at most made more balanced. It may be a comfort to those affected to know that Professor Balters spoke of the "intelligent overbiter" (the upper part, i.e., the upper jaw, being specially developed).

The most important aspect of orthodontic diagnosis is to make an accurate assessment of the present situation. This is done by taking plaster casts of the denture, which can then be observed and measured at leisure, without being impeded by lips, cheeks, tongue, and poor light. Putting the upper and lower casts together, it is even possible to look into the denture from behind, and again and again I am surprised to discover things I had not realized when looking into the patient's mouth.

It was a very sad experience some time ago, when numerous statements relating to the study of man made by our Dutch colleague Hooghoudt proved untenable, for they were entirely based on inspection of the mouth. More accurate information has since become available from casts and X-rays. It goes without saying that apart from analyzing the model, it is important to examine the mouth and its functions in detail, one main reason being that we must diagnose existing caries and institute treatment where indicated, and inspect the gingiva and the quality of dental and oral care.

If the relation of the dentition to the facial skull is abnormal, anterior and lateral photographs must be taken to investigate this. Distant lateral X-rays provide further information. To come as close as possible to parallel projection, the distance should be not less than 150 cm. These X-rays also permit some degree of prediction as to the growth direction of the face. It is important to know if there will be any appreciable further growth, especially in girls who have reached puberty, and X-rays taken by hand will provide fairly reliable information. The use of apparatus to stimulate and guide growth is only indicated while growth is still in progress, i.e., when the mandible and temporomandibular joint are still developing. Intervention needs to be early, and we have to work with the growth process.

A key factor with malocclusion and malposition, and therefore also the outcome of orthodontic treatment, is whether closure of the mouth is normal and natural, or if the patient breathes through the mouth, which tends to be open, and possibly even with the incisors positioned on the lip. A balanced bite is only possible if closure of the mouth is normal and natural, for otherwise pressures are not normal in the mouth. I always explain to the patient: The nose is meant for breathing, the mouth only in emergencies. In the nose, and only in the nose, we smell the air, and the fine hairs inside the nose clean it (the dust ends up in your handkerchief); the air is also warmed up in the nose, and actually given life because of the form of the air passages. It is easy to make someone realize how cold air actually is when inhaled through the mouth, if we ask them to pant with the mouth open like a dog. You can easily catch a cold if you keep your mouth open, and then, with the nose blocked, need to keep the mouth open even more in order to breathe. How do we break this viscous circle? I first of all show the children that they do not look nice, but rather stupid if they leave the mouth open. We used to call this "gaping." You hardly ever see adults walk around with their mouths open. Almost all of them manage to close them. But the sooner you learn, the easier it will be. I then often show them a series of denture models taken from a patient whose dreadfully displaced upper teeth and regressed lower jaw could initially be corrected, but then deteriorated again, because she always had her mouth open. In the end the position of the teeth was worse than it had been to begin with.

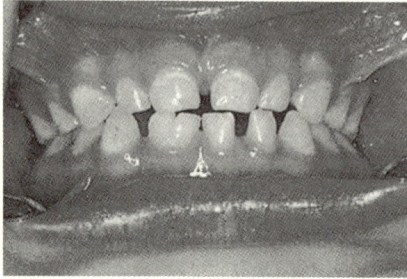

Fig. 4b, 4 years, 1 month
Notice the spaces between the teeth.

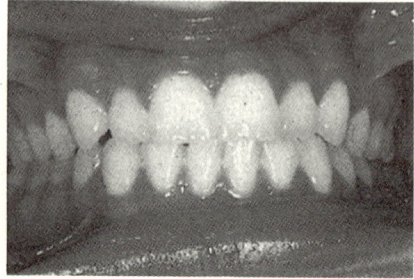

Fig. 4c, 14 years
Open bite has corrected itself once permanent denture has been established.

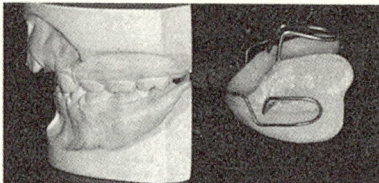

Fig. 5a, 6 years, 10 months
Malpositions due to sucking (upper jaw narrow and acuminate, i.e. incisors projecting: posterocclusion of lower jaw by width of a premolar). "Bionator" on right.

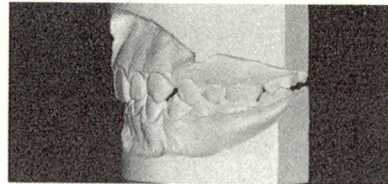

Fig. 5b, 11 years, 10 months
Result of orthodontic treatment with a single "bionator" after 3 years and 10 months.

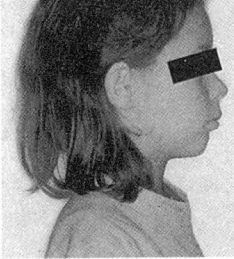

Fig. 6a, 8 years, 1 month
Patient at onset of treatment.

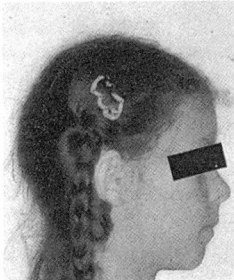

Fig. 6b, 8 years, 9 months
*Patient after 7 $^1/_2$ months course
of treatment with a single
function regulator.*

It needs practice and patience to change nasal breathing. I know of only one activity where the mouth is naturally kept closed because of the concentration required: balancing. It does not need to be a beam; a tree trunk or curbstone will do just as well. Otherwise we have to make a conscious effort. I tell the children to watch all the time if their mouth is closed. If it is not, they must close it immediately. Memory is aided by pictures put up in rooms where they spend a lot of their time, of a nicely closed mouth, for instance, or an open one looking far from one that is crossed out, like the cigarette in a non-smoking sign. Signals may also be put on the covers of exercise or textbooks, blotting paper or even a finger nail: "C" for "close your mouth," or a red "L" for "lips closed!" I also ask friends and family to give signals if the mouth is left open inadvertently: making the "V" sign for instance, and then bringing the fingers together, pointing to the mouth, etc. This can be done very discreetly, so that others won't notice.

A simple exercise is to take a sip of water and keep it in the mouth for as long as possible without swallowing it or spitting it out. One can also get the children to hold something in their lips during some quiet occupation such as a wooden spatula like those used by ENT specialists. You could also use a button, or a clean stone – using bigger and heavier ones as time goes on. Anything where breath is used can be helpful. e.g., playing a wind instrument, blowing out candles, or making soap bubbles. Other methods are to breathe in slowly for as long as possible, the outward sign of this a leaf or a piece of gauze held across the nostrils by the negative pressure, or doing the opposite, which is to take a deep breath to fill chest and abdomen and then exhale as slowly as possible, external evidence being provided by talking, counting, singing, whistling or, more tolerable for anyone else who happens to be around, humming. If the nasal passages are not clear, an ENT specialist has to be consulted who will remove any greatly enlarged pharyngeal tonsil (preferably not the visible palatine tonsils), also known as adenoids.

A common contributory cause to open mouths is a dentition so badly out of shape due to sucking that the lips cannot be closed. Children will suck not only their fingers and a pacifier, but also a corner of their blanket or a piece of clothing. The upper front teeth are generally pushed forward, and the whole mandible is pushed back in the process, resulting in the typical open bite. The sucking gesture is one of definite introversion, withdrawing into one's shell before an unkind world; it may also be regression, wanting to go back to the protection enjoyed in early infancy, for instance, when a younger brother or sister suddenly appeared and attracted most of the family's love and attention.

What can be done to overcome these and other undesirable habits (chewing nails, for instance)? We must help the child to take the necessary developmental steps, e.g., not to put their hands into their mouths but use them in the outside world. There is no point in shouting at them, but ignoring the habit may sometimes help. A doctor's wife once told me she suddenly realized she had stopped sucking when she left her parent's home at the age of 20. To have such a habit drop away like a ripe fruit is, of course, the ideal, except that in her case it was much too late. It is generally easier to wean children off their pacifier than their fingers, by "losing" it, for instance. If one has to give them a pacifier, it is best to use a specially shaped one that will at least prevent some of the damage.

If a child has only been sucking for a short period, is able to close his mouth easily, and there is sufficient room for all the teeth, the defect due to sucking may correct itself. If sucking continues for such a long time that the permanent dentition is also affected, orthodontic intervention is usually required. In simple cases, it is often enough to use a ready-made trial plate; difficult cases require an individually fitted appliance. An activator is most commonly used, or the greatly reduced form called a "bionator." It may be said to be a sucking body that acts in reverse. It lies loosely in the mouth, has a guide surface for the lower teeth and a wire brace above the projecting upper front teeth. Every time the mouth is closed, e.g. swallowing saliva, the mandible moves forward, wants to go back again and takes the upper teeth back.

This is known as a reciprocal action (going back, *re-* and forward, *pro-*, and is particularly effective. A seriously malformed denture has, of course, responded particularly well to the original sucking bodies and will, therefore, also respond well to the appliance which acts the other way round. The use of appliances lying loose in the mouth is the functional method. It does not impose force but offers an opportunity to change position, which influences the jaws, teeth, and joints via the muscles. Apart from the above mentioned classic activator and the smaller "bionator", a number of similar appliances are available.

In my experience, the "function regulators" designed by Professor Fraenkl in Zwickau, Germany, are the best appliances for effecting functional changes. With distoclusion (always referring to the movable mandible; with antero- or mesioclusion, or prognathism, structural reversal), the mandible is made to move in an anterior direction to avoid a wire arch or tongue shield. These appliances are attached to cheek shields positioned in the atrium or "cheek pouches". Small additional pads positioned behind the lower lip help to block external pressure from the muscles of the cheeks and lower lip. Internal pressure from the tongue muscles is thus given dominance and can help to widen and round the narrow dental arch. The special advantage of the regulator is that there are no impediments inside the mouth apart from a few wires and perhaps a tongue shield. Speech is possible, and it is important to speak while wearing it, speech being the primary oral function. To achieve a different position for the jaws and teeth it is necessary to wear the regulator while the mouth is functioning, i.e., speaking. We do most of our talking during the day and little at night, and this means that the regulator is intended mainly for daytime use. Once one has gotten used to it, it is helpful to wear it at night as well. The treatment can be supported by doing lip exercises, asking the patient to pull the upper lip down and bite it. This is particularly effective with the head tilted back. Many children do, however, find this exercise difficult.

It would be nice if such exercises were all that is required to correct a distoclusion, but experience has proved otherwise. The same applies to eurythmy therapy. I have found that years of experimentation with this meant orthodontic treatment was not initiated at the right time, causing more space to be lost in the dentition as the gaps left by the prematurely lost deciduous teeth were not kept open. Eurythmy therapy will, however, be useful as a baseline treatment. Even if money is no object, it is important to remember that any additional treatment may demand too much of a child's time and energy causing them to lose interest and not comply where it is most important and not to wear the appliance usually for years. I usually tell them that in orthodontics the saying is, "The end is always the hardest" because a person's patience tends to wear thin.

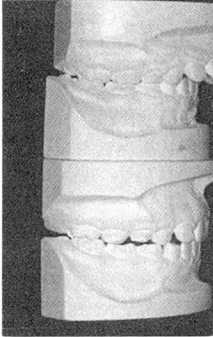

Fig. 6c,d,e

1. Dentition with mandibular retrognathism and premolar widening resulting from chronic sucking.

2. Following a 7 $^1/_2$ course of treatment with a single function regulator.

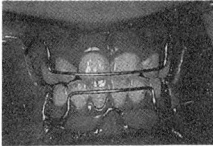

3. Function regulator in place in mouth.

Fig. 7a, 8 years, 9 months.
Guided eruption involving extraction, after Holz. No permanent teeth removed from lower jaw, therefore but 4 + 4 above.

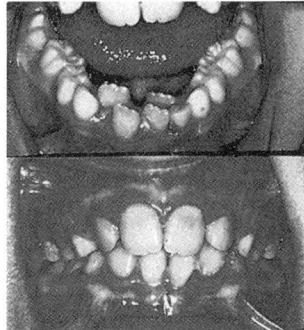

Fig. 7b, 10 years, 3 month
Lower front teeth well positioned without further treatment (only canines removed).

If there is lack of space, no matter where and in which direction, there are essentially two possible solutions: either we manage to stimulate growth and enable the dental arches to develop fully or stretch and expand them so that room is found for all the teeth, or we must redistribute the available space, i.e. dispense with some teeth. The latter is unpopular with orthodontists and their patients and is a method chosen only after careful investigation and thought. It is good to remember Wilhelm Balters' words, saying that with a vault it does not matter if it consists of 12 or 14 stones but only that it is a good arch.

I can understand people's concern over the probable relationship of certain teeth to specific organs, but so far I have seen no evidence of this. We are dealing with extremely hard facts in the case of teeth. They cannot be compressed to fit a gap that is too narrow. Sadly, the need to remove teeth is often people's own fault, having failed to save a full dentition of deciduous teeth (with fillings). The size of teeth and that of the jaws are inherited separately, and conditions may be so unbalanced that it is impossible to accommodate all the teeth. The opposite may also be the case: large arches and small teeth, resulting in gaps.

I have never actually regretted having removed teeth, but I have often been sorry I did not make my demand more urgent. The premolars are usually removed first, which provides space for the front and lateral teeth. In the upper jaw the premolars tend to have two roots and be among the most susceptible to disease. One often sees crowns, gaps, and bridges in that area. The lower premolars are more resistant. Sometimes the second lower premolars are also removed. Unfortunately, their posterior neighbors, the first molars (six-year molars), are sometimes so bad that they cannot be kept alive in the long run. There is no good orthodontic reason for their extraction, which can only be an emergency measure to deal with caries and usually has serious consequences, as neighboring teeth are apt to tilt. As one of the most renowned orthodontists has said, planned removal of teeth requires the greatest expertise in the field.

A word on the removal of wisdom tooth buds (germectomy), which is being done more and more frequently. It has to be advised if the X-ray shows that the wisdom teeth are very badly positioned and cannot possibly emerge and find a space. This includes situations where they are tilted forward at an angle, with the teeth generally packed tightly together, so that they will cause even more serious overlapping once they emerge. Removal is easiest at the time when the roots are just beginning to develop. Once they are fully developed and curved like a postillion's horn, which is common with wisdom teeth, extraction is difficult and time-consuming even for an experienced orthodontist, and the wound heals less easily. Unfortunately, full dentures rarely include well-positioned wisdom teeth. One would obviously only extract these after careful investigation and assessment of their potential value, remembering the words of the above-quoted orthodontist: "Where would I be in my old age without my wisdom teeth" (as bridge piers)? Teeth that have failed to erupt should not be left in situ, however. Their enamel is part of the skin organ and, therefore, belongs on the outside. Teeth retained in the jaw can act as foci of pathologic disorder. Nature actually shows us that fewer teeth can be adequate, for premolars and wisdom teeth are quite often missing.

Removal of the first premolars sometimes involves long-term planning, starting with the removal of all deciduous canines. The incisors will then usually erupt spontaneously and be well positioned. Later the first deciduous molars are removed and then their successors. The process is known as extraction-guided eruption of permanent dentures. I felt it was important to know that Rudolf Holz, the main protagonist of the method, also used it with two of his three children.

Another equally acceptable reason for extractions of this type is that in earlier times, when the food was coarser, containing particles of ground millstone, for instance, not only the occlusal surfaces of the teeth were worn down, but also contact areas between teeth, so that a row of teeth would be reduced by about the width of one tooth and could be accommodated more easily in a jaw that had grown smaller. The extractions are done to make up for the absence of this kind of wear and tear.

To return to prognathism. In both deciduous and permanent dentures it is normal for the upper teeth to lie anterior to and partly enclose the lower teeth. If the opposite is the case, we speak of prognathism. It is important to diagnose this early, as it will become more serious unless treated. Treatment should start not later than the changing of the incisors, taking care that the permanent incisors are in the correct position. It is, however, better to start at nursery school age. A regulator of reverse construction functioning, like the one used for teeth displaced by sucking, is often fitted. Marked prognathism can be very disfiguring and is the most frequent indication for orthodontic interventions. The surgical procedure is to split the ascending rami of the mandible longitudinally to change their relative positions. In most cases, pre-operative and postoperative orthodontic treatment is also needed to adjust the dental arches to each other. The procedure is difficult, protracted, and expensive, but it harmonizes the facial features as well as improves mastication. Prognathism also presents extremely difficult problems at the later stage when the upper front teeth need to be replaced, which is another reason for early prevention. Early treatment gives lasting results, except in a few cases where a new growth phase of the lower jaw occurs in puberty – something which cannot be predicted. I have treated a girl with severe prognathism whose front teeth were reversed, and in her case there was no recurrence. Her brother had only a mild degree of prognathism that appeared to have been overcome by the age of twelve. During puberty his lower jaw grew inexorably forward, so that surgical intervention became necessary at school-leaving age, fortunately with a positive outcome.

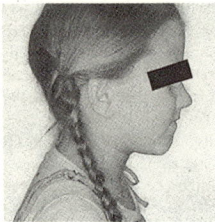

Fig. 8a,
8 years, 2 months
Before treatment.

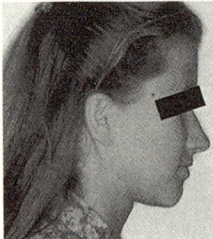

Fig. 8b,
15 years, 6 months
After treatment

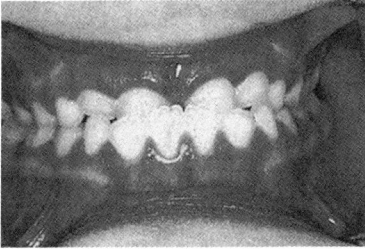

Fig. 8c,
8 years, 2 months
Hereditary prognathism
(frontal cross bite).

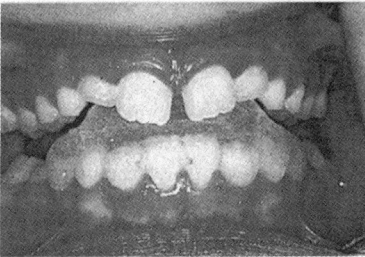

Fig. 8d,
Starting treatment with
"angled" glide plane 1/1
insertion (diastema).

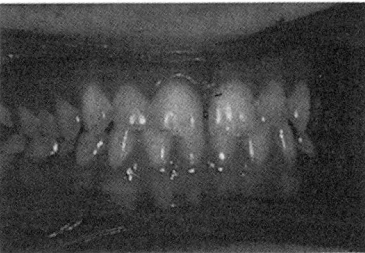

Fig. 8e,
Outcome after 46 months
of treatment using
appliance, with 17 months
interval between.

Crossbite is a form of malocclusion where the mandibular teeth are unilaterally or bilaterally outside the maxillary teeth, one arch crossing the other. It needs to be treated as early as possible, especially if unilateral and, therefore, asymmetric, which may also be due to a displacement of the whole mandible. Treatment will prevent the malocclusion from becoming fixed, and with the deciduous teeth this is relatively easy to achieve. Individual teeth hooked over the other arch on the inside or outside should also be corrected as early as possible. Working in collaboration with the Michaelshof Curative Education Institution, under the medical supervision of Dr. Hoefle, we found that overcoming the problem of caught-up teeth may also help to resolve an inner situation in which a young person is caught up. It is also desirable to have the centers of the jaws properly aligned, again also in relation to curative education. All these treatments should be given as early as possible, as they are much easier then.

Crowding of frontal teeth generally means waiting until all incisors have erupted, so that their exact size and, therefore, need for space can be established. On the other hand, it has proved effective to start earlier in cases where it is perfectly obvious that there will be problems. The "interceptive" method, using an appliance, will generally be indicated, but it needs to be interrupted as soon as possible in order not to overstrain the child's patience. Unfortunately, the appliance can only be removed if there is no danger of losing space in the lateral arch due to caries or even early loss of deciduous teeth, again demonstrating the importance of deciduous dentures that are healthy or at least well preserved by means of fillings.

If the crowding is moderate, it will always be best to avoid extractions if possible; if it is severe, it is definitely advisable to develop the dental arches as far as possible because it is not always sufficient to remove just one tooth from each half-jaw. Unfortunately, X-rays do not provide accurate information on the size of teeth lying within the jaw, and this is why orthodontists prefer to wait at least until the first lateral tooth has erupted before deciding for or against extraction.

It is also important to consider the background to crowding, something of which Wilhelm Balters has frequently spoken. The German term for it, *Enge* (closing in of walls), relates to anxiety and angina, which are typical signs of our times. People are constricted and coerced in so many ways that local measures will hardly suffice, and crowding will often develop where none has been before. It is comforting to know that crowding of the lower front teeth, which, of course, are particularly caries-resistant and tend to be retained longest, means no particular danger of caries or periodontopathy. Compared to the crowding of upper teeth, that of lower teeth is also less of an esthetic problem. It does, of course, have a distinct hereditary element.

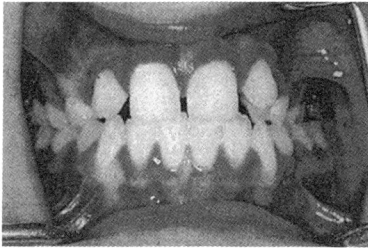

Fig. 9a, 9 years, 2 months.
Left lateral crossbite with slight
midline shift. Gaps between
incisors.

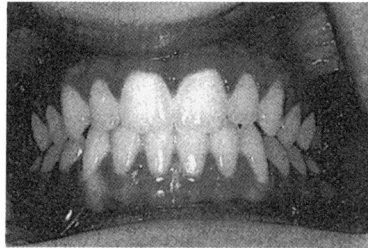

Fig. 9b, 11 years, 10 months.
After a year of orthodontic
treatment. Balanced position
of teeth.

Some functional orthodontic appliances have already been discussed with reference to malpositioning due to sucking. Others will be discussed below, starting with some that are removable. Active plates are attached to the teeth with wire clips. The active components are either sprung wires or devices with built-in male screw elements. This makes it possible to apply pressure or traction to specific teeth or parts of the dental arch, single or groups of teeth, and the relevant maxillary processes supporting them may be slowly moved as the bone is restructured. Functional appliances are thus intended to change form by changing function; the opposite is the case with active appliances. We change the form and hope function will also change. In either case, changes in form need time to stabilize. This is achieved by means of retention, using passive appliances to support the changes achieved. This does, of course, predispose closure of the mouth, as mentioned earlier.

Active plates will achieve quite remarkable changes, especially in the upper dental arch. The lower arch is less responsive but fortunately requires only minor correction as a rule. The lower canines in particular are known to resist change once erupted. If the intention is to widen this area, functional stimuli need to be set very early and for a long period, preferably using a functional regulator. Appliances which are half-way between active and functional are also available, e.g. the double propulsion plate with guide wires that engage in grooves and thus take the mandible forward each time the mouth is closed. The Crozat appliance is half-way between the fixed wire appliances, which will be discussed below, and active plates. It consists of a wire frame attached to the teeth with flexible wires welded onto it and acts only via the teeth and not like the plates, via the alveolar ridges as well. It takes up little room in the mouth, which means that it presents the same problems with mutual support of movements as the fixed wire appliances.

Other repositioning maneuvers are difficult if not impossible with removable appliances. This applies particularly to parallel repositioning of teeth within an arch, i.e. without tilting or rotation, extensive changes in the angle of the axis, e.g. moving the crown inwards and the root outwards (torque). Fixed appliances are used for this purpose. These are also known as multiband appliances, because the devices for holding the brackets were originally applied to the teeth with bands. Today the brackets are attached directly to the teeth in visible areas, using a caustic fusion process. This is less obvious than the metal bands, especially if plastic or ceramic brackets are used.

The action is based on the thin, highly elastic, light wires, which sometimes are also angular (edgewise arch) or twist and flex. They are fitted into the brackets and usually terminate in a small tubule on bands attached to molars. Spiral springs and elastic (rubber) rings are further energy sources in this type of precision engineering, which will also deal with many of the problems that can be solved by using removable appliances.

Orthodontists are increasingly giving preference to these "fixed" methods, mainly because they can be sure that the appliance will be in the mouth . This is not to say, however, that fixed appliances require less compliance than removable ones. Patients have to be highly conscientious with dental care, cleaning for about 3 minutes after every meal because the brackets, wires, and ligatures will retain food residues which may cause disastrous plaque and caries. Prevention consists in impregnating the teeth concerned with fluoride, a local protection against caries that has proven effective in this situation. As a short-term measure against caries, which after all is incurable and in the long run generally worsens, fluoride impregnation is certainly acceptable, even if its general use is regarded with skepticism. The complex orthodontic appliances affixed to the teeth make not only dental care but also eating, and especially mastication, more difficult. As a result the risk of caries is greatly increased.

To achieve certain goals it will frequently be necessary to support the appliance with headgear. This makes it possible to move upper lateral teeth posteriorly. For the opposite situation a "face mask" supported by the chin is available. A head-chin cap with elastic rubber to pull back the mandible is much simpler. It is mainly used for the early treatment of prognathism.

A very simple aid is the angled glide plane to align one or several wrongly interlocking teeth. It is usually cemented onto the lower front teeth for a period.

There are, of course, endless variations of the above appliances. What matters is that one knows "how to play the instrument", that is, the potential and limits of the different methods, which generally presupposes training as an orthodontist. It has no doubt become obvious that my personal preference is for the functional method, using a regulator. This does not use force but offers a possibility of change and addresses one of the main causes, which is wrong positioning and tensioning of muscles in the mouth (tongue) and around the mouth (above all lip, cheek, and masticatory muscles).

Having described malpositioning and methods for its treatment, let us consider the key question of the issue: when is orthodontic treatment indicated? Daily experience and a look in the mirror show that we shall manage even if our teeth are not the most beautiful. Still the desire for balance, beauty, and efficient function of teeth is perfectly natural and also common. On one hand, we hear again and again from parents and caregivers that when they were young, the war, the post-war period, or simply lack of money - insurance companies were not paying what they do today - prevented orthodontic treatment, and they are surprised that so many children are fitted with braces today, and ask if this is really necessary. News has got around that orthodontic treatment also has its problems.

Again, younger parents and others of their generation will often say that they had orthodontic treatment, but "it has all gone back to what it was before." They will often confess that they only wore their braces at intervals. We can tell them that orthodontics has made enormous progress since then and that, unfortunately, it is impossible to check the reported failures because no documents are available. In most cases it was probably crowding that was the problem, because the often considerable expansion that could be achieved was thought to be permanent in the past. Crowding of the lower front teeth is very liable to recur, as already mentioned.

The number of orthodontic treatments has undoubtedly increased, and conditions are much more favorable today. On the other hand, why should malformations of the teeth remain at the same level at a time when disharmony is on the increase in so many other respects? We only have to think of the widespread sucking habit and of the fact that we have not yet overcome caries. A highly experienced dentist of my acquaintance, who specializes in young people, has recently written that 80 percent of orthodontic treatments have become necessary because of caries, bad habits (sucking, mouth breathing) and "refined foods" that require little chewing, and that all of this is avoidable.

Again and again we see parents, who take great care over their children's mental and spiritual development seriously, fail to care for the children's teeth; often they do not even notice major malpositioning of teeth and even jaws. The children are only too glad to be left in peace, since too many demands are made on them.

The question is asked again and again if malposition of teeth and jaws is a purely esthetic matter. My answer would be in the positive if it was merely a matter of minor dental rotation and mild crowding. Yet children are brought to us exactly because of such "mini-anomalies."

The real problems in the mouth are often not apparent at first sight, because they are in the lateral region. Generally these are instances of misalignment, with a lower tooth engaging with one rather than two upper teeth (singular antagonism or cusp-to-cusp bite), or the bite is displaced by the width of a whole tooth. This will, of course, also mean that the front teeth do not relate properly.

In a well-developed, complete, balanced dentition, all parts fit well with each other, despite the fact that they have developed separately, with the teeth already mineralized and unchangeable when they erupt. Everything fits, making a single whole for mastication and speech; everything is arranged around a distinct mid-point with left and right mirror symmetry. Above and below are different but designed for balanced interaction of incisor edges, cusps, and grooves when the mouth is closed, that is, when closing the bite.

The same holds true for both masticatory and so-called "idle" movements. It is not surprising that we rarely see such perfect dentition today, though they are the ideal to strive for. Many things that interfere with balanced dentition composition can be greatly improved today, even if they cannot be entirely removed. As always, we have to compromise, and this is not so reprehensible if we are aware of it.

Let us now try and make a list of the most important indications for dentition regulation. When should we advise orthodontic treatment for children?

♦ Obviously in all cases of disfiguring anomaly, when teeth protrude so far that mouth closure is prevented. Experience has shown that such teeth are ten times more at risk from accidents than normally-positioned teeth.

♦ For all misalignments that come under the heading of prognathism, that is, with lower teeth overbiting the upper teeth, in severe cases with the whole mandible projecting forward; also for misalignments such as all types of crossbite and "missed bite" - a similar situation where upper and lower lateral teeth do not come together but go past each other. All these anomalies cause unfavorable stresses on teeth and periodontal tissues and may in the long run also affect the temperomandibular joints

♦ For very deep overbite, with the lower front teeth biting into the palatal tissues or the upper front length into the lower gingiva, especially if both are the case. Pain, inflammation, and regression of gingiva may result. The teeth are subject to abnormal stresses, which may cause them to loosen.

♦ For open bites, where some upper and lower teeth do not meet at all, often because the tongue is again and again coming between them. Here the biting function suffers and in severe cases also speech. Absence of functional stresses is as harmful in this instance as wrong stresses are with deep overbite.

♦ Marked crowding, one reason being that physiologic and toothbrush cleaning have poor access to the hiding places created by the condition. Crowding of the upper front teeth may also be unsightly, while barely noticeable in the lower jaw.

♦ For regression of the mandible, causing wrong relation of front teeth and alignment of lateral teeth, so that a lower molar does not bite between the two corresponding upper molars, with the bite displaced by the width of one or half a tooth width, with each tooth biting only against one other (singular antagonism). All this again causes harmful stresses. In severe cases the profile is markedly affected.

♦ For front teeth and molars displaced in the jaw, especially the canines, those vital corner-posts for the whole denture. Every effort to get a canine in position is justified.

♦ If the number of teeth is too small. Efforts will be made to close gaps by orthodontic measures where possible to avoid having to use prostheses for young people that soon have to be replaced.

♦ If the number of teeth is too large, and it is not enough simply to remove excess teeth. In most cases, the remaining teeth will have been displaced.

The basic precondition for all orthodontic treatment is that child and parent are willing to cooperate, usually for years. Support at school is most important since functional methods of treatment, especially using a regulator, require the appliance to be worn all day, that is, also during school hours. Once the child is used to the appliance, he is able to speak well and must be encouraged to do so. If only the dentist is convinced that orthodontic treatment is necessary, and the other parties involved do not see the need for it, the treatment does not work well and often fails. It goes without saying that the dentures - such a marvelous creation - should look, fit, and function harmoniously.

Karmic Aspects

In anthroposophical circles people often express concern that orthodontic treatment intervenes in destiny, a view I do not share. The idea is that it relieves the individual of the need to come to terms with an inherent physical malformation. For a physician, however, it is natural to do whatever is possible to promote the healing of physical disorders of whatever origin. By the way, health insurance companies have for some years now considered malposition of the jaws and teeth a pathologic condition and been prepared to pay for treatment.[22]

I would also say that common dental anomalies are not usually a matter of destiny, especially those caused by sucking or due to caries. Severe malformation of the jaws, above all cleft lip, jaw, or palate, are much more likely to impress one as related to karma. But no one would think of leaving such individuals, who are at particular risk perinatally, to their fate. From the beginning they are in the care of orthodontists and surgeons and later also of speech therapists who "rehabilitate" them so that the mouth functions as well as possible and their facial appearance does not cause social problems. If this is taken as a matter of course for individuals thus severely affected, why should we not be allowed to help also those with lesser dental anomalies?

Another reproach leveled at orthodontists is that they use mechanical means. It has to be admitted that in the majority of cases we cannot manage without wires and appliances. Malposition of teeth presents us with genuinely "hard facts." In orthopedics much can be done by exercises. Orthodontics also call for exercises, above all mouth closure, but also with the unattached "functional" appliances used to correct the position of the jaw. This changes the familiar relative position of dentures and usually makes room for vertical growth, i.e. letting teeth grow into a different position. I have been using these appliances, which create the conditions for harmonious development, for more than 33 years at the Curative Education Institute in Hepsisau, where orthodontics has effectively supported curative education. Balters was evidently right in saying: "No real change unless the whole person changes." When a curative teacher is unable to help a child to progress in a real way, orthodontic treatment usually also has little effect. We also try to contribute to the overall change that is required by using the means offered by orthodontics, e.g. by influencing the positioning of the jaw. This will usually fail if the new position is not in accord with the nature of the individual.

So this is where we find our limits, an indication that there can be no unwarranted interference in the person's karma. On the other hand, orthodontic treatment also offers something that is desirable in this context - exercise of the will. It always calls for an effort of will for patients to use unattached appliances or those that clip on and can be removed by them, and we are powerless if they do not do this regularly and reliably. Orthodontic treatment requiring an appliance to be worn is unlikely to be successful in spoiled children who have never been asked to do anything that goes against the grain. Even fixed bandelette appliances are no way out. They are certainly no more comfortable and, what is more, tend to collect food residues, so that the teeth have to be cleaned thoroughly after every meal to prevent caries. This calls for a considerable effort of will several times daily.

In conclusion, some attempts will be made to explain the situation in psychosomatic and anthroposophic terms. Dental phenomena have frequently aroused the interest of researchers. Wilhelm Balters actually went so far as to draw conclusions as to the personality of the individual from a study of denture plaster casts. This provided him with more reliable evidence than merely looking in the mouth. His conclusions are often graphic. With reference to deep overbite, for instance, he said that the individual concerned tended to cover up rather than be open about things, that "he had let down the shutters." Conversely, he spoke of a child with open bite as "open and unprotected." He also said with regard to frontal open bite that you'd never find a surgeon with such a bite, for surgeons have to use their front teeth to probe situations. Another of his statements was that people with frontal open bite always wanted to have the last word, something I can only report without comment.

Wilhelm Balters' opinion that open bite might also indicate unbelief induced me to make a declaration and substantiate it at a congress of the German Orthodontics Society. I referred to the threefold organization of the mouth. The maxilla clearly relates to the upper human being. It is part of the head, with the palate a vaulted structure similar to the cranium. The mandible is connected to the head by joints and is the "limb" of the head. The middle human being may be seen in the rhythmic movement of maxilla and mandible in speaking and chewing activities, in the sinus curve of the dentition and in the mediating function of the tongue. When above and below are no longer in touch, as is the case with open bite, we have a "loss of the middle." The relationship between upper and lower is upset. I might also say "God" or "world of the spirit" rather than "upper", and "the human being on earth" instead of "lower." It is difficult to say if the interpretation is correct, but it does make sense to me.

In cases where the open bite was due to pushing the tongue between the teeth, Balters was able to offer two further interpretations. It is normal for hard tooth to meet hard tooth in a bite, but some prefer to put the tongue in between as a soft cushion. They prefer to pull their punches. On the other hand we might take the tongue pushing in between as an image. The tongue, or metaphorically speaking the individual concerned, intrudes where not wanted. When I told a mother whose daughter was always pushing her tongue between the lateral teeth, resulting in a highly uncommon lateral open bite, about these two possible interpretations, she said spontaneously, "We call her 'the wedge in our marriage'." Again, the interpretation would make sense to me. By the way, everything turned out well for Karin, partly because she did not continue as the only child in the family.

It is also graphic to speak of someone who is always clenching his teeth and does not relax them, as "dogged" or someone who has to fight tooth and nail.

If teeth are thus subject not only to pressure but also to grinding, they are evidently getting worn down, even in childhood. Grinding the teeth may also be interpreted as autoaggression, biting oneself. Conversely a relaxed jaw, someone who is too lazy to chew, would indicate that the individual does not want to be seriously involved in his food or in the environment, lacking the necessary awareness for this. Eugen Kolisko commented: "When we chew, the conscious mind goes for a walk on the food."

Balters once used a military analogy with reference to posterocclusion, where the lower jaw is too far back and the lower front teeth bite into empty space. He said: "At the front, there are no punches pulled. You (the patient) are not at the front, you are behind the lines. It is time to go forward and engage the enemy!" We use our limbs to realize the will. Everyone can push his lower jaw forward if he wants to. Posterocclusion is a matter of holding back. If, however, the lower front teeth actually bite into the palate, then, according to Balters, it is better not to damage oneself. That would indeed be masochistic.

Balters and his students, above all Fritz Bahnemann and Hubertus von Treuenfels who took over Bahnemann's practice, also established connections between jaw position and body posture, calling this the "gnathovertebral syndrome", and devised exercises for this. Their goal is holistic orthodontics. Fraenkl, who designed the function regulators, is of the same opinion. Years ago he wrote: "It is extremely difficult to get people to understand that we treat not only the dentures but really the whole human being. What is more, the head and face of the individual are unique, and measurement based on mean values will not serve the purpose." Some people take an oversimplified view, however, thinking it is holistic therapy just to fit a child with a Balters bionator or a Fraenkl function regulator. On the other hand, we must beware not to let our enthusiasm for a holistic approach go to extremes.

We have to keep our feet on the ground and develop a feeling for what we may ask of a child, considering the domestic and school situation. Plus it is always sad to see how an impending or completed divorce seriously puts our orthodontic efforts in jeopardy. Help comes from anything that creates order. In this sense, orthodontics is a treatment that establishes order in the meaning of the term given by Bircher-Benner. For fatherless children it is a help if the orthodontist is male.

To come back to the tongue once more: apart from pushing it between the upper and lower jaws and letting it rest there, another more active habit is to push it in a vertical position between teeth within a row. This creates gaps. This soundless gesture of the tongue (compared to speech with its sounds) may also be regarded as body language and interpreted accordingly. The tongue is breaking through the fence (of teeth), rotating through an angle of 90°. According to Balters, and my observations confirm this, the area where the tongue is pushed through means something. In the upper jaw we are dealing more with higher elements relating to soul and spirit, in the lower jaw with the physical basis. The middle of the row of teeth indicates a central problem. The individual's general laterality probably influences the laterality of the phenomenon. Experience has shown that this kind of diastema usually disappears again in children. If it persists, an effort should be made to discover the reasons. We might try and make the individuals conscious of the mood in which they make this initially unconscious gesture (also recommended for those who grind their teeth). However, this will probably work only for individuals who are able and prepared to work on themselves. On the other hand, if a trace of former habits remains in the dentition and does not disappear of its own accord, it should be regarded as a fossil record, signifying no more for the individual than an aspect of the past that has been left behind.

"Myofunctional therapy" has been developed by the American speech pathology expert, Professor Garliner, to deal with malposition of the tongue between the jaws; it involves a program of tongue exercises that require a great deal of patient compliance. The Brazilian speech pathologist and former Waldorf teacher, Mrs. Padovan, suspects that these problems are partly due to developmental deficiencies in early childhood. Her treatment program, therefore, includes going back to infant movements such as crawling. Another problem going back to early childhood has been pointed out by Dr. Wellmann, Waldorf school doctor in Wuerzburg, Germany. He noted that children who prefer to lie in the prone position are liable to develop crowding of teeth. He would be grateful for substantiation of this.

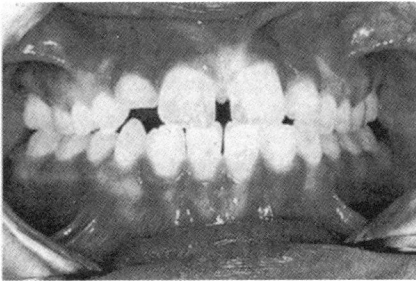

Fig. 10a, 7 years, 6 months.
Distema 1 + 1 caused by
insertion of the tongue.

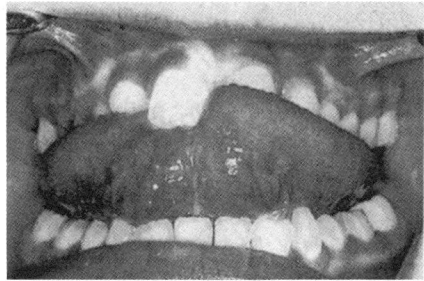

Fig. 10b, 7 years, 6 months.
Tongue between teeth
(habit, "parafunction") .

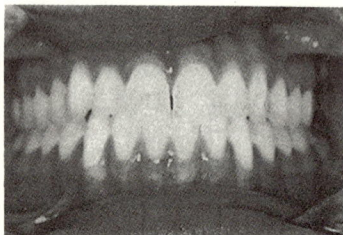

Fig. 10c,
15 years, 2months.
Spontaneous recovery

Finally, I'd like to emphasize that extreme caution is indicated in establishing this kind of connection and interpreting it. With interpretation, I stick as far as possible to imagery and never impose my views on others. What matters, I think, is not to have great thoughts about these things nor a theory, however magnificent, but the encounter, always unique, with human beings who may come to see me on account of their teeth but should not have a label attached to them, just because of certain dental phenomena.

Let us recall the words of our doyen, Dr. Angle, who called the dentition a *secretum apertum* – an "open secret." It is for us to increase our understanding, not by applying "screws and levers." Goethe himself considered these inappropriate, although they are justified and necessary for some of the mechanical problems that have to be solved in orthodontics. But to uncover the mysteries of human dentition we need a different tool and that is a good, Goethean way of thinking.

BIBLIOGRAPHY AND NOTES

1. Steiner, R., *A Social Basis for Primary and Secondary Education* (GA 192)
2. Lindenberg, C., *Waldorfschulen,* RoRoRo, Sadebuch 6904, Dokument 1, 5, 167.
3. Steiner, R., *Boundaries of Natural Science* (GA 322), Sep. 29, 1920.
4. Steiner, R., *The Younger Generation* (GA 217), Oct. 7, 1922.
5. Steiner, R., *The Spiritual Ground of Education (*GA 305).
6. Steiner, R., *The Spiritual-Scientific Aspect of Therapy* (GA 313)
7. See handbook *Die Zahn-, Mund- und Kieferheilkunde,* Munich, Berlin, 1955.
8. Goebel, W., Glöckler, M., *A Guide to Child Health*, Anthroposophic Press.
9. Steiner, R., *Waldorf Education for Adolescence,* (GA 101) Kolisko Archives, 1980.
10. Steiner, R., *Man, Hieroglyph of the Universe* (GA 201) Rudolf Steiner Press, 1972.
11. Steiner, R., *Background to the Gospel of St. Mark* (GA 124) Anthroposophic Press, 1985.
12. Steiner, R., *Pastoral Medicine* (GA 318) Anthroposophic Press, 1987.
13. Schulze, C., *Lehrbuch der Kieferorthopaedie*, 3 Band, Preface, 1981.
14. Steiner, R., *Spiritual Science and Medicine* (GA 312), London Rudolf Steiner Press 1975.
15. Author of: *Medizinischer Index zum Vortragswerk Rudolf Steiners*, Stuttgart, 1976.
16. Steiner, R., *Curative Education*, London: Rudolf Steiner Press, 1981.
17. Schad, W., *Zahnwechsel und Schulreife*, in *Erziehung ist Kunst,* Frankfort 1986.
18. Ref. 10, July 5, 1920.
19. Wicke, K., *Ueber die Durchbruchszeiten der Milchzähne bei Wuerzburger Kindern*, Dissertation. Wuerzburg 1934 , Rostock, 1967.
20. Husemann, A. J., *Der musikalsiche Bau des Menschen.* Stuttgart, 1989.

21. Hoerauf, K., *Form und Stellung der Frontzaehne ihrer Beziehung zu den Koerperbautypen*, Munich, 1958.
22. This may mean a temptation for patients to want to and for dentists to actually 'overdo' things. To limit abuse, the insurance companies in Germany now only pay 80 percent of the cost, or 90 for additional children in the same family, with accounting done quarterly. The rest has to be paid in advance by the insured and is only reimbursed when treatment has been concluded according to plan.

CHAPTER 4

THERAPEUTIC PRINCIPLES IN THE CURRICULUM IN THE ARTS AND IN CRAFT LESSONS

by

Sylvia Bardt
Translated by Johanna Collis

Classes 1 to 5

After a eurythmy lesson with the third grade one of the small boys, Christian, met me in the corridor. "Where are you going?" he asked. "I'm going back to the eurythmy room to do some more eurythmy," I replied. "Who with?" "With the big children in class 11." "But you've already done eurythmy today, with us. Do you always do eurythmy?" He fixed me with a stare. "Well then, you can't be a proper teacher!" So Christian already has ideas about who is and who isn't a proper teacher. What does this mean as far as we are concerned? In the first lecture in *Waldorf Education for Adolescence* Rudolf Steiner pointed out:

". . . You set going in the child a hygienic – yes, even a therapeutic activity. That was not probably your original intention; and indeed the activity is perhaps all the healthier if you do not go about it in the spirit of amateur doctors, but simply leave it to your own natural, healthy feelings and outlook. It is, however, good to know that as teachers working together we really do work for one another . . . . It is good if we can in this way see the work of the school as a connected whole; for then, if anything shows itself to be out of order in a child, we shall make a point of seeing how we can cooperate with other teachers to put it right."[1]

We have to ask ourselves the crucial question: How can we work more closely together? Armin Husemann appealed to us to see how the lesson content suggested by the curriculum relates to the facts of the children's mental, spiritual, and physiological development, for instance, in the way we use music in lessons with classes 1, 2, and 3. You'll get nowhere nowadays if you still expect the children in class 1 to sing "*The Happy Countryman*!" Similar discernment is needed in relation to main lessons, language lessons, and especially eurythmy.

All the teachers in a school must strive to co-operate, joining forces in their attempts to work both with the curriculum and with what the children bring towards us out of the times in which we now live.

We have all noticed how children even in the youngest classes no longer like standing. You can be sure that four or five of them will always be leaning against something while they speak the morning verse, even in a class that appears to be quite strong. This is a phenomenon we ought to be concerned about. It is not easy to find a eurythmy room without a tell-tale gray smudge around the walls made by children who cannot stand up properly.

Most schools now have benches or chairs for the Sunday service so that the children do not have to put up with standing for the whole of the 20 minutes the service takes, but can sit down at intervals. Why do children no longer want to stand up?

I think it is very important to investigate this matter of being strong enough to stand up properly; and there is another phenomenon that can be very upsetting, especially for teachers without much experience. Young teachers beginning with a new class for the first time will come to grief if they base their confidence on the children doing what they are told. This is no longer in any way a matter of course. "I don't want to!" is a sentence with which class teachers soon become very familiar. As for the other teachers, for instance, when trying to get the children to go outside during break time – is there anyone who has not been confronted by a small person declaring: "You can't tell me what to do. You're not my teacher!" Even if the class teacher succeeds in building up a relationship based on authority, other adults aren't seen in a similar light merely by virtue of being adults.

I find myself asking whether there is a connection between these two phenomena. Have our children not had enough opportunity before reaching school age to move in an upright way led by the ego? Is this why they are unable to respect authority? Did not Rudolf Steiner speak of the power of uprightness as an organ for the sense that perceives the ego? Or have those in authority been so weak that the children have been unable to gain enough strength from them with which to achieve uprightness? I think the time has come for some research into this.

To return to young Christian's question: "Are eurythmy teachers, or handwork teachers who do nothing but knitting, proper teachers, or is my class teacher, who teaches me my letters and numbers, the only one?"

How can we combine all the things that happen in the different lessons? What influence do we have on human beings when they are nine or ten years old? How can what we do with them help us discover who these children are? And once we know who they are, how can this teach us what we ought to be doing with them?

I shall describe and compare eurythmy, handwork, and gym in classes 3 and 4. For the ninth year of life Rudolf Steiner gave us the picture of the Rubicon, a word that has become a technical term for Waldorf teachers. The image of the Rubicon River provides us with a rich source of ideas, for it played an important part in the history of human evolution. What is a river, what is this Rubicon, Julius Caesar's river?

A river has two banks with movement taking place in between. I can submit to the current and allow it to carry me downstream while I experience the speed, see what is on the banks, and let myself be swept along. Or I can try to swim against the current, and if I succeed, I shall arrive at sources. I need plenty of energy to do this. I can stand on one bank and find out what is going on here, or I can look across to the other side with a burning interest for what might be going on over there.

When we meet class 3 pupils on this side of the river, we must never forget that they want to get across to the other side and become class 4 pupils.

It is our task to prepare them by becoming bridge builders or by giving them excellent swimming lessons, so that they can conquer the river.

Here are two pictures drawn by class 3 children.

In the first a class 3 child has drawn himself and his world in a wonderful way. We see a flower with red petals growing upward to the sun. Many golden stars appear in the red chalice of the flower, and these carry another sun in which yet more flowers grow. The whole of life is as though enclosed within a sun-filled living sphere. A more beautiful depiction of this age is hard to imagine; the picture gives us an inkling of what a nine-year-old child is.

The second picture invites us to become guests at a school festival. We see a stage in a great hall, and many, many children. A class is passing across in front of the stage with their teacher; presumably they are waiting for their turn. On the stage the young artist's class is performing "*Rumpelstiltskin*" in eurythmy. This picture is much more "earthly" than the other. The outdoor shoes of the waiting children are huge compared with the eurythmy shoes of the children on the stage. While this is quite realistic, a good many other details are quite different from reality. The piano is really on the left in the hall, but in the picture it is on the right because it fits in better there. Left and right aren't yet particularly important for this child in class 3. Now look at the brightly colored costumes the children are wearing. Actually they all had their green eurythmy tunics on. And what about the spinning-wheel? There was none on the stage, but it lived in the child's soul where "straw is spun into gold". The child sees the world but arranges it to fit her inner picture.

If we were to look for an image with which to depict this age, we would find one in the archetypal image of the sphere. This is the inner motif out of which we work during the first three years at school. Kepler described the essence of the sphere as follows: "The sphere represents the Trinity: the Father is the center, the Son the surface, and the Holy Spirit the distance from center to surface, which is always the same – the radius."[2] In class 3 this is the ordered whole out of which we live and work. But now we come to the point at which the sphere begins to crack open.

In eurythmy we live and work with the interval of the fifth for two years. This is the "great bell" that resounds in every eurythmy lesson in class 1 and 2, and even at the beginning of class 3. Then one day, when the eurythmy teacher senses the time is just right, the lesson begins with the sound of the major third. The same happens in the next lesson and in the one after that, so that the children begin to expect what is coming, moving their arms accordingly. The children's ears become accustomed to the major and the minor third, yet when a fifth puts in an appearance, they smile: "We know that ever so well. That's what we used to have!" We lead them into their first experience of independent listening and feeling, and carefully take our leave of the space where the fifth resounded. Now comes the time when the children experience their inner life more and more strongly and begin asking the kind of questions quoted by Armin Husemann: "Am I really your child or did you find me somewhere? Was I abandoned perhaps?" The children ask about death; they see the world and experience themselves. They turn towards the world in the major third, while sensing their own inner being more in the minor. This is what we have to let them practice, so that they can practice with themselves.

Here is another example of how this new departure in the ninth year of life is taken up in the eurythmy lesson. In classes 1 and 2 the whole class made its way around the room; we followed "paths", with the teacher leading and the whole crowd of 36 children following on behind. We went round the room, climbed a mountain (in-going spiral), climbed down again, walked round in a circle or rather "in actual fact" round a big lake, and we weren't just pretending. If a child strayed from the "path", another was sure to call out, "Watch out, you're getting your feet wet!" This had to be done in every eurythmy lesson, but if it were to continue now we would make the children dependent.

This is an important point to note for all lessons. We must not make the mistake of wanting to go on working until class 12 with the children's willingness to imitate. Becoming independent has to be practiced, very slightly already in class 1, but firmly and concretely from class 3 onwards. How can we do this? The classes have not yet been divided up, and so we have quite a crowd to work with. Hitherto the children have been accustomed to watching the teacher and following wherever she led them. But now, as they stand in a circle, all of a sudden the teacher says: "You stand still and watch what I'm going to do. I'm showing you a path; who can see what shape it is? Which of you can see the path I have just shown you?"

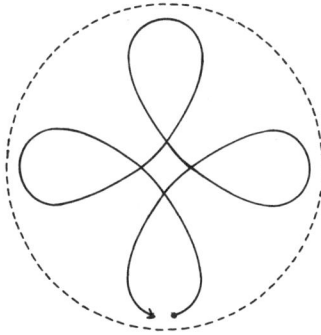

Instead of following the teacher, the children now do their forms individually, within a group, each child moving to the spot where another is standing, who then moves on to the next, so there is always a definite point to aim for. I am not talking about the way the curriculum is built up but about principles that emerge, and it seems to me that the manner in which moving in great swarms is transformed to moving individually in class 3 is a very significant step at which we have to work.

Another important element we now have to introduce with plenty of patience, quietness, and love is the gestures for the speech sounds. So far the children have copied the gestures we have made without knowing what they were doing. The gestures for sun and stars fitted in with their picture of these things. Now, in class 3, we can begin to do the sounds for quite long texts with the children standing and working with us on discovering the gestures from the pictures the words give us. Harking back to a main lesson in class 2, we might take St. Francis's **Canticle to the Sun**, beginning at the start of the new school year when the weather is still sunny:

> Praised be God for Brother Sun
> Who shines with splendid glow.
> He brings the golden day to us,
> Thy glory doth he show.
> Praised be God for Sister Moon
> And every twinkling star.
> They shine in heaven most bright and clear,
> All glorious they are.
> Praised be God for Brother Wind
> That storms across the skies . . . .
> (English by Lawrence Edwards)

They do not realize that I have made a sweeping S for the storms, but they recognize the picture and feel confident in being able to make it, too.

It is important for the children to recreate independently the images that live in their soul. Then, by class 4, they will begin to recognize the sounds as such, so that, for example, a small B gesture can be a ball, or a basket. By then we shall have detached the sound from the image. We must begin this clearly in class 3.

The sphere is the basic motif in handwork in class 3. The children work on spheres of the most varying kinds, and they use their hands to do so. In connection with eurythmy, I spoke of the children becoming more independent. Another way of putting this could be to say that more ego needs to come into their work. Speaking to architects about the relationship between ego and sphere, Rudolf Steiner said:

"There is a form we can make through which egohood or self-hood can be sensed. When we pass from purely mathematical conception of a form to really feeling what the form is, a perfect circle will give us a sense of egohood, of selfhood. To feel a circle means to feel selfhood. To feel a circle in a plane, or a sphere in space, is to feel the self, the ego."[3]

Children in Waldorf schools make wonderful balls in handwork in class 3. A gift of one of these lovely balls is far more thrilling than any number bought in a shop. It will have taken many weeks to make. In the center is a piece of cork wrapped in paper. This is wound round and round with a network of thick cotton. Then comes another layer of paper, then more winding of cotton until the desired size is reached. The intricate cotton network is now embroidered with colored lines. How interesting that in the elementary school the line makes its appearance in the way the color is shaped. These lines have to be made into surfaces in such a way that you can tell the many kinds of movement a ball can have. A red ball with white spots can surely only bounce, while a ball with a curly pattern will only roll in one direction. This one here can fly and also be rolled; it can be bounced, and all this is emphasized by its decoration. It'll be good fun playing with it. While they work on their ball, the children keep feeling it. Again and again they press their hands around it. The balls the children make differ tremendously from child to child. One is small and hard, another large and soft. What does this tell us about the children?

There is also another article that helps the children feel their way toward the sphere in class 3. In class 1 they knitted, in class 2 they crocheted, and now they take up crocheting again. The children begin to make garments for themselves, beginning at the top with one for their very own "sphere". They learn double crochet and it looks as though they are making a mat. "But we aren't going to crochet a mat, children; we're going to make a hat." It would be fun to be a fly on the wall in the coming handwork lessons and watch the children blissfully trying on their hats. After every round they put on the "mat" to see whether it fits yet, each time feeling the shape of their own head with their fingers. "What is my head like; what am I like?" It is a process of getting to know themselves that gives them the strength to "swim across the river" and become independent in class 4. When the hats are finished, we should study the color schemes. What colors have the small-headed children chosen? How do the temperaments show up? How strongly do the teacher's own colors impose themselves? Our study of the hats should be warmhearted and kind, so that sometimes we might even remark to one another, tactfully, of course: "Your class's hats are wonderful, but I can always tell that you have been the teacher in charge!" Of course, this is bound to happen, and rightly, for surely each of us must have our own handwriting. But how much room do we leave for the children to add their own nuance? It really is a balancing act!

Now let us have a look at gym. We have reached an interesting point, and it seems to me that gym is like a bridge or a leap across the river. As you will see if you read the **Conferences with Teachers**, Rudolf Steiner originally intended gym to begin in class 4. However, somehow it started in class 3 and has done so ever since. Our schools are so fixed in the way they are organized that we are unlikely to succeed in doing what would be really ideal, which would be to let every class begin doing gym when it is ready for it. They shouldn't have to start at the beginning of a new school year. We ought to be able to detect when the children have begun to experience a first degree of separateness in the feeling they have for their bodies and for space. This is the foundation on which gym lessons can build.

Let me describe a gym lesson in class 3. The children file into the empty gym from the changing room wearing their gym clothes. They sit down on the floor in a circle. I thought I knew these children, but as they sit there in their little shorts with bare legs, or wearing those close-fitting body suits, I feel that my nice rounded harmonious class 3 children have turned into puny little creatures. In eurythmy the shape of the body is much more covered since the children wear their eurythmy tunics over their clothes. In gym the body is revealed, and the sight is immensely touching. With their baby fat gone and their muscles not yet developed the children are small fry indeed. The gym teacher joins them in their circle and chats with them for a while, asking how they are and whether anyone isn't feeling well, creating a bit of a warm envelope around them. Then the lesson begins. The teacher goes to one side and calls out, "Children, run and hide!" They jump up from their orderly circle and hide, and watching this we can tell exactly which children are ready for gym and which do not yet need it, although it won't do them any harm. Some will hide behind the wall bars with their face to the wall; others slip behind the curtains, so many of them that there is not enough room. Their main concern is to hide their head. But there are others who are set on really hiding themselves, and this tells us a lot about their state of readiness. Now the gym teacher takes a tambourine and begins to speak: "Here we come from afar, running and jumping," and the children emerge from their hiding places and run about in the gym. "Gallop, gallop, trot, trot, trot . . ." and now they all return to stand in the circle. You get a feeling that somehow the glow of the sphere still surrounds them. This is how this Bothmer game is played and danced in class 3.

Bothmer gave a different game for gym lessons in class 4. Instead of calling "Here we come from afar, running and jumping," we now say:

> I stand and I walk and I follow my course,
> I jump and I jump and I jump and then stop.
> I jump up on the wall, I swing up to the tower,
> I ring its bells as loudly as I can.

This is an entirely new gesture, and it always begins with "I". Feeling the sphere with the fingers was a way of feeling the ego. In this circular figure the ego element now appears in force.

Look closely at the difference between eurythmy and gym. In eurythmy we do:

> We are born from the light,
> from pure heights of heaven,
> we come down to earth,
> and stand here firmly.

We have an inner image, and we go into this image when we have strongly created it inwardly. In gym we come from afar and find ourselves in the circle: What a good thing that we belong together. We do something, and this is the fulfillment. We must be very aware of these polarities. Gym teachers and eurythmy teachers, language teachers and class teachers, who also play games with the children during the rhythmical part of the lesson, must all know each other and be aware of what each is doing. We must clarify our point of departure. Is it more like eurythmy when I start in the soul realm and breathe the soul into the body, or is the body my starting point, the muscles and the blood from which a sense of strength and delight emerges? Here, where it is a matter of "crossing the Rubicon", gym and eurythmy have contrasting points of departure. In the teachers' conference held on March 1, 1923, Rudolf Steiner put it this way:

> "I can make this clearest by pointing out that eurythmy has to do essentially with everything involved in the breathing process. That is, whatever an arm, leg, finger, or toe does in eurythmy is in direct contact with the inner breathing process in which air passes into the blood; whereas gym is essentially the process underlying the movement of blood into muscle. That, basically, is the physiological aspect, and at the same time it makes perfectly clear what has to be developed.[4]"

These are thoughts we ought to be working with. As far as is humanly possible, we should let both gym and eurythmy come alive equally strongly in Waldorf schools. The one cannot do without the other – I cannot do gym without breathing, and I cannot do eurythmy without muscles.

Let us now look at handwork in class 4. The spherical shape worked at last year gets turned inside out. This image can throw light on a number of aspects. The hat provided protection from the outside. Now a bag is to be made. A bag does not envelop the child; its purpose is to let in the world. The world has to come towards the child, and the child has to go towards the world. We no longer have a long, unbroken thread out of which something larger is fashioned in knitting or crocheting. Now all kinds of things get broken or break open. The sphere breaks open and becomes a bag. The children each get a large piece of canvas and a pair of scissors. After careful instruction and preliminary discussion they have to cut into this nice piece of material. Have courage, make your cut, spoil something, so that something greater can come out of it! The handwork teacher won't actually say it like this, but it is what lies behind it. So each child cuts out a rectangle, and then they are quickly shown that many things in the world get broken, but it is up to us as human beings to make sure that something new can arise from the broken parts. The children sew up the seams and learn various stitches, such as over-and-over or blanket stitch, and each of these has its proper name, a technical term. Then the moment comes when the children draw a pattern on their bag. The pattern must show what the bag can hold – heavy stones, juicy grapes, or perhaps feathers. All these things must find room in it without coming to any harm. So the children draw on their bags to show this. Then they choose colored wool – the question of color again! – with which to embroider the pattern. The heavy objects go at the bottom where the dark colors are, while the light and delicate things are better placed higher up where the colors are bright and jolly.

In such things we find the therapeutic principles in the curriculum. The children embroider their bag in cross-stitch. In the parlance of eurythmy, they make hundreds of E-gestures in their embroidery; in handwork they do an exercise hundreds of times that gives their ego a firm hold in their astral body. The finished embroidery is like a whole layer of beautiful new fabric. Both sides of the bag are embroidered, and then it is lined as well. How proudly class 5 children – or their mothers – carry the bags they made in class 4. This cross-stitch work in class 4 holds mysteries that we should realize are deeply therapeutic and healing suggestions. Handwork teachers give the children a strong dose of medicine by letting them do the E-exercise week after week without interruption – blue E, green E, red E, on and on. In addition the bags are masterpieces of accuracy in which the pattern is exactly matched on both sides of a central axis. They are never-ending mirror exercises, exercises of completion. Each bag consists of two symmetrical parts. In a lecture on November 21, 1914, Rudolf Steiner said:

> "Had he not two ears, two eyes, and two noses, the human being would not attain to the perception of his own I or ego. Correspondingly, we also need two hands for the ego experience. When we clasp our hands together and feel the one with the other, we immediately get something of an ego experience . . . The fact that we have these two directions of perception, left and right, and bring them together – to this fact we owe our Ego-nature as human beings . . . ." [5]

This is what happens in handwork in class 4.

Where do we find the same principle in eurythmy? Where does the sphere get broken so that the intact form followed by the children in a crowd has to be changed? The children begin to feel: "I am here; the world is out there." How do we practice confronting the world like this? We face up to it! This means the children now have to develop a sense for an audience. They no longer follow their noses but face forward, toward the audience. They face up to the world!

In the musical element of our lessons we initially allowed ourselves to be entirely enveloped in the fifth. Then we accompanied the first stages of experiencing ourselves against the world with the interval of the third. In the songs we used to sing, the divisions were dictated by the length of a breath, so that the melody line had a swing that harmonized with human respiration. Now a new educational element enters into music, the beat which "splits" the music up. Working with the beat, the children are turned back on themselves. A musician who cannot keep time but relies on the others when playing in a quartet slows down the tempo. We have to be able to beat our own time; it has to be anchored in our bones. This is what we practice with the children in class 4. Again, this gives us a chance to observe which of them have reached the stage of having arrived in their bones that give them their own shape, and which have not yet got there.

In the middle of class 4 I like to make the following experiment: "Now I'm going to set you a riddle. I'm holding a ball in my left hand. Now watch, and tell me afterwards what I've been doing." As the accompanist plays the music, I throw the ball from one hand to the other, for four bars on every whole note (semi-breve), for four bars on every half note (minim), for four bars on every quarter note (crotchet) and for four bars on every eighth note (quaver). Here are some of the answers: "You always had the ball in your left hand when the music stopped." This is a wonderful answer, and it's true, but it has nothing to do with "There is the world and here am I." Or: "Every time you started it was quicker." Or: "It was like in fractions, whole, half, quarter, eighth." Quite a wide range of answers. I wish the class teacher, the school doctor, and all the other teachers could watch this, for these answers make it quite clear how we can go on working with a difficult child or even a delightful one, which children need holding back and which need drawing out.

There is another riddle I set the children. We listen to a piece of music, while they watch my movements. There is only one right answer.

(Throwing the ball from hand to hand, I step the rhythm of the lower voice with my feet.) What have I been doing? "You did something in two parts." Finally the correct answer comes: "You've been singing a round." Quite right. Now I do it again together with the children. First they use a "ball of air" and then a proper ball. This is a very difficult exercise, but the children learn to do it. By the end of class 5 we are so good at it that we can perform it in front of an audience to whom we say: "Look, eurythmy is really the most wonderful thing for it enables me to sing a round with myself. There's no other way this can be done."

DEVELOPMENTAL INSIGHTS
Discussions Between Doctors and Teachers

How do we work with the speech sounds in eurythmy in class 4? We have to reach a stage at which the children as a group know all the sounds. We stand in a circle and make the gestures of the alphabet. One child begins with A, the next forms B, and so on, up to Z. By the end of class 4 the alphabet runs quickly and smoothly round the circle. It's a festive moment when this is achieved, and we are reminded of what Rudolf Steiner said: "If you were to repeat the eurythmy gestures of the alphabet from A to Z ... you would find the human etheric body standing before you."[6]

So we have an etheric human being before us as we make the eurythmy gestures of the alphabet in quick succession. Such exercises give strength and form to the etheric forces, and we must start to do them energetically in class 4.

For the children facing the "Rubicon", overcoming the river means departing from Paradise. Out of the unblemished realm of fairy tales, legends, and Old Testament stories, the children are driven into the world. They ask of us: "Please tell me what it's like here on the earth. How can I build myself a house and become a capable human being here?"

Here are two pictures drawn after the same gym lesson. Some apparatus had been set up: mats, box, and horse. The children pretended they were at the edge of a precipice and had to swing across to the other side on a rope. This takes a good deal of courage. One child has already reached the other side and draws quite factually everything as it really is in our world. The other still lives and plays on the apparatus on the Paradise side of the abyss; we see the landscape as it is experienced inwardly.

The same can be found with equal clarity in the house-building period in class 3. The task is to model a house out of clay in which it is nice to live. One child will create a cave, a hollow sphere of clay without any windows and with a little slit for going in and out and a chimney on top. The whole thing looks almost like an apple, and there is someone living in it. The child has made a little ball of clay and put it inside – a sphere within a sphere. Another child will model a firm, rectangular house with straight walls and a roof, and around the whole will be a strong wall to keep the world at arm's length. What will these children be like in class 8? If we read the signs, we will be able to teach in a therapeutic and healthy way.

As teachers we are faced with a double task. We have to concern ourselves with the children and the material we want to teach them, and we also have to pay attention to ourselves, so that we can put our whole self as complete human beings into what we do. We can only comprehend ourselves as whole human beings when we move. So we must not do all our preparation sitting down, and I do not mean only eurythmy teachers. If all of us, teachers in both the Elementary and the High School, were to prepare our lessons while walking about the school, movement would have come many steps further by now.

Rudolf Steiner gave the teachers of class 4 a verse. This verse – which can be found in various places and in different forms – was handed down by Isabella de Jaager, one of the first eurythmists. At Rudolf Steiner's suggestion she first did stage eurythmy, then directed the eurythmy school at Dornach, and later gave decisive impetus to the further development of eurythmy therapy. "This verse," she said, "was given for the class teachers of class 4. Please immerse yourselves long and carefully in it before doing it with the children. This is a sphere that needs our special protection." I believe it can be a great help to us in our preparation, if we can enter the world inhabited by the children of class 4 where the ego-being gains an entirely new relationship with life, with suffering, and with the world. Here is the verse:

> Firmly I take my place in existence,
> Securely I tread the journey of my life,
> In the center of my being I cherish love,
> All my deeds I mold with hope,
> I place my trust in all my thinking.
> These five take me to my goal,
> These five give me my existence.

Classes 6 to 12

What happens when a new teacher enters the classroom? The first lesson poses no problems. It is the second and third that determine whether he or she will sink or swim, whether the necessary conversation between pupils and teacher will come about, and whether the teacher will be able to take up the pupils' questions in order to show them the way.

We have been trying to reach an understanding of how children live in the landscape through which the Rubicon river flows. We have turned our attention to children in classes 3 and 4 and experienced with them a significant new departure. Now we have reached class 6, when history lessons tell of Julius Caesar and his crossing of the Rubicon. The stories should be so gripping and lively in the way they are told that one or other of the children might quite likely throw a school bag at the wall out of sheer indignation at the death of Caesar. In class 6 knowledge must be profoundly experienced.

Seeing the outdoor shoes of a class 6 outside the gym or eurythmy room, we are often astonished at the range of sizes. Is the lesson for fathers and mothers as well as children? And what is the musical sound that comes to meet us when we open the door? It is the octave. We must never forget the octave so long as we are involved with children in their twelfth year. They are octave-beings. What impulse does this give us for our work with children living in a world in which the octave resounds?

The octave comes up in various contexts in main lesson. The curriculum for class 6 brings new subjects to which the children look forward with great anticipation. There is much they have already encountered, but now it takes on entirely new forms. Geometry is a new subject, yet we have been doing geometry with the children from their very first lesson. We have lived in straight lines and curves, in circles and lines. Now this is taken up in a new way in main lesson. Physics is another new subject, yet what the children meet here is not new to them. They already know that great bells have deep voices while the tiny bells on the tassel of their hat sound high and tinkly. Children in class 1 marvel at the deep growl of the double bass and know quite well that the little violins have much higher notes. But now the time has come to learn about the laws that govern these things. What note does a whole string have? What note results when I divide the string exactly in half? What do we hear when we divide the string in a ratio of 2 : 3 ? This is what we investigate with children in class 6, when they are in their twelfth year. Geology is another new subject. Yet the children have been familiar with stones from their earliest days. They collected them in their pockets and played with them. In class 5, in lessons about their local environment, they learned to observe what stones we walk on in our town. What do the stones of the old castle or the town hall look and feel like? In class 6 they learn to distinguish between the quality of granite or limestone or sandstone. They learn names and compositions. This strong encounter with mineralogy gives us the keynote. And what is the octave? Rudolf Steiner told us what it was when he said we should study astronomy with the children. The keynote is mineralogy, the octave astronomy. In the teacher lives awareness when he sees a child: What is your zenith? Where you are – that is also your nadir. You have your own, and no one can deprive you of it. Neither does anyone else share it with you. Where you are – that is where your octave is.

We tell the children about the Romans, their history and laws, and about Roman Law. In ourselves we carry the awareness and experience of this being the time when humanity reached rock bottom; that is the keynote. We speak to the children about the birth of Christ and about the Crucifixion; this is the octave sound of all humanity. We speak to our twelve-year-olds about these things. In their own biography they have reached the point mankind reached then, with the Here and the There encompassed in one experience. In the main lessons these young people are surrounded by the sound of the octave.

Now let us turn to eurythmy, handwork, and gym in class 6, after which I shall follow eurythmy through the remaining stages to class 12. How does the octave show in gym? In their physical bodies the children have reached a stage of wonderful harmony. Breathing and pulse are in perfect balance. Schiller's lines can provide a motto for this age: "Do you seek the highest, the greatest? The plant can teach it to you. Where it is without will, be you full of will – that is the crux!" Whatever etheric forces there are in the world now need to be invited into the lessons and treated there.

I have been a guest in class 6 gym lessons. The children entered the gym; some were small, delicate figures, others much larger and more developed. They had come from main lesson where perhaps they sat for a good while, so now they lounged about. The gym teacher began the lesson with the words: "Let's walk to get ourselves going." With serious faces the children walked round the oval gym room, such a variety of figures, large and small, fat and thin, yet harmonious. They walked about, following their noses. The tambourine speeded up; they began to run. There was a pause, and then they ran again. "Go on running – we're running ourselves in!" A large, heavy boy, red in the face, stepped aside: "I can't keep going." "You can," said the teacher with an airy movement. And he could. A well-developed boy wailed, "I've got a stitch!" "Never mind," said the teacher, "you must have been breathing wrongly; carry on running!" The boy's complaint was pushed aside with an entirely friendly but stern objectivity. What they were practicing was: "Find your own rhythm, find what is asleep inside you, what is like a plant inside you and grows of its own accord. Learn to handle it consciously with hands and feet and body by running here!" After a few minutes I noticed that now everything was fine; the children had breathed themselves into a new frame of mind and body. "Children, today we're going to practice something very important for when we do relay racing in class 7. We're going to practice starting off; it's very important to be able to get off to a good start. Those who start off late can never win the race!" They got into position in three rows behind the line. With great accuracy they practiced and tried out the correct position for their hands along the line, fingers pointing frontward or sideways – "Try it out and see how you feel comfortable." They bent their knees and experimented with the way they placed their hands. Silence reigned as they worked seriously, soberly, expertly. "Now look what you're aiming for. The wall bars are the goal!" Step by step the sequence was built up. At the first command, "On your marks", heads were bowed. At the second, "Get set", the rear leg was straightened and the head came up to face forward. At the third, "Go", they shot across the room towards the wall bars. Row by row they practiced the start. All they wanted was to arrive at the goal, and they were not in the least bit interested in who got there first. This is how the octave was practiced over and over again in a gym lesson: start – finish, keynote – octave. This is what these youngsters have to achieve; they have to have their eye on their goal. Between the point they are at and the goal there should be no overlong stretches, no boredom. Especially when working with twelve-year-olds this is the archetypal image we have to refresh constantly in our minds: Do not let things get boring, keep them active without interruption between their starting point and the goal they are aiming for.

What principles apply to handwork at this age? A class 6 will have a tremendous variety of hands, just as we have already noticed with the feet. There are tiny, delicate hands – often belonging to a boy; and there are girls who have hands that are large, strong, and well-formed, ready to get going on making something new and working creatively. In class 3 we saw the children make a garment for their head. By class 5 they had come down to earth sufficiently to embark on knitting socks with which to clothe their feet. This task involved a rather interesting alternation between sleeping and waking, being present and going off in a dream. The children know how to knit, but now they have to do it on five needles. This can be quite fiddly, but they learn it. After knitting the top of the sock they can go straight on for a long time, dreaming as they go. But a moment arrives when something has to happen if a proper sock is to be the result rather than an endless tube. To get round the heel you have to wake up. This moment of waking up and becoming aware is something that brings us close to class 6. The teacher explains how the heel is turned. The description is so exact that the children can do it and write down what they are doing. Then, once they have got round the heel, they can go back to sleep for a while – the larger the foot, the longer the sleep. But then they have to wake up again to do the tip. Here, too, they can write down what they do. Soon we shall see whether the teacher has applied a scientifically competent method here in class 5, whether the process is repeatable, since it is to be hoped that the second sock will bear some resemblance to the first! If the children go by what they have written down, they will soon be holding the result of the scientific method, of their awakeness, in their hands; or rather, they will be wearing it on their feet.

This is the preparation in handwork that leads on to class 6. Now they are faced with a new task: "Draw your favorite animal!" Each child draws his or her favorite animal, often surrounding it with a beautiful landscape. Somewhere in the shade of palm trees and coconut palms an elephant grazes. It is the elephant we are after. "Now draw the elephant so large that it covers the whole sheet of paper!" So the elephant is drawn again, and as most people find it easiest to draw animals from the side view, this is probably what will appear on the sheet. "Now cut it out!" Cut it out? This is something quite new. The palm-trees disappear, the water disappears, the mood vanishes. The children notice that things are getting decidedly sparse. "How can we make this into an animal for you to give your little brother?" Of course, these animals are never given away, but there's no harm in putting the proposition like this. So now a second elephant is cut out.

"What can we do to make the elephant plump and round? Elephants are plump, aren't they? If we sew these two parts together the result will an elephant bag, at best." So we have to use our intelligence and try to make a paper pattern for the elephant. Where must gussets go to make the animal plump and give it a proper shape? Busily the children try it out. Every child makes a different animal and every animal has a different paper pattern. You can imagine how busy the handwork teacher is now. With the socks all the children were doing more or less the same thing. Only the sizes and colors differed. But all this endless variety of elephants, horses, and bears makes heavy demands. The parts are sewn together with neat, expert stitches. An animal like this will have to be able to take some rough treatment later on when it is played with, but first also when it is being stuffed. This process of stuffing the animals from the inside is precisely what happens to us at night when the etheric world fills out what has wilted during the day so that we can bloom afresh. This is what the children are doing; they are using etheric forces – "Be you full of will." Here again we discover subjects and questions for research. How do you stuff your animal? So thoroughly that all the seams burst or so thinly that it will never be able to stand by itself? Who are you? Are you following your own instincts or are you seeking balance for yourself? Are you looking for the other? We can read the children by studying their artifacts.

In these handwork lessons a strong appeal is made to the children's sense for the astral, which in turn is modeled to conform with the etheric world. The fact that the same result can be achieved by making dolls, or by some other means, is irrelevant as far as this example goes.

The woodwork teacher works quite differently with this class, as though bringing out the octave in the curriculum. The task is to make a moveable toy, perhaps a waddling duck, or a water-wheel that turns and is actually strong enough to scoop up water. Which way must the wheel turn? What is the correct angle for the paddles? Or: now that I have carved this duck, what kind of wheels must I give it so that it will waddle nicely and not sail along like a swan on the water? I must use my intelligence; I must work out what to do and send my thoughts into the mechanics of this object. In order to make an animal or useful article in woodwork, I am not concerned with stuffing the shape as I was in handwork. I have to follow the opposite path. I carve, I whittle away some of the substance, I make concave shapes; speaking anthroposophically, I'm working as a craftsman on the astral plane. Whittling away and breaking down have a very strong effect when combined with thinking. In classes 3 and 4 eurythmy and gym appear to complement one another all the time. The same appears to me to be the case with handwork and woodwork in class 6. We ought to see these things in combination.

In the eurythmy room, where earlier we looked at the shoes and listened to the musical sounds emerging, we now see the children in their circle and gain a strong impression of their standing properly on the earth. They have arrived; they stand on the earth but not yet heavily. We ought to make use of this lightness in all subjects. It helps us practice skipping and jumping in all kinds of ways. Including the Kiebitz (lapwing) M in every lesson with class 6, skipping exercises, hopping, running fast, generally making use of the children's lightness – all this seems to me to be the most important task for the eurythmy lessons.

Let us try once more to experience keynote and octave. What has happened? First there was the sphere in which the children lived and which now turns inside out. The sound of the octave is in essence a turning inside out of the sphere we had before. It is the task of class 6 to enter into the quality of the octave in this way. This is connected with jumping. We all know that our gait is different when we are sad. If we then experience something that turns us inside out by making us infinitely joyful, we want to jump up into the air. Small children still do this. In class 6 we have to succeed again and again in turning the children inside out into the brightness of the world in skipping, jumping, and with octave movements in every eurythmy lesson. But there is also something else that ought to be thought about and taken into account both in eurythmy and in gym during this year, and that is the children's skeletal structure. We know that a good jump needs a good launching pad; you can not launch yourself satisfactorily from a soft mattress. Rudolf

Steiner spoke about the system of muscles and bones in the eleventh lecture of the Christmas course for teachers:

"Towards the twelfth year a new situation arises . . . the muscles, previously closely allied to the rhythmic system, now become entirely oriented towards the bony system. In this way the child adapts itself more strongly to the external world than was the case before the twelfth year. Formerly the muscular system was more directly connected with the child's inner being, and the rhythmic system, because of its relative independence, played a dominant part in the growth of the muscles. The child moved in harmony with the muscular system, and the skeleton, embedded in the muscles, was simply carried along. Now towards the twelfth year, the situation changes rapidly. The muscular system begins to serve the mechanics and the dynamics of the bony system."[7]

"The skeleton . . . was simply carried along." But now the children take hold of their skeleton. At this stage it is perfectly natural for them to do this. "Be you full of will . . . ." Do it consciously, child, and you will be educating yourself! Obviously the time has now come to embark on specific work with the copper rods. Once the children can take firm hold of their skeleton, we can say to them: "Make sure your arms are properly horizontal." "Make sure that your right hand comes to rest in front of your right shoulder, so that the middle space here remains free." When we do this basic exercise with the children – up, down, right, left, right, up, down – we should bear a strong awareness of the octave within ourselves. If I go down with the rod and think "down" at the same time, I drag the children down instead of suspending them between up and down. And if I think about "up" when the rods go up, I let them fly away. But if I go down with the rod while thinking of up, I experience the octave, and if I go up with the rod while feeling my feet, the octave is there again. If we balance sending the rod to the right by being aware of the left, keeping the middle free, then this rod exercise is a strong therapy, a eurythmy therapy for all children of this age.

We have to see a turning inside out in the gesture of the octave. To work rightly at this point we adults have to bear this in mind. We hear music with a constant rhythm: short, short, long; short, short, long. Now we try clapping the opposite rhythm: long, short, short. It's a bit like singing a round. First we have the long note while the instrument plays two short ones, and then the opposite happens. This is another exercise we do with class 6.

We often conclude the lesson with a saying, for example: "Who is it, say, that achieves the greatest?" making a question gesture, which is like a great ear ready to catch what comes in. "Who conquers the lion?" – question gesture. "Who conquers the giant?" – question gesture. "Who overcomes this one and that one?" – question gesture. Now I'll tell you: "It is the human being, who can control himself!" This gives us a preview of the soul gestures. This theme is gently introduced during class 6. At first it is a matter of a feeling in the soul that is not yet heavily weighed down or colored by one's own strong astrality.

In classes 3 and 4 we experienced something like being driven out of Paradise. In class 8 the children are driven out of the intact realm of the Elementary School. Now things become dramatic. The soul gestures are very much a part of this age, and the rod exercises gain in importance, because the growth of the bones must be cultivated and guided. An exercise that is like a bridge for children of this age is the rod exercise in which we throw rods to each other and catch them.

Drama is the main theme of class 8. In *Eurythmy as Visible Speech* Rudolf Steiner said: "Making the forms of eurythmy – this is to continue the divine movements, the divine forming of the human being."[6] Look at the pupils of class 8 and consider what it means that we eurythmists must continue the work of the gods. There are many things hidden in this sentence and the image it presents. Often the children are drastically dramatic in what they say about eurythmy. We have all met this. But what they say and what they do are worlds apart when they really enter into doing eurythmy. We have met this, too, and the memory of it provides a support to which we can cling.

When you enter a eurythmy room where a class 8 has just had a eurythmy lesson, the first thing you want to do is open all the windows. The smell is quite different after a class 1 has been doing eurythmy. We can smell the children, and we ought to do so. We should ask from the anthroposophical point of view: "What are my perceptions of a whole class that is being born into the astral?" We need to practice soul gymnastics, soul gestures, plenty of

120

drama. One exercise may be based on Conrad Ferdinand Meyer's **Beggars' Ballad**: All the beggars have been invited. They sit on magnificent marble seats and feast on hare, chicken, and wine. Then Grummel enters. The children, 20 strapping class 8 boys and girls, are forming a loose group. Now someone comes in, moving rapidly through the group from behind to the front. What do the others do? They react! "A beggar rushes into the room" – tension arises. "Grummel, what brings you here?" What is he going to say? "Having been given a bed at the imperial palace, I happened to hear ..." What did you hear? "Your uncle is sending a band of murderers ..." The groups goes through it again and again. "Is it really true, what you are saying?" Working on a dramatic piece with the children, we practice soul gymnastics. I get to know my own feelings and sensations. Am I really afraid? Am I excited? How do I react when someone suddenly appears and finds me in a place where I don't belong? First I have a bad conscience, particularly if I'm a pupil in class 8. Such things have to be expressed.

What seems to be especially important now is that in eurythmy lessons as well as all the other subjects we should teach "out of the joints." I mean by this that we should take as our starting point those places where externally there is nothing, where the physical recedes so that something spiritual can begin to work. Our joints are the most spiritual part of our limbs. In class 8 we need to practice everything that is like joints – the switching places in music and speech; we need to let what lies between the notes or between the lines come to the fore and begin to work.

In class 6 we practiced the octave, and in class 8 we now take it up again. Brightness in thinking must be guided down into the will. There is an exercise that works with the archetypal rhythm of pulse and breath. The rhythm of the hands is two shorts and a long while at the same time the feet do a long followed by two shorts. The result is an octave within one's own human body. The exercise is difficult; we have to build it up gradually and work on it repeatedly. But when the children succeed in doing it, you see how all of a sudden a higher being enters into them; they grow bright and light.

In our search for therapeutic principles in the curriculum, what does it mean when we are so concerned in class 8 with the way soul and spirit work in the body, particularly the soul? We study the soul in a living way when we practice the soul gestures. Youngsters today have an urgent need for this when their soul being begins to free itself. They get to know themselves through this way of studying the soul: I can hate, I can be in despair or only sad, I can be incredibly clever or insatiable; – all these attitudes are in me. I can handle them and learn to control them. If we can succeed in this, we will, I believe, have created the strongest possible prophylactic against the temptations that beset youngsters today. We must let the children seek out soul experiences at various levels; we must let them practice and also come to grief over such experiments so that they can grow strong. If we can practice knowledge of the soul right down into the body – in its purest form in eurythmy, but also in all the other subjects – then we shall have made a contribution that will perhaps prevent young people from seeking drug-induced soul experiences of a lower kind.

The curriculum for class 9 presents us with a peculiar phenomenon: much of the material for class 8 is repeated. In class 8 Schiller and Goethe were studied; in class 9 we now read *The Sorrows of Young Werther*. History in class 8 brought us up to modern times, and the same goes for class 9. What is the reason for this? Up to now individual facts have been presented. Now they are linked together, so that interconnections become visible. In music eurythmy the intervals with which the children have long been familiar are built up into chords. That the gesture for the major third is made more to the right, or how the gesture for the fifth is formed, this we learned in class 8. Now the major chord asks for both gestures simultaneously. Major and minor chords, the six-four chord and dissonances present us with plenty of work for class 9. In speech eurythmy we also take up what we did before, but now we say, "Do it yourselves! Bring me a poem you think is really good and do your best to draw an appropriate form." Of course the initial reaction is, "I can't." So the youngsters have to be encouraged to try. Here, for example, is a form made by a small, delicate, curly-haired girl in class 9. It comes straight from her soul. The poem is by Wolfgang Borchert [roughly rendered into English]:

I want to be a lighthouse
in night and wind,
for cod and smelt,
for every boat,
yet I myself am a ship in
distress!

P.

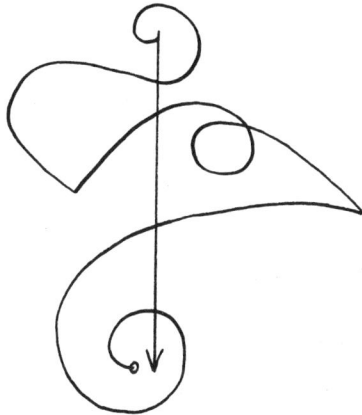

Rudolf Steiner never tired of challenging us to get to know the children, to read the children. We can read a form like this one and ask: How does it sit on the page? What are its links with the text? Does it ring true? We only study the laws of form with the children later on in the year. But what is expressed here, what can we all read in it? "I want to work into the world: 'I want to be a lighthouse . . . yet I myself am a ship in distress.' " The form begins at the back of the room, goes forward toward the world and ends by going back into itself. It is beautifully done. The class 9 youngsters endeavor to live in their own newly-developed octave space. Let every child make a form like this, and we shall get to know one another in an entirely new way. Do we hear the questions the youngsters ask of us, loudly or perhaps only whispering, or merely with a glance? Do we take up the challenges in the high school?

Returning from the summer holidays and encountering a new class 10 confronts us with a specific problem. How to make the transition, in German-speaking countries from addressing them by the familiar "Du" to using the more distant and formal "Sie".

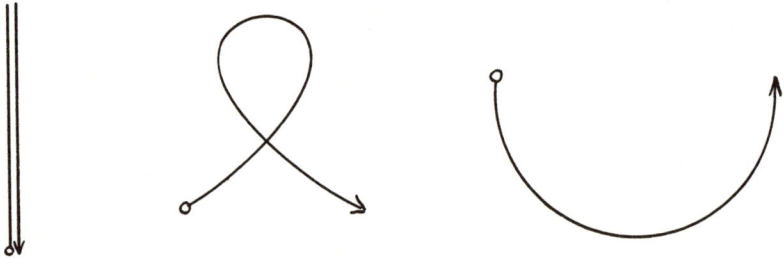

Earlier I referred to the aspects which Kepler related to the three qualities of the sphere. In class 10 we come to Kepler again. He described the sphere as representing the Trinity and its radius the Holy Spirit. My own ego is the radius of my own sphere, my circumference is the same size as I am. "God the Father is the center," said Kepler.[8] Younger children live out of the element of the Father as though in the center of the world. "The Son is the surface [of the sphere]" – the Christ power that leaves us free yet encompasses us.

Returning to school after the summer holidays, don't we all ask ourselves: "What am I doing? Where is my deepest impulse?" In Rudolf Steiner's Mystery Dramas there are words addressed to teachers and physicians, indeed to all those who help to educate human beings out of the wisdom of anthroposophy. In *The Soul's Probation* Felix Balde says:

> What stands before us as a human being,
> what we experience as the soul,

what as spirit shines for us –
a multitude of Gods have seen before them
already since eternities;
and it was their intention to unite
powers from every world,
which form, when they are joined, the being of man.[9]

These words could very well provide a motto, a starting verse, for our teachers' meetings. But they might equally well be a motto for the work in eurythmy lessons with class 12: ". . . to unite powers from every world, which form, when they are joined, the being of man."

Dear class 12 pupils, this, surely, is what you want. You go out into the world in order to gather powers from it, in order to search for powers with which to build your lives. Each one of you is different as you stand before me today; and the powers that each of you will take up in your lives will be just as different. You have ideals; how will you bring them to the world? Have you had a good look at your teachers? When they were young, they also had ideals. Have they succeeded in realizing any of them? Realizing ideals is something that can be practiced. We shall be doing it over the next few weeks as we work on the signs of the Zodiac. We shall begin by bringing into the world in all kinds of ways the ideals we have in us, what stands behind us and above us. You all know someone who has great ideas and is capable of putting them into words. If you scatter these words over people, they sometimes begin to form new thoughts. This can happen! One or another of you might do it at some point in life. Your thoughts and ideas are up here. Go and fetch these thoughts from the spiritual world, bring them down to earth and formulate them accurately. It is an art. Then the idea will be resurrected in new thoughts.

I might say the same in signs:

DEVELOPMENTAL INSIGHTS
Discussions Between Doctors and Teachers

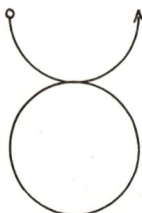

We take our departure from the world of thought; we carry the thoughts down to earth; new thoughts arise. It is our task to bring movement into what is at rest. To follow this path is one way of realizing our ideals.

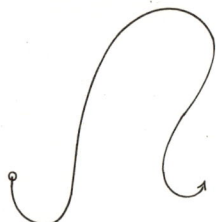

But something quite different can also happen. There are individuals who have difficulty in realizing anything down here because their thoughts and ideals keep on snatching them up to the heights. These people are small on earth but great in the realm of ideas, and they find it hard to keep on coming down to earth.

Then there are people who are in danger of being boring, but they have a great capacity for bringing balance into things. Their spiritual impulse and its realization in the world are harmoniously balanced. It is difficult to pick a quarrel with such people!

Or there are those against whom we constantly feel we need to protect ourselves a bit. Something of this is in all of us and makes us need protection in ourselves. We must not think that everyone else should be obliged to understand our great and wonderful ideas.

These signs, runic pictures, become pictures for life when we fill them with movement. We follow these forms with class 12 pupils, and doing this is the same as practicing life. It is very impressive to see groups of pupils simultaneously following the forms of the four evangelists. We all share the same space; we have to accommodate ourselves and be aware of one another, so that the Scorpios finish stinging at the same time as the Water Carriers

126

complete their form. We practice on the basis of these facts, because these facts are within us, and because this is a way of practicing life.

In our journey through the ages of childhood we have seen the children of class 1 each still living in his or her own "sphere." This sphere broke open and turned as though inside out in class 8, while in class 12 each pupil gained a new space.

BIBLIOGRAPHY AND NOTES

1. Steiner, R., *Waldorf Education for Adolescence* (GA 302). Tr. not known. Forest Row: Steiner Schools Fellowship Publications, 1993. Lecture of June 12, 1921.
2. Steiner, R., *Christ and the Spiritual World and The Search for the Holy Grail* (GA 149). Tr. C. Davy & D. Osmond. London: Rudolf Steiner Press, 1983. Lecture of January 2, 1914.
3. Steiner, R,. *Ways to a New Artistic Creation* (GA 286). Tr. rev. J. Collis. London: Rudolf Steiner Press (planned publication 1997). Lecture of June 28, 1914.
4. Steiner, R., *Conferences with the Teachers of the Waldorf School in Stuttgart* (GA 300). Tr. P. Wehrle. Forest Row: Steiner Schools Fellowship, 1986-89. Vol. 3. Conference of March 1, 1923.
5. Steiner, R., *The Balance in the World and Man* (in GA 158). Tr. D. Osmond & M. Adams. Vancouver: Steiner Book Centre, 1977. Lecture of November 21, 1914.
6. Steiner, R., *Eurythmy as Visible Speech* (GA 279), Tr. V. & J. Compton Burnett, London, Rudolf Steiner Press, 1984. Lecture of June 24, 1924.
7. Steiner, R., *Soul Economy and Waldorf Education* (GA 303). Tr. R. Everett. New York & London: Anthroposophic Press & Rudolf Steiner Press, 1986. Lecture of January 2, 1922.

8. The next 3 paragraphs of the text are omitted. They describe exercises practiced in eurythmy lessons with class 10 to help with this transition in German-speaking countries.

9. Steiner, R., **Four Mystery Dramas** (GA 14). Tr. A. Bittleston. London: Rudolf Steiner Press, 1982. *The Soul's Probation*, Scene 5.

CHAPTER 5

METHODOLOGICAL AND THERAPEUTIC ASPECTS OF FORM DRAWING

by

Hildegard Berthold-Andrae
Translated by Christian von Arnim MA, M.Litt, FIL

The forces which build up the organization of the child acquire their individual characteristics in the period leading up to the age of seven. The will is constituted internally in all movement; the feeling in learning to speak; and, finally, the imagination, previously linked with the whole body, is individualized as the child approaches school age. The etheric formative forces affect the physical body in a specific way within this process. At this age human beings incorporate forces from the body into the nervous organization in the head. In this context Rudolf Steiner also refers to the "nervous and will organism" into which every motion of the limbs is integrated.[1] Rudolf Steiner expressly referred to the need to deal with the formative forces which are released in this period of the child's life one stage at a time. They have worked in a sculptural and musical way to build up the human organism. In their transformed state they have to be treated in the same way, in other words, not intellectually but artistically.

The first lecture in *Practical Course for Teachers* describes how the performance of artistic activities raises to the level of the nervous and sense being – the "upper human being" – those things which are predisposed in the whole person.[2]

On the basis of these thoughts about the nature of the human being, the basics of form drawing made up the content of the first day's exercises: straight and curved lines and their various combinations; then the basic order of their appearance in space: continuous movement

~~~→ or movement round a center; ⊙ and finally, the inner laws which govern form and which give it the beauty of its appearance.

How can form drawing exercise a harmonizing influence on the developmental disorders which are evident in increasingly serious form in almost all children of school age? Form drawing has a harmonizing and healing effect in very different ways in the first years of school when the life of the will and of the nervous and sensory sphere are being transformed.

From Outer to Inner Movement

Every day we see the children moving through space: trudging with heavy steps or gliding along lightfootedly, acting swiftly or deliberately, using their hands and feet skillfully or clumsily. When they are at work, we experience them as quietly concentrated or volatile and fidgety – the latter being much more frequent nowadays. The same group of children, playing round games, will swing backwards and forwards and around in unison, carried rhythmically by a song. That is a beautiful sight, but the movement is guided more from the outside than the inside. Beat and rhythm of the song, the given form, and, not least, the feeling of group cohesion, together create order here.

Quite a different form of movement is observed in the orientation exercises performed on their own body. The children are asked to perform, with rapid presence of mind, movements on their own body which they have to think about. Rudolf Steiner placed great value on this exercise and described it as: ". . . becoming dexterous on oneself using vividly pictorial thinking." He went on to explain: "If a child carries out such exercises at around age eight, it learns . . . to think for life."[3]

It is the purpose of this process to unite touch and movement with thinking. Anyone who frequently carries out this exercise with children can observe something quite remarkable. By touching one's own body, something like assurance in one's own presence, a kind of existential feeling which has a calming effect on the children's feeling of being alive, is created. The senses connected with the will and how to strengthen them were the focus of these exercises and the subsequent discussion.[4]

The Line as a Pattern of Movement

As regards form drawing itself, grasping and making visible a pattern of movement, Rudolf Steiner gives an example which directly engages the newly developed powers of thinking: "A feeling should be awakened in the child as to what it means when a circle is drawn around a point."[5] Anyone who does this exercise, starting with the waving, circling, semi-dreaming movements of the infant,   and moving on to the   cited above, will notice clearly what is going on inside him or herself. This exercise has a strongly harmonizing effect on the inner aspect, the will and the thinking, and the outer aspect, perception of the form as it is created. The connection with the external world is created where the hand guides the pencil in tracing the form, the eye accompanies the line at every point of its movement, and our feeling inwardly accompanies the form itself as it curves or straightens; at that point we find the external control over our internal thoughts and intentions as they appear externally.

"Being Wholly Present" as a Means to Create Harmony

The signature of his/her newly developing abilities can be seen in every line that is drawn by the school-age child: too firm or too light, too tight or loose; everything is an expression of what is going on in the soul. At the same time we have to be aware, however, that it is always the present state which comes to expression in a drawing. All learning, like growth, is a temporal process. Thus, the effort of the child to co-ordinate the activity of hand and eye is very important. Practicing, too, needs to be practiced and requires patient guides!

Whenever Rudolf Steiner speaks about learning to write as it develops out of form drawing, he urges that the children should receive guidance, that their activity should be accompanied "with interest."[6] This remark contains the reason for all learning, for interest is an essential instrument for strengthening the etheric organization.[7] Every mechanical movement entails a weakening of the etheric body because the physical body dominates.

In drawing the forms and letters, it is not only the hand which is active but the eye, and the sense of movement in the eye in particular, is active together with the hand. In "being wholly present"[8] the interest in the process itself, in the process of creation of a form, grows; in other words, this is a thoroughly artistic process. The whole of the human being is challenged to participate. Notes on form drawing.[9]

Stimulating a Feeling for Space:

Children encounter space with their physical limbs in the early stages of their lives. After the age of seven they want to conquer their inner soul space in thinking, feeling, and willing. Form drawing can help in this, because it is able to arouse a flexible feeling for spatial relationships. Every line appears in its spatial context which is experienced as the line is drawn. This occurs initially on an unconscious level but can increasingly be made part of the child's awareness.

The feeling lives in the oscillation between up and down.

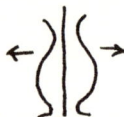

The symmetrical forms initially establish the difference between right and left and are then united again in their continuation. This is done by the thinking. The will moves actively from the back to the front. It is more difficult to represent this in drawing form, and the child can only grasp it after age nine. Unconsciously, it happens before then, of course, with every loop for instance in which the later movement goes over the top of the earlier one. Equally, there is symmetry in most forms even if this is not experienced consciously.

This can lead to the establishment of something like a guideline for the way that the drawing process is constructed:[10] Up and down in all its variations is largely appropriate for the initial years of school. Symmetrical forms are given particular prominence at age eight and nine. After age nine plaited forms can be used to help the will unite even more strongly with the imagination.

Rhythm and Structure of the Pattern of Movement

The rhythmical element exercises a harmonizing influence in form drawing as well. But it also contributes much to the beauty of a form. Linear forms are beautiful if they reveal inner laws such as the orders and relationships of a number or of space. This beauty is often misunderstood. It is hidden by being colored in, by being wrapped up in a soul covering as it were. That reduces the clear statement of the line tremendously. Furthermore, the creative process which has just been completed cannot continue to work in the child.

Dissolution and Concentration

The basic elements of the line are introduced on the first day of school: straight lines and curves. The steps which are built up on these elements may be compared with breathing in and breathing out, alternation and interaction of formative forces.

Oscillating shapes release and enhance this dynamic. A strong imagination has to accompany and guide the dynamic will here, otherwise the form will disperse into chaos.

The drawing of forms with straight lines has a concentrating, but also a consolidating effect. Every angle requires sustained alertness for the conscious change of direction. No rounded angles, no "sort of like this" should be allowed to go unnoticed. Cross-overs and reversals of direction contribute to strengthening attentiveness and concentration in the same way that angles do. Linking dissolving and concentrating form elements produces ever new exercises to stimulate the children. "It is not so much the passive element, but the active way in which we approach things with our will which is important for the sense perceptions of the eye and the ear." [11]

BIBLIOGRAPHY AND NOTES

1. Rudolf Steiner, *Erziehungs- und Unterrichtsmethoden auf anthroposophischer Grundlage*, GA 304, 1979. Lecture of November 23, 1921 in Oslo.

2. Rudolf Steiner, *Practical Course for Teachers*, Rudolf Steiner Press, London, 1988. Lecture of August 21, 1919 in Stuttgart.

3. Rudolf Steiner, *The Kingdom of Childhood*, Rudolf Steiner Press, London, 1988. Lecture of August 15, 1924 in Torquay.

4. Rudolf Steiner, *The Boundaries of Natural Science*, Anthroposophic Press, New York, 1987. Lecture of September 29, 1920 in Dornach.

5. Rudolf Steiner, *The Younger Generation*, Anthroposophic Press, New York, 1984. Lecture of October 12, 1922 in Stuttgart.

6. Rudolf Steiner, *A Modern Art of Education*, Rudolf Steiner Press, London, 1981. Lecture of August 13, 1923 in Ilkley.

7. Rudolf Steiner, *Erfahrungen des Uebersinnlichen. Die Wege der Seele zu Christus*, GA 143, 1983. Lecture of January 11, 1912 in Munich.

8. See Note 1, lecture of November 24, 1921 in Oslo.

9. These remarks about form drawing represent the briefest of brief summaries of a four-day training course.

10. See also E.M. Kranich/M. Jünemann/H. Berthold-Andrae/E. Bühler/E.Schuberth, *Formenzeichnen*, Stuttgart, 1985.

11. Rudolf Steiner, *Study of Man*, Rudolf Steiner Press, London, 1981. Lecture of August 23, 1919 in Stuttgart.

CHAPTER 6

READING AND WRITING DIFFICULTIES AND THEIR TREATMENT[1]

by

Heike Schuhmacher
Translated by Christian von Arnim MA, M.Litt, FIL

It is clear that there are increasing numbers of children in Waldorf schools who present class teachers, parents, remedial teachers, and teachers in curative education with problems which are difficult to resolve. These children are not able to gain any pleasure from reading or to become confident in handling German grammar. It is noticeable, however, that they often display a marked cleverness in the fields of mathematics and geometry and have an engaging ability to tell stories and recite texts. This facility with language often hides for a considerable length of time the fact that they cannot read. In spite of great efforts, these children are unable to make sovereign use of the instruments of reading and writing in English or in a foreign language without mistakes.

The participants – almost exclusively people involved with this problem area on a practical level – considered the educational and therapeutic assistance which was available for these children to be inadequate. There was a unanimous wish for concrete information about ways to diagnose and treat the problem.

The first of these two days was wholly devoted to the process of diagnosis, which was divided into three sections:

I. Phenomenological examination of reading and writing as a sense activity.

II. Examination of the human sense organism from the perspective of Rudolf Steiner's teaching of the senses; the division of the twelve senses into the lower ones – related to the will; middle ones – related to the feelings; and upper ones – related to the thinking. The relationship between the lower and upper senses and the relevance of integrating the senses of life, touch, movement, and balance with the activity of the sense of vision, which forms the basis of the seeing process in reading and writing, were examined.

III. Phenomenological examination of a complex disorder of sense-perception in children with reading and writing difficulties.

Against the background of the above examination of reading and writing within the context of the physiology of the senses and from the perspective of a sense-organism comprising twelve senses, results of neurophysiological research conducted on people with reading and writing difficulties, which investigated the finer functions of binocular vision, opened new avenues of understanding. Considerable disorders of the vision processes in both eyes can be shown to exist in a large number of children with reading and writing difficulties.

In spite of outstanding visual ability in each eye individually, there were considerable disorders in the autonomic accommodation of both eyes to the text (properly distanced accommodation and convergence) and the ability of both eyes to scan the lines of text without trouble and without loss of a sense of balance. The fusion of vision in each eye into a single sense impression (three-dimensional vision) is possible in principle but keeps being interrupted by temporary loss of vision (scotomata) which alternates between eyes.

This brain-induced disorder of the visual process can be shown to exist by means of orthoptical investigations and through the measurement of visually evoked potentials over the visual cortex of both hemispheres. It only takes place with binocular vision. The feeling of "I am looking at" which is tied to the functions of the inner part of the retina and which arises as a result of the harmonious interaction of both eyes, only occurs for a short time and keeps slipping from consciousness. At the moment when this happens, a sort of shadow (functional scotoma) is thrown across the center of the visual field of the one eye, only to disappear again quickly and reappear blocking the vision of the other eye. Right and left eyes – as well as the feelings "I am looking at" and "I" am conscious of the activity of looking as a nervous and sensory process in both brain hemispheres, which accompany the visual process – are not coordinated harmoniously in simultaneous and calm vision which is fully in the grasp of ego-consciousness. For children who suffer from this visual disorder, which has few external symptoms (but is often accompanied by frequent blinking and rubbing of the eyes, headaches and stomach pains while reading), it means constant uncertainty in recognizing closely spaced letters. Letters or parts of words persistently disappear from vision with the result that there is uncertainty about the order in which letters occur; the development of secure internal word images and reliable recall of word images is made extraordinarily difficult. The ability to observe how a word is written is, after all, an essential prerequisite for learning to spell in German (and there can be no more disastrous piece of advice in this context than "write what you hear").

A conspicuous number of mistakes when copying texts and the bunching of mistakes towards the end of a page at the same time that the script becomes contorted are not always caused by lack of concentration but are frequently a sign of a visual process which is no longer working despite great effort. Insecurity in the perceptual functions of the senses of touch, balance, and movement are evident almost always from the beginning classes onwards and can range from an inability to distinguish subtle differences to disorders of specific or even overall motor coordination of the lower and upper limbs. The remedial care of the lower senses by the class teacher in the rhythmical part of the lesson is, thus, a very important and often extremely helpful form of preventive treatment for the later development of learning difficulties. It can be so effective that, as I know from my own observations, visual disorders in some children had disappeared completely after two Waldorf years.

The subject of the second day was an examination of reading and writing lessons in Waldorf schools for children just starting to read and write, with particular emphasis on the symptoms which can alert class teachers at an early stage to the need of a child for special help. A therapeutic program for children who have already developed reading and writing difficulties, which has been in use for some years, was also presented.

It is clear that this could only be done in outline, since each child presents the therapist with completely individual issues. In general, we may say that the basis is almost always provided by medicinal treatment of the child's constitution within the context of anthroposophical medicine. Questions concerning care for the life sense always involve detailed conversations with the parents on the way that the day is organized, food, sleeping and waking rhythms, and so on. It has also become increasingly clear in therapeutic practice that many children require rhythmical massage to begin with, before the curative eurythmy exercises may be started, which play such an extraordinarily important part in any treatment. The focus of the latter is on the large "E" exercise, the "I" exercise, and especially the lemniscate exercise.

For older children, a therapeutic program has proved itself which consists of exercises for one eye to begin with, for only under such conditions can the continuity of consciousness relating to the visual process be developed without interruption. This requires that one eye be covered for three to four hours per day. Playing ball with large and small balls at various distances, throwing at targets, archery, embroidery, and delicate modeling work form the enjoyable part of the exercises. This is supplemented by spelling out the letters while reading with one eye in order to acquire the delicate visual scanning movements over a page of text. Italian texts, for example, have often been used to begin with, since the practiced readiness of the child to supplement its approximate perception by guesswork has often become too deeply ingrained in habit. Soon the reading of German texts, spelling them out aloud, follows, whereby seeing and hearing have to be recognized as complementary perceptual processes (see "Meditativ erarbeitete Menschenkunde").[2] Here the therapist has to perform the important function of reflecting back to the child's sense of hearing through speech the words which the child has perceived visually and spoken. The process is then concluded by short dictation exercises based on the two to three lines of text, which have been worked at in this way.

The additions or intermediate steps which might sometimes be necessary in individual cases cannot, of course, be discussed. The blind eye during the exercises (which should not, incidentally, last more than ten minutes per day) is obviously fully involved in the therapeutic process. In the vast majority of cases there is an improvement in the visual disorder relating to binocular vision, with a very clear increase in reading and writing ability, within a few weeks or months.

BIBLIOGRAPHY AND NOTES

1. Report of a working group led by Heike Schuhmacher and Peter Zimmermann. The report on the approach to reading and writing difficulties by the psychologist Peter Zimmermann was unfortunately not ready in time so that this additional material is missing.

2. "Meditativ erarbeitete Menschenkunde" in: Rudolf Steiner, *Erziehung und Unterricht aus Menschenerkenntnis*, GA 302a, 1983.

CHAPTER 7

MATH DIFFICULTIES
DIAGNOSIS, SYMPTOMS AND THERAPY[1]

by

Ernst Schuberth
Translated by Christian von Arnim MA, M.Litt, FIL

Difficulties with arithmetic, like those in reading and writing, cannot be classified within a single, uniform syndrome. A wide variety of different causes can lead to similar patterns of either overall or specific "weakness." The study of the manifold causes of difficulty with math is not made easier by the fact that many differing schools of thought generate literature on this subject.

Extensive research has, firstly, been undertaken by subject specialists into mistakes commonly made in arithmetical processes. Such research chiefly examines the mistakes made in computations and in set tasks, such as choosing the wrong arithmetical operation, or using mistaken rules: adding two fractions, for example, by adding the numerators together and the denominators. Such studies draw our attention to the particular difficulties children may have in solving certain tasks. To combat these, a large number of methods have been thought up and tried out. But in general, this research has little to say about more fundamental difficulties that people may have with arithmetic. As well as this approach, there is also the research done by general educational psychologists into the problem of mathematical inability; in addition, there is the literature produced by those who work within the wide field of special needs, psychiatry, and neuropsychology. Of particular significance are the studies of psychomotor disturbances by Kiphard and his colleagues.

I will begin by touching briefly upon several types of arithmetical difficulty and distinguishing them by their root causes:

1. Difficulties caused by teaching method

a) A particular form of mathematical weakness has resulted from the introduction of logic into school mathematics. In the 60's, the reform of mathematics teaching was begun by presenting mathematical set-theory to the youngest classes. In the 70's, this became compulsory for all pupils taught according to the state national curriculum. The idea was that the logistic approach would enable the child to understand the psychological origin of mathematical concepts; but this was largely untenable and in certain cases led to a specific type of inability, which had no basis in the child's actual constitution.

There are several aspects that could be mentioned here, but I would like to address one in particular that seemed important to me in certain cases. Having pondered it for some considerable time, I believe it to be of deeply spiritual significance. At the time that set-theory was introduced, there were children who refused to adopt the required thought-processes. These processes, derived from logic, were supposed to lead the child to think in patterns of formal logic made "material" through logical blocks. There were – although it might be hard to give any outward proof of this – children who were particularly sensitive to the spiritual, who did not wish to hinder their own destiny by harming the development of their brains in this way. They took refuge, therefore, in mathematical inability. Such children could be recognized by the fact that they responded immediately and capably to a teaching method imbued with a spiritual approach. Such phenomena gave one a certain glimpse of the battle being waged for human thinking and intelligence.

b) Another difficulty caused by teaching can come about through a change of method. We may suspect this cause where a child has had a change of school or even just a change of teacher. The risk is greater if a teaching method relied heavily on a specific visual teaching-aid. If, for example, a child has learned to do arithmetic by using Cuisenaire rods – small sticks which represent number by means of color and length – and then another teacher comes along who uses a different method, the subject will sometimes seem unrecognizable, and the child fails to understand what is required.

c) Closely related to this cause of failure is a narrow, exclusive reliance on a particular form of representational method when a sudden transition is made to abstract arithmetic. The child who feels unable to cope with numbers and processes without resorting to their tactile or visual manifestation is likely to fail. If, for example, children have been taught the low-order numbers, to the power of one, two and three, using respectively linear, 2-D or 3-D visual-aids, numbers to a higher power will remain an abstract conundrum for them. The failure in teaching method resides here in a one-sided, geometrical representation of arithmetical relationships.

d) In Germany there is currently a problem for immigrants who have a different mother-tongue, caused by the change of language. I first became aware of this in the case of a Waldorf school pupil, who had German parents but had attended an English-speaking school in South Africa. The family returned to Germany in the child's second or third year of school. The child had no problems with normal speech, since the family had always spoken German together. But in arithmetic there were considerable difficulties, which had not been apparent in the teaching medium of English. I continued to observe this problem in other children in Bielefeld, who had come from abroad. A large number of them had an unexpected weakness in math.

Anyone who has contact with foreigners will observe that even when they speak good German, they continue to do most math processes in their mother-tongue. It might be a waiter in an Italian restaurant who adds up the bill in Italian, or an English person who dials a phone number while murmuring the digits in English. Arithmetical processes are not embedded in ordinary speech and do not develop simultaneously with it. Habits picked up in the first years of school usually determine math abilities for most of our lives. Special training is needed to achieve a sound re-orientation.

For immigrant children we have developed initial programs of language-free math. Tasks were set using drawings, or were given in ordinary colloquial speech. These trials were very successful and encouraged many children who were struggling. Since Waldorf schools, in particular, often have pupils with foreign parents, some attention should be paid to these programs. This is particularly so for children who join a school not in first grade but at a later stage. We should not underestimate the difficulty caused even by the altered position of words making up a number: twenty-one in English becomes einundzwanzig (one and twenty) in German. It is useful also if numbers in language teaching are dealt with to some extent in parallel Main Lessons, so that any difficulties can be picked up, and the children helped to become aware of them.

e) There is, unfortunately, a specifically "Waldorf" math difficulty, caused by children remaining dependent on rhythm. As is known, we use many different rhythms in math teaching, which we stamp, clap, or otherwise express. If this method is employed too one-sidedly, it can lead to specific difficulties, which I would like to examine here more closely because of their topical relevance.

Through the years I have had experience of many children who showed marked weakness in some aspects of math, although they were otherwise of normal ability. Such weakness becomes unavoidably obvious from grade three onwards. In such a case, I would first test the child's motor development - of which more later. If, as far as I can judge, everything is normal, I ask: "What is 6 x 7?" and observe the child's response. If he or she recites the 7 times table - perhaps even with the help of fingers - then stops at 6 x 7 and answers: "42", I ascertain a mistake in the teaching method. By third grade, or with good teaching by second or even first grade, a third of the children will have realized that it is not necessary to repeat the whole seven times table in order to find the right answer. Many teachers take this transition for granted – and their lessons will at least appear successful to the extent that a third of the class will achieve it without much guidance. But a child who continues to recite the whole table will fall hopelessly behind, and will cope only with multiplying small numbers. Soon he or she will stop responding, through inability to do what the teacher is asking.

To overcome the barriers which have arisen, I ask the child: "Which times-questions can you answer straight away?" "None, I can't do that!" says the child. "I'm sure that's not so", I say, "let's see what you can do. Can you tell me straight away what 1 x 7 is?" "Yes!" "Can you tell me another that you know?" "Yes, 10 x 7 is 70." They also usually know that 11 x 7 = 77, 7 x 7 = 49 and 2 x 7 = 14. Then I write down the tables in order under each other, and underline the answers which the child can give me straight away. Then I say: "Right, now just have a look at this: 35 = 5 x 7 (or 5 x 7 = 35)." In this way I encourage the child to remember another answer. I include this one with the other answers the child knows, and keep asking and testing until he or she is sure of it. That can lead - at least it has done so many times in my experience – to the child suddenly looking at me and saying: "Is it all right just to say the answers like that?" The child has been suffering failure for ages. Why? Because the transition from "rhythmic memory" to "time memory" has not occurred properly and consciously.

We all rely on rhythmic memory to recall language, songs, sequences of numbers, etc. This form of memory is closely connected with speech and movement. The specific, individual elements of knowledge that we need conscious access to, are something altogether different. In the first lecture of December 24, 1923, of the Christmas Conference cycle, *World History in the Light of Anthroposophy*, Rudolf Steiner speaks of the historical and evolutionary aspects of localized, rhythmic, and time memory.[2] It is right that we should base our initial math teaching on the fostering of rhythmic memory, but we must not halt there. When Rudolf Steiner – as so often in his pedagogical lectures – speaks of the task of developing the capacity for memory by means of mental arithmetic and the tables and additions from 1 to 10, he is talking of modern, time memory. This is, unfortunately, often neglected. Particularly in math the teacher needs to make a careful transition from the motor activity called upon in rhythmic chanting, to individual and specific knowledge. This involves raising the process from the limbs and the middle region up into the head. The child must have a certain grasp of the fact that 7 x 5 = 35 without having to recite a little verse to get there. If we succeed in establishing this whole process of head-memory by carefully lifting it out of the rhythmic system, then we are provided with a wonderful means of working upon the relationship between the soul-spirit and the physical body.

Arithmetic then leads to that invigorating alertness and secure ability which is the sign of good math teaching.

All these difficulties result in psychological barriers. They are not constitutional weaknesses, in the real sense of the word, in the child. To overcome these barriers, we need an insight into their causes, a pedagogical and psychological approach to the difficulties encountered, and a strengthening of the child's confidence and ability through positive affirmation of his or her achievements.

2. Difficulties caused by emotional disturbance

Alongside the barriers to learning created by inadequate teaching methods, there are also the difficulties caused by purely emotional factors. These are not connected with the teaching itself, but with the social environment. Children can, for example, become very discouraged when their mistakes and failures are continually highlighted. They may also be under pressure from the parents to succeed; or may be anxious because they feel they are failing – as a result, perhaps, of a mistaken teaching method. These emotional difficulties can lead to them seizing up altogether - sometimes to a near-physical paralysis – when they are required to solve math problems. I once encountered this in a Waldorf teacher-training seminar: an experienced colleague, who had already been teaching successfully for several years, was overcome by paralyzing fear when I directed a math question at her. I found out in conversation with her that the cause of this had been a change of school and teaching method in her first year of schooling. This damaging trauma had not yet been healed.

Once aware of such problems, one starts finding them to be more widespread than would at first appear. I cannot give an absolutely reliable estimate, but I suspect that in every reasonable-sized group of adults, more than a quarter will exhibit signs of damaging trauma resulting from failures in the way they were taught math. More than almost any other subject, math is very liable to cause experiences of failure, resulting in a refusal to learn, anxiety, and life-long "switching off" whenever faced with a math problem. The term arithmophobia describes this. In school this is particularly serious, since the child is not in a position – unlike the adult – to find ways of evading the problem. I believe that the only remedy is by way of strong emotional reinforcement and encouragement.

Georg Hartmann, who has since died, once gave me an important piece of advice: "When you take on a ninth grade in the High School", he said, "be careful not to emphasize what they don't know; show them how much they know! You could, for instance, talk to the class about what they think the simplest task in math is." The pupils will usually reply to such a question: $1 + 1 = 2$! Then you can ask for a still simpler calculation. They may then suggest $1 \times 1 = 1$, which is simpler in some respects because only the number 1 appears in it. In $1 + 1 = 2$, there are already two numbers – 1 and 2 – to be considered. Is there a task that is simpler still? They may come up with $0 \times 0 = 0$, $0 + 0 = 0$, $0 \times 1 = 0$, $1 \times 0 = 0$. This question of the simplest possible math task can give rise to discussion about nought and one. I have frequently introduced this at the beginning of ninth grade, and the pupils have always shown great involvement and interest. Almost everyone can contribute to such a discussion, and the math teacher can draw double benefit from it: firstly, he can praise the class for their enthusiasm; and secondly it gives him an opportunity to speak of the neutral element – one and nought – in addition and multiplication, which is an important aspect of mathematics.

In passing I will also mention the great importance for teachers of language, music, etc., to draw positively on what the pupils already know. It is a poisonous habit to want to show off one's own superiority over the previous teacher of a class by demonstrating that the pupils have learned nothing; to really accept such a view, the children would have to negate their own previous biography. In contrast, you win over a class of children by positively affirming their abilities - which will in every case be present. This may not flatter your egotism as much as putting down your predecessor, but it creates a better relationship with your pupils. They will go home feeling deeply satisfied, and will look forward to the next lesson in which what they already know will be affirmed. This is not of least significance for the high school teacher in relationship to the work of the elementary class teacher!

I can only make passing reference to the wide field of mental abnormality which some researchers have investigated in connection with math ability. Their results show that some people suffering from particular syndromes – especially epilepsy – are extremely gifted at performing math calculations. Curt Weinschenk describes many such cases. His book, *Rechenstörungen*, came out a good while ago but is still useful. I would also refer you to the book by Hans Grissemann and Alfons Weber, entitled *Spezielle Rechenstörungen - Ihre Diagnostik und Therapie*, which arose out of their work in psychology and child psychiatry.

3. Math difficulties caused by constitutional problems

These kinds of difficulty require a therapeutic and curative-educational approach. I would like to say at the outset that we have an enormous need for more research in this field. We do not, though, have the capacity within our institutions to conduct these investigations to a sufficient extent. We lack the staff and the means. Therefore, I can do little more here than sketch out the concepts underlying such research.

The basic question we must ask as a prerequisite of all research and therapeutic work is this: What is mathematical ability, or upon what does it depend? This, in turn, is connected with the question: What is mathematics? Different schools of thought have very different answers to the question of the origin of math. Many theorists point to its connection with logic; math then appears to be a particular branch of logic. Besides this approach, there are also the theories of constructivism, etc. As we saw from the attempts to reform math teaching, these approaches do not provide a sustainable basis for the development of mathematical thinking in the child.

A quite different approach is taken by the Geneva psychologist Jean Piaget, who has done intensive research into the development of mathematical thinking in the growing child, along genetic and developmental-psychological lines. In his collaboration with the math educationalist Erich Wittmann, a detailed attempt was made to construct a method of teaching math that would draw on the results of developmental psychology. These attempts were not really successful, and Piaget later distanced himself from them. Although he was able to distinguish separate developmental stages in children's thinking, he could not derive from an interpretation of the nature of mathematics any methodologically useful approach to developing math ability. I emphasize this point, although in many countries math teaching in the primary curriculum is still founded on a basic math method devised by Piaget. The importance of his research to our theme, though, seems to me to lie in the way he relates the internalizing of math operations to the formation of number concepts and arithmetic ability.

One can also find important pointers to the origin of mathematics in some of the work on neuropsychology, for example, of Luria and his school. In his book, *The Working Brain*, Luria mentions the – to him astonishing – fact that spatial orientation and math ability are both affected by brain damage. These, and other seemingly unlikely connections (or also non-connections) of various capacities, become understandable through an anthroposophical view of the senses.

If one reviews, as far as possible, the whole spectrum of neuropsychological, developmental-psychological, and logic-based approaches to the content and origin of mathematics and its relation to the human constitution, Rudolf Steiner's indications about the underlying human, physical basis of mathematics, come sharply into focus; they provide real points of departure for both math teaching and curative education in the case of specific difficulties. I would like firstly to formulate a thesis about the origin of mathematics, and then try to substantiate and clarify it.

Math arises from the internalized activity of the sense of movement.

I will provide an example from actual experience, which everyone can inwardly test for themselves. When I was a (still rather naive) class-teacher in Munich and was teaching sixth grade, I drew two "straight lines" on the board one day and asked: "Do these two lines intersect?" (diagram 1). An extremely sanguine child immediately put up his hand

and, to my surprise, said: "No!" I had not long ago taken my math degree and did not expect a child to be able to say "no." But another child followed with another "no", to my dismay. What should a teacher do in such a precarious situation? Try to help himself out with another question: "Who thinks they do intersect?" A usually quiet girl put up her hand and said: "They do intersect!" Then the first boy called out: "Where then?" The girl pointed to a place just off the board. The boy laughed aloud and said: "Well draw it then!"

It would be interesting to tell you how the same class of children, in the tenth grade, discussed infinity in projective geometry. It was again this particular girl who helped the class take a step forward.

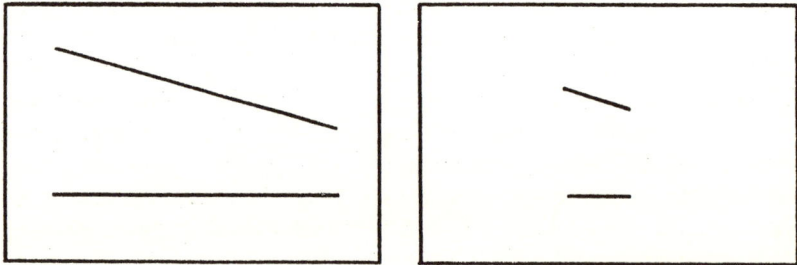

Let us look more closely at the problem of intersecting straight lines: to what extent were the boys right to say that they did not meet, and to what extent was the girl right? Let us look at this in detail. Colored surfaces are perceived on the board: the gray-green board surface and the white chalk lines. The thin, bright chalk surface causes me to make a movement with my eyes, which is coordinated by the sense of movement and balance. The eye-movement is immediately related to my body by the sense of balance. I suspect that a disturbance to the sense of balance will make it impossible to ascertain an intersection point somewhere beyond the board's surface. The girl was able, like us, to ascertain it, because she herself continued the movement stimulated by the white chalk, and therefore freed herself from the color-impression.

We can determine the intersection point even if only a small bit of "straight line" is drawn (diagram 2). The sense of color allows us to differentiate between different color qualities. At the border between different color areas, we are stimulated to movement. This is coordinated by the sense of our own movement (kinesthetic sense), and brought into relation with the position of our own body by the sense of balance. The sense of movement is no longer orientated to the colored surface but to the motor activity of my own eye-balls. "Mathematical perception" does not, therefore, reside in the outer world, but within one's own organism. This is why one can have access to a perception which is no longer provided by the sense of color (e.g., off the board). The difference between the children clearly lay in the fact that some of them were perceiving mainly through their color-sense, while the girl, by projecting the experience of movement beyond the board, could base her thinking upon it.

Although our sense of vision is of outstanding importance for us, it is nevertheless not decisive for the perception of mathematical qualities. To understand any concrete, spatial aspect of geometry, we need only to activate a process of movement. How this actually occurs is not so important. For three years I taught a blind girl, to prepare her for her school-leaving exams. She had to learn a lot of geometry. A friend of hers drew all the constructions in the palm of her hand. From this time-sequential experience of touch, she could grasp all the shapes: straight lines, circles, ellipses, hyperbolas – and their intersection points, etc.

The sense of our own movement, by means of which we simultaneously create and perceive mathematical content, depends upon one or more senses which are directed towards the outer world. Those of us with eyesight rely upon the dual or even multiple function of the eye. The organ of sight is the bearer of several sense-functions. It not only perceives color, but is at the same time a highly sensitive organ of movement. Leaving aside such things as creasing of the forehead, etc., it is the highest placed organ of movement in the body. If we examine the chief organs of our motor-organization from below upwards, we pass from the legs to the arms, then the organs of speech, and finally the eyes. Our legs are involved in willed movement through three-dimensional space;

our arms in the active grasping of the spatial environment; our eyes, with their capacity for rotational movement, convergence, and focusing, are involved in spatial perception.

Mathematics arises within the human being where outer movement is continued inwardly. The boys in my class, whom I mentioned, were very sanguine, motor-active children who lived in their outer senses, but were therefore less able to step back from outer impressions and carry out purely inward movements. This was caused both by their strong connection to the sense of sight and their disinclination to be physically still, which would have allowed them to create and perceive internalized movement. Ascertaining an intersection point beyond the board relates still to the actual spatial circumstances; but it also requires us to project and imagine something that is not evident to the outer senses. In the same way, mathematical activity as such also has to free itself from what is given in outer spatial relationships, and work with internalized concepts of movement.

In actual fact, a chalk line has never been synonymous with the mathematical concept of a straight line. What, then, does geometry consist of? Of what are geometrical forms composed?

They are the will impulses of the movement I create within me, which I relate to the ego incarnated in my physical body through the sense of balance. It is only by means of this ego-activity that I can establish a conscious relationship between my body and its environment, bringing outer configurations into inward imagination and permeating them with thinking. If the sense of balance does not function properly, the "I" becomes exiled from the physical body. In past times people said that the heavens were "crashing down all around them" to describe a dysfunction of the sense of balance. In such cases, mathematics becomes at least temporarily impossible.

I have been speaking of the basis of mathematics in connection with geometry. But how do we develop awareness of number? Concepts of number draw upon our power of judgment in a different way. If, for instance, I say that three people are sitting over there, the process is as follows: by saying "there", I both encompass and exclude. I first form the unity of the number which is to be counted. Every perception of number is therefore preceded by the creation of a unity.

Let me mention something here in passing: In Waldorf circles one continually encounters the idea that One is the largest number. This idea has also been circulated in print and so has gained a certain currency. But no one who champions this idea would swap his hundred dollar bill for my one dollar! Not even if I reminded them that One is, after all, the highest number! What is true – and Rudolf Steiner also made this point – is that unity precedes all processes of counting. A modern formulation for this is that overall quantity is determined before counting takes place. The overall quantity represents the unity of the counted objects. When we say, therefore, that "three people are sitting over there", our thinking is conducting a process of simultaneous encompassing and exclusion. The sense of life is somewhat involved in this, even if the unity is only established through a concept or a judgment. The concept formed can either be orientated more towards the senses, or towards other concepts. In the first case we determine the number of perceived objects; the second case comes about when, for example, we determine the amount of prime numbers that exist between one and a hundred. But as I have said, every process of counting depends upon conceptual thinking. The concept we use determines the resulting number. If we ask: "How many people are here?", we get a different answer than if we ask: "How many men are here?", or "How many chairs are here?" The space in which we dwell does not encompass a quantity as such, but allows us to determine a number according to a particular concept. Once we have created the unity of objects we are concerned with by means of a concept, we begin the individualizing of this concept: we ascertain how often the concept presents itself to our perception or to other concepts.

When I say that a group of people "consists of seven", I am creating a conceptual and spatial context, in which the unity is provided by thinking. By encompassing the objects before me with the concept "people", this concept is individualized in the case of each separate person. Wherever the concept attaches itself to a perception, it receives an individual coloring that is not contained within the overall concept as such. But by attending to my perception, I exercise a time-sequential motor activity in the process of comprehension. If I now wish to focus upon the number rather than the particular qualities of the people concerned, I must, it is true, carry out the individualizing of this concept, but also attend to the process of comprehension itself, rather than its content. This may explain why mathematicians are so frequently introverts! They are less interested in the intrinsic qualities of the objects under their consideration, than in the form and number qualities which they deduce from the process of comprehension itself.

A more accessible way of putting this is to imagine I have a telescope; you watch me as I view things through the telescope which are invisible to you. The telescope is turned in three different directions. You, the watcher, cannot see what I see, but you can observe the process of movement with which I perceive the distant objects. This process occurs here, where you are observing me. You can deduce from my movements that I have looked at three different objects – but not that they were, perhaps, three distant ships on a high sea. The ships are experienced out there in the world, the number is experienced in ourselves, in the process of active comprehension.

Mathematics is, then, experienced through our own activity. But the marvelous thing is that by drawing back what we perceive into our own very individual activity, we also grasp laws active in the outer world. We all know how subjective our judgments about taste or smell can be. If one person says: "Herring tastes awful!" , it does not seem like a very objective statement. In reality, the speaker has merely described his own relationship to herring. But if someone says: "Here are three herrings" , this is true – whatever our other judgments about herring may be - as long as we have perceived correctly. Indeed, people with views which may otherwise be diametrically opposed nevertheless agree on these issues.

I have had to speak at some length – although still not in nearly enough detail to do justice to the subject – about the origin and basis of mathematics, because a reasoned therapy or diagnosis of math difficulty cannot get anywhere without knowledge of how mathematics arises. Whoever thinks that math is an abstraction from sense perception does not understand it, and cannot make any headway in therapy or diagnosis. The starting point for getting to grips with math difficulties is observation of the way the senses work in both children and adults; of particular importance is the way the outer senses – like the senses of color and touch – work together with the inner senses, such as those of balance and movement.

To gain an overview of a particular child's constitutional capacity for the development of math ability, I believe that we must first examine a sequence of developmental stages – which do not, of course, occur completely independently of each other.

First Stage

Our first task is to diagnose the degree to which the senses in general have developed and matured. Some senses are fairly advanced at birth already (smell, taste), while others only gradually develop (balance, movement). Motor development plays a particular role in mathematical capacity. I will confine myself here to a few salient points.

First of all there is the whole realm of overall and specific motor functions. We can tell a great deal just from the way a child walks. How does he or she run? How do the feet meet the ground? How do the arms move? In curative homes one can often distinguish the healthy children from those in need of special care just by the overall image of their walking movements. Even slight disturbances express themselves in a rather inharmonious interplay of individual movements. The development of patterns of movement in the human being seems to be highly susceptible to psychic disorders. A simple test of the condition of interplay of movements – coordination – in a child, is to ask him or her to take off a shoe. If there is a motor disorder, he will prefer to sit down to do this. One then asks: "Can you do it standing up?" The child will perhaps lean against something while trying to take the shoe off, for he will have had much practice in compensating for difficulties. If one then says: "Now try to take your shoe off without leaning against anything", he may well fall over while trying to lift his foot. It becomes noticeable that he just lifted the foot up and made hardly any other balancing movements. Normally when we lift up our leg, our whole body is involved in the movement. We move in an overall, coordinated way. The muscles of the neck, chest, back, stomach, and feet are all actively involved. If I were to stand on one leg on a board fitted with pressure sensors connected to a screen, and we could observe the activity of my left leg while I moved my right leg about, we would see a veritable multiplicity of data: it would become clear how much is going on at other places while I move my right leg. Learning to walk is not just developing the ability to put one leg in front of the other; it is a manifestation of the harmonious interplay of our whole sense of motion. It means establishing the unified basis of our sense of motion.

This overall sense of motion is "disconnected" in children with math difficulty. That is the first symptom to look for in a child who has a constitutional weakness in math.

Another important aspect of motor development can be tested in the following way: ask a child to climb up on a chair, and watch the movements which he makes with the rest of his body. Do the movements of his arms help him, or are they unconnected with his efforts? Watch also the head movements or even the facial expression and the position of the fingers. So-called "associated movements" are often indicative of developmental disorders; these are movements which do not usefully contribute to an intended movement, or are unconnected with it.

A small degree of associated movement, though, should not be counted too important. Many of us, for instance, make a small motion with our tongue when we bang in a nail or take a photograph, etc.

Also of importance for developing math ability, as has been demonstrated a good while ago already, for instance by Johnson and Myklebust, is awareness and control of body position. Much is done in the Main Lesson in Waldorf schools to develop this – for example when children are asked to make quick body orientations: touch the left ear with the little finger of the right hand, touch the nose with the forefinger of the left hand, etc. I don't need to elaborate on this here. But it is important that teachers should have an insight into the therapeutic significance of much that is done daily in the teaching situation.

Observing laterality also forms part of the diagnosis of a child's motor development. In the book by Eggert/Kiphard, *Die Bedeutung der Motorik für die Entwicklung normaler und behinderter Kinder* (The Significance of Motor Functions in the Development of Normal and

Handicapped Children), there is a study by Friedhelm Schilling called "Determining Laterality." Empirical research shows how difficult it is to form a sound diagnosis in this area. Laterality does not depend only, as is commonly believed, on the specifically tested organs (eye, ear, hand), but also on the nature of the accomplishments required. Schilling comes to the conclusion that there is an uninterrupted continuum between right and left laterality, in which one must also take account of the requirements of a specific task.

Delacato also contributes much to this theme; he did intensive studies into the connection between reading and writing difficulties and motor development, and in the process encountered the role of laterality. I cannot go into detail here; I would just like to draw attention to the complex nature of laterality and its development. From the anthroposophical view of the human being, this can be seen in terms of the ego taking hold of the body, and also of the etheric forces as they become free at the change of teeth. There is already a good deal of anthroposophical research available on this subject.

Interestingly enough, motor abnormalities can derive from over-intellectualization at an early age. One is tempted to say that a certain kind of parent can bring this about. It can result in a range of symptoms from slight to extreme tensions, a tendency to poor spatial awareness, to bumping into things, etc. In such cases there may either be an inability to progress beyond a fixation on particular number-processes, or, more positively, an unusual ability for math. In the first scenario, the process of internalization – which we will shortly speak of at greater length – seems to lack an insufficient foundation in the child's constitution; in the second, the child becomes strongly fixated on an inner involvement with concepts of space and number. Adult mathematicians, in particular, often display a lack of motor co-ordination. This seems to me to be connected with an over-emphasis on the conceptual life – as opposed to dwelling more in outer perceptions. Undergraduates used to say, at any rate, that they could tell math students apart from others, even at a distance – by their pallor, lowered head, flat-footed walk, and taciturnity. Although this may be true, it should not be used as an argument against the thesis that mathematical ability is connected with healthy motor development. It tells us, rather, that we need to examine a second stage in the development of ability in math.

Second Stage

At first grade age, the part of the child's etheric body primarily connected with the nervous system becomes relatively free of organic processes, and can therefore form the foundation for the soul-life of imagination and memory. This stage, which we also describe as the "birth of the etheric body", or of the intellect, does not yet represent the transition to causal thinking, which occurs in a marked way at the time of pre-puberty. It is the task of education to enable the child to take hold of these etheric forces with the will and ego. Piaget's researches very clearly show the changed nature of the child's physical and emotional constitution at this age. The "internalization of operations" which he speaks of shows in an increased independence of the power of imagination from sense-experience. He has observed that in some cases a conceptual sequence can be reversed in a way not possible in physical reality; or also that different means for achieving an aim can be thought through, etc. If the ego does not properly take hold of the forces of imagination and memory at this age, there is a danger that a purely associative thinking develops. In this case, concepts just lead on from one another, in the following kind of way: "What is 3 x 7?" Oh yes, 3 x 7 – I had that sewn on the front of a jersey once, it was black and white – it was given to Claudia eventually; Claudia had a friend who was Greek. I'd like to go to Greece. . . ." This exaggerated sequence depicts how concepts are threaded one to the other, from association to association, in a continuous, completely pathological way – without direction from the will or ego. The pedagogical task of mental arithmetic is to bring order into conceptual life and allow the ego to permeate it.

What Piaget describes as "internalization of operations" is an inner involvement with qualities of space and movement. We can speak, therefore, of an internalization of the motor sense-processes. At first grade age it becomes possible – though this differs in extent from child to child – for many different senses, not only the motor senses, to be internalized and inwardly imagined. This is true of concepts of color, sound, smell, taste, and many others. Whoever wishes to be a cook must be able to "compose" meals by imagining taste and smell; the painter must inwardly imagine color, the musician tones and sounds. In the same way, the mathematician must work inwardly with concepts of space and movement. It is not enough just to reproduce outer spatial and movement sequences; he has to work with them actively.

If we are going to make use of these two stages in basic math teaching, we should, each lesson, begin with physical activity, and end with stillness in which inner spatial and number concepts can unfold. This is the starting point for a math curriculum based on an understanding of the human being.

An interesting – and for numeracy, very important – intermediate step between perception and the process of purely inner movement, is to be found by using one's own body. If we draw a shape on a child's back, the sense of touch is activated, but the sense-impression must be followed by an inner process of movement if the shape is to be recognized. It is not possible for the body alone to accompany and reproduce the movement. It would be interesting to test whether a form drawn on the back is perhaps accompanied by fine muscle-responses, for example of the eye-muscles.

The movement is accompanied in a still more inward way when fingers or toes are used in counting. This inner grasping by means of the body is sometimes very deficient. I will mention an extreme example that I encountered in a special school in Herford. I was asked to test a 15-year-old girl in the sixth grade. Her level of math ability was that of a first grader. What was the problem? I asked the girl to put her hand on the table, then I covered up three of her fingers and asked: "How many fingers are hidden?" She looked at me astonished and said: "I don't know." I took my hand away, then she counted with her other hand, "one, two, three fingers" , as though they didn't belong to her. Then I covered over only two fingers and asked her the same question. Again she answered: "I don't know." I took my hand away, and once more she counted her own fingers as though they were objects separate from her: "One, two – two fingers!" Try to feel what sort of inner relationship this girl had to her own body, obviously not one that could form the basis for inner conceptualization. It was as though her hands were bandaged up. It is interesting to note that such children who lack "finger-awareness" often draw stick-figures devoid of fingers (see diagrams 3a and b).

Fig. 3a

Fig. 3b

We can get some faint idea of what this lack of awareness is like from our own toes. If we were to use them to aid counting-processes, we would make quite a few mistakes. Many people find it particularly difficult to distinguish between the third and fourth toes.

A simple finger test involves finding out if the child can name individual fingers when they are touched, then seeing if he can move a particular finger when it is named. Games with fingers and toes can help develop this awareness from an early age; the child then becomes conscious of his own periphery. This awareness develops at the point in the body where it divides and multiplies. It is, surely, wonderful to observe how the single bone of the upper arm divides first into the duality of ulna and radius, then into the wrist-bones, and then still further into the many finger bones! Ernst Michael Kranich has written a very beautiful essay about math and our inner connection with the body. Some aspects that I can only mention briefly here are there described in greater detail.

The foundation of math functions on inner movement processes which continue the immediate impressions of other senses, and is connected with a further series of exercises which can be of particular help to children with math difficulties. Every child has its own individual interplay of senses. Just as a horse-chestnut absorbs different substances from the earth than an oak, so different people take in sense-impressions in a variety of ways. Children, for example, who are visually orientated, experience the world in a different way from those whose sense of hearing is more pronounced. When we are trying to stimulate in the child a concept of number or a process of computation, we must, of course, first approach this task through the outer senses. The resulting sense-impressions then need to be worked upon by the inner sense of movement. This process can provide us with a wide variety of different exercises according to the individual nature of different children. In some cases we will only be able to arouse the child's interest in any aspect of number by addressing particular outer senses. Number processes can be practiced not only by means of visual, acoustic, and tactile senses, but also through impressions of temperature and taste. We call such exercises "number-guessing." It is possible to arouse even a very impassive child's interest in numbers by showing him a tray on which are three small pieces of Camembert, two small pieces of lemon, one small piece of milk chocolate, and a small piece of black chocolate. The child is blindfolded and allowed to eat everything on the tray; then he must say how many different tastes there were, or how many different kinds of taste. That is how you can stimulate number-concepts through taste. Another exercise would be as follows: blindfold a child and ask three or four other children to circle round him and give him their hands, one after the other. Their hands are all of slightly different shape, warmth, and softness. The children keep circling until the child in the middle can say how many they are. Such an exercise calls on the senses of touch and warmth, and other senses as well. Children also get very involved if you blindfold them, sit them on a chair, and let them count a number of pebbles with their feet. Such exercises connect the first with the second stage of developing math ability: direct sense-impressions are accompanied by an inner picturing of movement, which gives rise to concepts of number. It is striking to observe the effects of these exercises: on the one hand, children enter into their outer perception; on the other hand they also concentrate very hard and try inwardly to connect the many impressions they receive. This is, then, a focused way of repeatedly exercising both perception and inner picturing.

We can add another very important process – which as far as I am aware has until now received very little attention – to the inner working with sense-concepts, something which becomes increasingly possible from first grade on. The internalization of sense-activity makes it possible to gain willed, ego-directed access to a single sense-quality. The world directly addresses the multiplicity of our senses. In each individual situation there may be greater emphasis on specific sense-qualities, while others remain more unconscious. If, for example, we look up at the night sky and see a star shining, we are primarily aware of brightness and color. More unconscious is the relationship we establish to our own spatial position through our sense of balance: we see, perhaps, a star in front of us, high up on the right side of the sky. Our willed, ego-directed control over the sense-realm can express itself in our choice either to concentrate on the impressions of color and brightness or on our spatial position. The boys whom I spoke of in connection with diagram 1 had only a weak capacity to separate spatial and movement qualities from color impressions, while the girl was clearly able to do this. The ability to internalize and work inwardly with sense-qualities only reaches its culmination when a capacity is developed for separating sense-impressions from each other. It usually takes until the age of twelve before concepts of space and form, for example, can be dealt with separately from each other. The theorems of congruence in elementary geometry depend upon grasping form independently of spatial position. If a child does not yet have the capacity to understand this distinction, there is little point in trying to teach him such theorems. An extensive description of the connections of the senses with geometry can be found in Ernst Schubert's *Geometrische und menschenkundliche Grundlagen für das Formenzeichen* (The Basis of Form-drawing in Geometry and the Human Being) in the book on form-drawing edited by E.-M. Kranich.

Third Stage

Once a healthy motor development and a willed capacity for drawing on inner concepts of movement, space, and number have provided the constitutional foundations for math activity, then conceptual thinking can recognize and express relationships between objects. That is the point at which math really starts - no longer only depicting and describing specific forms, but also relating them to one another, formulating general laws, and examining their logical interdependence. The latter activity is often of prime importance for the mathematician.

We have thus outlined three main stages in the development of math capability: firstly, the training and coordination of the physical senses, then the more inward, soul-capacity of internalized sense-activity and conceptual picturing, and finally, a mental grasping of objective laws. At each stage there exists the possibility of distorted or retarded development. The conceptual framework I have sketched out can enable us to recognize the widest variety of problems, and derive from this recognition the therapeutic means to tackle their causes. Let me very briefly recapitulate on the key observations and exercises. I am assuming the presence of partial or overall math weakness and leaving aside barriers caused by teaching methods and psychological factors. First, motor development is tested by examining:

+ motor development in both its overall and precise, specific functions;
+ the development of coordination. (Are there any signs of "associated" movements?);
+ control of body and finger orientation;
+ laterality (left/right emphasis of hand, foot, eye, ear);
+ any muscular spasms or similar abnormalities.

At the next stage one tests the extent to which the sense-processes and concepts have been internalized. Normal accomplishments will vary with the child's age, for example:

+ Can forms in various spatial positions be recognized as identical?

* Can the child separate the concept of number from an outwardly visible quantity?
* Can number-operations be carried out independently of a visual or other sense-concept?
* Are there signs of any particular interconnections between certain senses?

In short, we need to test the degree of mental flexibility in the handling of forms and numbers.

The transition to actual math operations as the expression of number relationships is the beginning of math as such, as an intellectual activity. In Waldorf schools we start from the unity of all things – the One – and from it derive all the math processes. As we do so, we can test whether the child has any difficulty in producing the necessary inner activity, whether, for example, his inner picturing is still too dependent on outer stimulus.

Both aspects – motor and inner flexibility – provide us directly with constitutional therapy procedures, in which we take account both of coordination and the conscious distinction between sense-impressions. Once healthy development has been achieved, or once therapy has brought order into a disordered state of affairs, then the mental faculties can permeate and order the math content that is worked upon by inner picturing.

To conclude, I would like to turn my attention to a question that concerns the spiritual dimension of math teaching.

One can often observe, particularly in curative education, that math concepts are made very material and sense-bound, in order to try to get the children to understand them in some form at least. Those working with children with special needs have always tried to rely on material methods of operation, to an even greater degree than modern math teaching with its logical blocks, Cuisenaire rods, and many other sense-orientated, math visual aids.

It is for this reason that I would like to quote a passage by Rudolf Steiner from the second lecture in **Universe, Earth and Man**, in which he speaks about the connection between math teaching and the healing forces within the human being:

"To uplift oneself in this way to the spiritual was, in ancient times, of healing value; and it would be good if people could learn to understand such things, for by so doing they would also grasp the great mission of the anthroposophical movement. This mission is nothing other than to guide human beings into worlds of spirit, so that they can once more perceive these worlds from which they descended! In future times human beings will retain their full self-awareness, they will not sleep-walk through their lives; but a strong spiritual power will nevertheless take effect within human nature. When this comes about, the possession of wisdom and insight into higher worlds will have a harmonizing and healing influence on human nature. Nowadays this connection between the spirit and healing is so veiled that only those who have somehow been initiated into a deeper Mystery wisdom know anything much about it, for otherwise they cannot begin to perceive the minute and delicate facts of the matter. Those who can see deeper know the profound inward sources from which healing can arise. Let us imagine, for example, that someone falls prey to a certain illness, one that has an inner cause – not a fracture of the femur or an upset stomach, which have outer causes. Anyone who wishes to understand the deeper aspects of things will soon realize that a person who likes to occupy himself regularly with mathematical concepts, will have access to quite different sources of healing than someone who does not want to pursue such activity. This is a fact which can demonstrate to you the remarkable connection between a person's mental life and the circumstances of his outer health. Of course it would not be true to say that mathematical thinking heals people. We must be more precise and say: a person who is receptive to mathematical concepts requires different healing forces from someone who is not. Let us assume there are two people suffering from the same illness. In fact this does not happen, but let us assume it for a moment. One person has no interest in mathematical concepts, while the other occupies himself intensively with them. It would be possible in such a case that the non-mathematician would fail to respond to all treatment, while the other person would, given the right medicines, be cured. This is a real possibility.

Another example: two different people, one of whom is an out-and-out atheist, the other a deeply religious person, have quite different potential for being healed. It could very well happen that if both suffered from the same illness and were treated by the same means, the religious person would be cured while the atheist would not. Such a suggestion seems absurd to the large majority of people nowadays. Yet it is the truth.

Why is this? It is because the human being is quite differently affected by sense-free as opposed to sense-bound concepts. Just consider for a moment the difference between someone who hates math and someone who loves it. The first thinks it is a waste of time, preferring to involve himself only with his sense impressions. Yet, it is of great value to dwell upon concepts which are not outwardly visible. In the same way it is of value to dwell upon religious ideas, for these also have to do with things that one cannot grasp with one's hands, which have no outer, material, sense-bound aspect. These are things which, when people once more become aware of the spirit, will one day come to exert a great influence on pedagogical principles. Let us take the simple concept of 3 times 3 equals nine. It is best if children relate to such a concept without basing it on the senses. They can perhaps first of all – but not for too long – count with their fingers; but then get used to conducting such a process in the realm of pure, mathematical thinking. Then it has a healing, ordering effect on them. Nowadays people understand so little about such things – that is clear from the fact that in education the exact opposite occurs. Just think of the calculators which have been introduced into our schools, which are supposed to make tangible the processes of addition and subtraction, etc., by means of all sorts of visible beads. People want to draw down to a sense-perceptible level what should be grasped only by the mind and spirit. That may be a convenient method – but whoever thinks it is pedagogical knows nothing of a deeper, healing education that is rooted in the power of the spirit. A person who has become used, from childhood on, to dwell in sense-bound concepts, will be far harder to cure of an illness – for his nervous system suffers from conditions conducive to illness - than someone who has always been used to sense-free concepts. The more you accustom someone to think independently of outer objects, the easier it will be to heal him. That is why it was part of ancient traditions to focus upon all sorts of symbolic forms, such as triangles, and combinations of numbers. Apart from their intrinsic interest, this also had the aim of uplifting people from concern with what is just in front of them. If I place a triangle in front of me and just look at it, it has no particular value. But if I see in it a symbol for the higher threefold nature of the human being, then it is a healing concept for the spirit." [3]

This passage can give us pause for thought, if we wish to educate on the basis of an anthroposophical understanding of the human being. Should we not be doing all in our power, even with children who are hampered with difficulty, to try to follow the three stages sketched out here: from a training of the physical senses, through internalization of sense activity and concept, to the purely inner, mental math content? Mathematics is, from the deepest pedagogical point of view, an education towards the spirit. More than any other subject it can give a young person the certainty that, within himself, proceeding from his own absolutely individual activity, he can gain access to an objective, universal reality that never comes to him passively from without, like a color or tone. This real content has clearly defined parameters and proves itself to be a far-reaching instrument for grasping the laws of the outer world. What we acquire in a purely inward way gives us access to the objective laws of the world. The important anthroposophical mathematician Louis Locher-Ernst spoke of mathematics as a "pre-school of spiritual knowledge." Even when working towards the healing and progress of a child hampered by constitutional weaknesses, we should never lose sight of this great aim: that spirit should shine out within earth existence!

BIBLIOGRAPHY AND NOTES

Grissemann, H./Weber, A., *Spezielle Rechenstörungen, Ihre Diagnostik und Therapie*, Bern, 1982.

Kranich, E.-M. (Ed.), et al., *Formenzeichnen, Die Entwicklung des Formensinns in der Erziehung*, Stuttgart, 1985.

Kranich, E.-M., *Mathematische Früherziehung im Vorschulalter als psychologisch-pädagogisches Problem*, In: Der schweizerische Kindergarten, 3/1970.

Luria, A.R., *The Working Brain*, London, 1973.

Weinschenk, C., *Rechenstörungen, Ihre Diagnostik und Therapie*, Bern, 1970.

Steiner, R., *Universe, Earth and Man*, Anthroposophic Press, New York, 1985.

1. Based on a lecture given on October 24, 1989 at the Kolisko Conference in Stuttgart.
2. *World History in the Light of Anthroposophy and as Basis for Knowledge of the Human Spirit*, GA 233, 1991.
3. *World, Earth and Man; their Nature and Evolution, and their Reflection in the Connection between Egyptian Myth and Contemporary Culture*, GA 105, 1983, lecture of August 5, 1908 in Stuttgart.

CHAPTER 8

WORKING WITH "DIFFICULT" CHILDREN[1]

by

Hans Friedbert Jaenicke
Translated by Johanna Collis

The questions and themes discussed in this group included: What symptoms mark a child as difficult? Are children more difficult now than they used to be? What do children bring with them and what is caused by their environment? When there is an accumulation of difficult children, what can be done to ensure that they can remain at a Waldorf school? What is the meaning of early learning in kindergarten? How do we work with parents as a prerequisite for positive integration? Particularly conspicuous children are: aggressive, "unreachable", hysteric, hyperactive, have motor dysfunctions, psycho-organic problems, etc. Is there any ongoing research into diagnosis and therapy? The case conference as an important aid.

Difficult children are usually those who disturb their fellow pupils in kindergarten or school class to such a degree that proper lessons become almost impossible, while the other children suffer psychologically or physically, and teachers are pushed to their limits. The other type of difficult children are those who cannot cope with the social situation in their group or class, or are permanently overtaxed by the material of the lessons to the extent that they develop psychological problems culminating in learning difficulties or complete failure to handle the school situation. The ratio of those making problems to those who suffer from them is generally regarded as being 1:4. The ratio of difficult boys to girls is also approximately 4:1. Bernard Lievegoed's book ***Heilpädagogische Betrachtungen*** is an important source of help for teachers in understanding and diagnosing the problems of difficult children.[2] Lievegoed uses Sigand's four constitutional types (the cerebral, the respiratory, the digestive, and the motor-muscular) as his point of departure. Basing his insights on the one hand on developmental phenomena (acceleration and retardation) and on the other on the polar syndromes in Steiner's ***Curative Education*** (epilepsy and hysteria)[3], Lievegoed describes the various possible disorders in such a clear, and lively way that class teachers studying the book carefully will find a description of every problem child which will help them reach a deeper understanding of that child, and also discover ways of tackling the problems educationally and therapeutically.

The increase in the number of difficult children is noticeable. Whereas a meeting of ministers of culture from German federal states in 1972 arrived at a figure of 10%, special education circles now consider the number to be nearer 25%. A congress of child psychiatrists in Düsseldorf found that half the children seen by school doctors before starting school had developmental problems to a greater or lesser extent. Although class sizes are decreasing in state schools, the number of problem children is increasing. This is also a serious challenge in Waldorf schools, especially those more recently established. It is often suggested to parents of difficult children that they might try a Waldorf school since this type of school is especially suited to help such children. While this is true and is likely to transform the lives of a good many parents, Waldorf schools are increasingly having to ask themselves how many difficult children they can possibly integrate into a class. How can we do justice to these children? What kind of remedial or special education do they need? Are our teachers sufficiently prepared to work with difficult children in relatively large classes? Where are the limits of what can be done for a child, and how do you part company with a child you cannot keep in your class? Is the Waldorf curriculum still up to date now that children with accelerated development and precocious intelligence want to determine the rate of progress and the mood in a class, and parental expectations and the requirements of high school teachers pressurize the class teacher to achieve more?

Developmental problems are not caused solely or even primarily by environmental or social and cultural factors. It is obvious that many of them are in fact the consequence of difficulties while incarnating. Children arrive from the spiritual world with a constitution that favors either acceleration or retardation (precocious attachment to the earth caused by overdeveloped nerves and senses, or else a cosmic dreaminess). Whichever the constitution, it tends to be compounded in early childhood, leading in many instances to a loss of integration that manifests as behavioral problems or learning difficulties. Rudolf Steiner frequently referred to this phenomenon.[4]

Knowing that just now many children are being forced into incarnation prematurely and insufficiently prepared, and that it is necessary to rescue these souls,[5] we realize how important Waldorf education is in our time. If we take this challenge seriously, we have to accept that one of the most important tasks of Waldorf education is to find ways and means of meeting the needs of these "difficult" children. This means teachers have to be adequately prepared. In the first lecture in *Curative Education*[4], Rudolf Steiner said he expected curative teachers to have a fundamental knowledge of education for normal children. In the same way teachers in Waldorf schools ought to have a thorough knowledge of developmental disorders and ways of treating them. This will need to be considered at our training establishments.

Especially in the elementary school one prerequisite is that the artistic and imaginative aspects of the curriculum must be fully realized. Constitutional acceleration needs to be counterbalanced by broadly based general artistic and musical activity in lessons as shown in the curriculum. Many younger Waldorf teachers report that children in Class 1 do not want to listen to fairy stories any longer but try to set the pace of the class by pushing forward intellectually. Teachers who go along with this fail to realize that these accelerated children are the very ones who need the mood of pictures, fairy tales, fables, or the interval of the fifth in Class 1. Waldorf education as it is designed to suit children of this age is a therapy for these accelerated children and works against the tendency of hyperactive children to be too awake in their nerves and senses.

It must be possible to organize schools in a way that can enable difficult children to be integrated. We cannot solve the problem by founding remedial Waldorf schools for the purpose of off-loading the difficult children. The comprehensive aim of the original Waldorf School must remain our guiding light and goal. This means that we shall have to include remedial measures during Main Lessons, or in separate remedial sessions, or after school. Just as every Waldorf school ought to have a school doctor, a curative eurythmist, and a speech teacher, so should the post of remedial teacher be a firm one on any faculty. Class teachers ought to have two to five remedial lessons a week, in addition to their Main Lessons, in which they can divide their class and give individual attention to the children. There ought to be a possibility for subject teachers (eurythmy, languages, music) to send difficult children who make it impossible to hold orderly lessons to suitable remedial teachers who can help them gain the skills that will enable them to return to normal lessons.

Children with weak reading and writing skills should not have to wait until Class 4 or 5 before they are noticed. Early recognition of this problem is particularly important, and training of the lower bodily senses can achieve more than focusing specifically on writing and reading. We shall have to work very hard to expand the Waldorf school's ability to provide remedial help.

There will be consequences as regards personnel and finances, of course, but surely there must be means and methods by which these problems can be solved for the good of the children (and also the teachers). Connected with every school there are educationally trained and capable parents or friends who could be brought in. A number of schools have let us know that they have developed "care groups" consisting of parents, friends, therapists, and the school doctor who concern themselves with individual children, with play and therapy groups or with advising parents either during school hours or afterwards.

Collaborating with parents – always an important ingredient in the Waldorf movement – is especially urgent where a disturbed child is concerned. It is essential for us as Waldorf teachers to refrain from getting on our high horse or pointing an admonishing finger at parents as we lecture them about all the things they have done wrong and how they ought to treat their child. The parents of difficult children often approach us with much trust and hopeful expectation. Some are already extremely unsure of themselves and feel quite helpless about their child's problems. We should treat them as partners in the work of bringing up their child and help them understand our reasons for suggesting specific educational or remedial measures. During parents' evenings or when making home visits, it is not a good idea to quote what Rudolf Steiner might have said about soccer, etc., or to criticize the family's lifestyle. Rather than wanting the parents to believe us, our hope is that they will recognize what is right and helpful for their child.

An example of what can be done is to be found at the Christian Morgenstern School in Wuppertal. For many years this school has been running a very special seminar for parents. A few weeks after the beginning of the school year, the parents, children, and teachers of Class 1 go on a "retreat" at premises on the edge of town, where they all live and work under one roof. The children have their lessons as usual and can then play in the surrounding woods, while their parents experience what eurythmy, speech, pentatonic flute music, water-color painting, form drawing, and so on are like, what they mean and the effect they have. As the week goes on, they sew marionettes and at the end put on a performance of a fairy tale told by the parents and accompanied by suitable instrumental music. In the evenings they work on the ideas underlying Waldorf education, make music together, and embark on deep discussions lasting far into the night. This venture places great demands on the faculty as a whole. It is like a gift to the class teacher from all his or her colleagues, and for the children and parents it provides a deep experience and an intense introduction to Waldorf education. The experiences of this seminar live on throughout the rest of the children's time at school and lead to further communal events connected with the class (children's birthdays, reading groups, eurythmy groups, and so on). Important foundations are laid for a trustful working relationship between parents and teachers.

Another important area discussed in our group was the child study held in the care group. Many varying reports were given, right down to the fact that this important aid to educational, anthroposophical, and therapeutic understanding did not exist at all in many schools. There was controversy on many points, including whether the child and/or the parents should be present or not, whether a small or large group of teachers should be involved, whether such conferences should be a regular feature or convened on an ad hoc basis, and whether they should take place on one day or be spread over two to enable the night in between to play its part. The discussion is summarized in the following:

The child study in the care group is an important element of the anthroposophical and educational work of the faculty. Its main purpose is not so much to discuss difficult children but rather to be a combined endeavor, on one hand, to reach general anthroposophical insights, and on the other, to gain an understanding of the destiny situation in which individual children find themselves in the context of home and school. The latter, of course, means that the child and the parents should be present for part of the time, if possible. A good many participants thought that this would make too many demands on both parents and child, but on the whole, these objections were more of an emotional kind. If a case conference has been properly prepared and carried through, parents have confirmed in follow-up conversations that although they had been nervous beforehand, in retrospect they were grateful for this experience of a united effort being made on behalf of their child. For the teachers this work shared directly with the child has various positive consequences. On the one hand, a case conference is an extremely effective method of further education for all concerned, while on the other, working together at encountering the individuality of a child changes attitudes to that individual. Teachers have frequently reported that problems formerly experienced with that child have become relatively mild after the child study was held. The children are usually the least worried by the whole affair. If the class teacher encourages them in a meaningful and loving way, they are usually the least embarrassed participant. It is most important and helpful for the child to be met with a friendly openness that in no way generates a sense of having been called before a tribunal. The inner and outer attitude of the adults is, of course, extremely important. Outwardly, it would be wrong to sit there with arms and legs crossed, creating an inquisitorial atmosphere and openly demonstrating one's antipathy. Inwardly, there has to be an attitude of reverence for the individuality and a conscious wish to learn what it is that this child has brought from former incarnations. A case conference based on reports – however lively the descriptions by the class teacher and the others might be – does not lead to a common awareness and experience of the child's individuality. A case conference in the absence of child and parents is a make-shift.

A report from the Christian Morgenstern School in Wuppertal showed how the teachers there have been guided by Johannes Bockemühl for many years in their efforts to carry out case conferences that are meaningful and helpful for all the participants.

Here is the way a child study may proceed:

Phase One: Presenting the child (20 to 30 minutes).

The class teacher works with the child doing things he or she enjoys (playing ball, playing the recorder, singing, knitting, drawing a picture on the blackboard, etc.). Subject teachers do eurythmy or gym, etc., with the child. The child presents his or her exercise books and articles made in handwork, after which leave is taken by saying the verse from the child's report or perhaps by shaking hands round the circle of those present. The teachers have been asked to observe the child without categorizing or making judgments.

Phase Two: Now comes an endeavor to look at the picture together. The participants summarize what they have observed, and the teachers in question give further observations they have made during lessons. The parents report on how things are at home or speak about the child's pre-school days, and the school doctor presents relevant information arising from his examination of the child. There is still no judgment and certainly no criticism. The purpose is to bring together as many aspects as possible to create a picture. The child is usually not present during this phase.

Phase Three: Partly with and partly without the parents, the aim is now to reach a diagnosis. The diagnosis then leads on to the educational, remedial, and social measures necessary for the child, the parents, and, not least, for the teachers.

There have been case conferences after which the participants felt they had achieved nothing and which left the class teacher and the others dissatisfied, because no helpful practical ideas had emerged. However, only a short while later it became clear that obvious methods and measures are not the only aim. Class teachers find themselves developing and having to develop a new attitude toward the child, and the child can gain an inner sense of the strength that emerges from such an intensive effort on the part of so many people.

Thus, *Phase Four* of a case conference turns out to be the most important one. It takes place when the participants are no longer physically gathered together. The spiritual and psychological strength and help that can arise from a case conference come about when night-time experiences lead to non-physical encounters with the child's individuality.

Some reports stated that several schools allow a week to elapse between *Phases Two* and *Three* in order not to arrive at results without sleeping on things first. In every instance stress was laid on the importance of including the parents in the process. A follow-up conversation between them and the class teacher or school doctor must not get pushed aside by other pressures. Also, this conversation with the parents must not have the character of announcing the conclusions reached by "those in the know." The ideas for remedial measures, therapy, or youth counseling arrived at during the case conference should not be presented to the parents as a "final decision" or "order." They need to be discussed together on the basis of all the participants' observations and consultations. The parents are more likely to accept our advice and help if they understand the reasons than if they are given the feeling of "receiving orders."

Children with developmental problems present the Waldorf movement with a destiny-related challenge. To the degree in which we succeed in doing what is right for these difficult children, the Waldorf movement will be making an important contribution to humanity as the present millennium draws to a close. By knowing and recognizing the meaning of a disturbed incarnation process, by being enthusiastic and positive in our attitude toward the individualities of difficult children, and by knowing that we can also learn from difficult children, we teachers and therapists will gain the means that will help us to save the souls of such children. Waldorf education will let them develop the strength and skills they need for unfolding their personality and for shaping human society in the coming millennium.

BIBLIOGRAPHY AND NOTES

1. Report from a group working with Hans Friedbert Jaenicke, Uwe Mommsen, and Eckhard Wellmann.
2. Lievegoed, B., *Heilpädagogische Betrachtungen, Verlag das Seelenpflegebedürftige Kind*, Wuppertal, 1984.
3. Steiner, R., *Curative Education*. (GA 317). Tr. M. Adams. London: Rudolf Steiner Press, 1981.
4. As in Note 3. Also: Steiner, R., *Balance in Teaching* (in GA 302a). Spring Valley, New York: Mercury Press, 1982; Steiner, R., *Deeper Insights into Education* (in GA 302a), New York: Anthroposophic Press, 1983; Steiner, R., *Education as a Social Problem* (GA 296), Tr. L. Monges and D. Bugbey, New York: Anthroposophic Press, 1969; Steiner, R., *Curative Education*, op. cit.
5. Steiner, R., *Education as a Social Problem*, op. cit. Lecture of August, 16, 1919.

DEVELOPMENTAL INSIGHTS
Discussions Between Doctors and Teachers

CHAPTER 9

THE CHANGE THAT COMES WITH MATURITY –
VITAL PROCESSES AND BIRTH OF THE SOUL

by

Wolfgang Shad
Translated by A. R. Meuss, FIL, MTA

When we discuss the third 7-year period, we have to ask: Is the 7-year rhythm in human development a reality? Do we actually see it in children and young people, for instance as the ether body being born around their seventh birthday? And is it true that the change from childhood to youth comes at age 14? Surely much of this has changed in the course of the century? Considerable deviations may be seen when we consider an individual child or young person. Going into the matter we even find that it is not possible to establish a statistical mean for this 7-year rhythm. If it were, the rhythm would also have been discovered in descriptive developmental psychology, a field where human development is divided into entirely different phases. The question asked over and over again in anthroposophic education is: what is this concept of 7-year steps really about?

Rudolf Steiner himself said on one occasion that this 7-year rhythm as such is not easy to detect, and that he was not speaking of diagnostic findings based, say, on mean developmental rhythms among our young people. He said, however, that it was infinitely helpful for the whole biography if this 7-year rhythm could be conveyed to children and young people in their education. The rhythm is thus a therapeutic challenge. A child reveals its individual karma in deviations from the 7-year rhythm. If it proves possible to connect with the rhythm again, with the help of an adult teacher, the individual destiny can relate again to the human element that is common to all. This is a profoundly karmic therapeutic element. The 7-year rhythm would exist for every member of the human order, if it had not been for the intervention of Lucifer and Ahriman in human evolution. Guiding those in our care back to it, we help them in the struggle to overcome the powers that go against all that is truly human.

How would children and young people grow up today if it had not been for those interventions? Rudolf Steiner spoke of this in a lecture he gave in Stockholm on 16 April 1912:

"Considering the different aspects of the human being in relation to reality, we find that if only progressive powers had intervened in human evolution at a particular time in earth evolution, in Lemurian times, the development of young people would be very different today, for it would be in step with "I"-development. Psychological development would always be exactly in line with physical development. Human beings would then inevitably have developed in accord with the ideal demanded in my small publication *The Education of the Child in the Light of Anthroposophy*. If only progressive powers had been active at the time, the strange result would have been that people would have been much less independent in the first twenty years of their life than they are today. This lack of independence is not meant in a negative sense but in a way that you would all find totally acceptable. The fact is that for the first 7 years of life human nature is entirely designed to be imitative."[1]

Rudolf Steiner went on to say that this is in fact not the case, for the child's discovery of its own I in the first phase of defiance, when he experiments to see what happens if he wants something different from what those dear old grownups want, breaks into this. This is no longer pure imitation.

In the second 7-year period of life, the authority principle would prevail, but today it is not just a national but indeed a world calamity that people want to be independent at age 7 to 14, and are actually educated to form their own opinions. Adults would have been the natural authorities for the children. From age 14 to 21, people would have looked even less to themselves, into their inner life; they would have turned to the outside world. The power of ideals, the power to enter into life's dreams in a living way, would have become tremendously important to them. Life's dreams would sprout from their hearts, and full "I"- consciousness would have developed in their 20th and 21st years. And so there would be the period of imitation in the first 7 years, then a looking up to authority figures in the second 7 years, and a sprouting of ideals that would bring the human being to full "I"- consciousness in the third 7 years. Humanity was deflected from this line of development in the course of human evolution by the sum of powers called the luciferic powers, which are also active in evolution.[1]

Human nature has suffered injury. It no longer lives the 7-year rhythm as a matter of course. In the 13th lecture of *The Study of Man*, Rudolf Steiner speaks of our mission in a way that touches the heart:

"You have to be a good friend to [the child's] nature as it develops."[2]

The teacher must take note that children not only have to learn during their school years but must also grow. Our teaching must not interfere with the child's nature, and we must endeavor to encourage the processes of physical growth in a healing way as we teach. Yet how can we take note of the child's nature if we do not know how we influence it? Rudolf Steiner spoke of teachers having a certain influence on childhood growth by developing the children's fantasy on the one hand and their memory on the other, causing them to be either tall or short and stocky later on. Our school doctors have been working a great deal with this subject in earlier years. Hanno Matthiolius[3], for instance, considered the connection between prolongation, with young people getting taller and taller, and a faster rate of development. Is there a connection with the way we teach? He was able to show that teaching does influence the degree of acceleration. It was found that the effect is only seen in children who enter a Waldorf school before class 5. After this, no direct effect on onset of puberty has been recorded. What a teacher does in the first four years at school, the way he works with the powers of fantasy and memory, shaping the newly born ether body, has a definite effect on the growth processes connected with puberty a few years later.

In the second 7-year period, the ether body is particularly open to the effects of education. In *The Essentials of Education*, Rudolf Steiner referred to pathological dispositions in later life that may unfortunately be caused if a teacher does not get proper control of his temperament in some way.[4]

DEVELOPMENTAL INSIGHTS
Discussions Between Doctors and Teachers

Children of ages 9 and 10 are most sensitive to this. What happens is that the children's need for authority is blocked, and they distance themselves. Questions arise that do not come to full conscious awareness: Are those really my parents? Is this a teacher I can really trust? The wish for authority is disrupted. In this unstable state, when the children are as though wrenched out of the healthy progression of the second 7-year period, they are particularly sensitive to unhealthy elements in our approach as teachers. This will have consequences in the 40th or 50th year of life, when rheumatic conditions, heart diseases, etc., develop.

The ether body's greatest achievement at the end of the second 7-year period is physiological sexual maturity. The organism has once more been restructured in a very special way where its growth principles are concerned. Here we get a tremendous phase of generative force activities that cause the whole metabolic and limb aspect of the human being to be enhanced, also providing procreative potential. In principle the individual is now able to produce physical offspring, and this makes him an entirely earthly human being. Earth maturity is reached.

Earth maturity brings out the important aspect of differentiation. Development is now differentiated in all kinds of directions – physically, mentally, and in terms of destiny. The most obvious physical differentiation is into female and male organization, with the development of secondary sexual characteristics at sexual maturity. Girls characteristically start a year earlier than boys – which also marks a difference between the sexes. The process now comes about two years earlier in Europe than it did 70 years ago, and in Nordic countries several years earlier, so that later the characteristics of sexual maturity show in class 6, particularly among girls, and sometimes in class 5. In the past, this was more the norm in Southern European countries. A kind of geographical gradient existed then. In Central Europe menarche came at 14 or 15, in Scandinavia at 17, 18, or 19. This was entirely normal at the last turn of the century. Meanwhile, development has accelerated in the direction of the "Mediterranean" timing.

It is often said today that it is no longer correct to speak of a 14-year threshold. Why is this so? We also have to consider that mental maturation, changing from a child's mental attitude to that of a young person, has been correspondingly delayed. In his **Occult Science,** Rudolf Steiner wrote that the birth of the astral body was not a brief event around the 14th year, but took from the 12th to the 16th year.[5] This is now clearly evident. Physiological maturation has moved forward to the 12th year, mental maturation now extends to class 10, when pupils are 16. One can only be grateful if the most acute signs of puberty are extinguished towards the end of class 10, and the wonderful evolution of the young person's soul then follows in classes 11 and 12.

What lies behind this? We hear that before World War I and even in the 1920s, the change from child to young person proceeded much more quickly.[6] Mental change went closely together with physical change, so that physical and soul aspects were still more directly connected. They have gone further and further apart in the course of this century. They do still overlap, but it is remarkable to see how the well-turned-out young "ladies" and "gentlemen" still take a child's delight in the family celebrations at their confirmation, for instance. It is difficult to imagine that there have been times – even at the turn of the century – when confirmands had profound scruples: Am I ready to be confirmed? Deep inner struggles were gone through, as shown in Charlotte Bühler's study of the diaries of young people, for example.[7] Psychological problems would then come as young people went through the physical changes; today they tend to be delayed, only emerging fully in class 9, persisting strongly in class 10, and not infrequently dragging on for some time after this.

The dissociation of physical and psychological existence, the soul aspect and the bodily aspect, has been frequently referred to as something that is getting too powerful. It is no doubt a negative element if we consider that maturation of the soul involves much greater risks if it does not go hand in hand with physical maturation which will always take its course. Happening as an extra process that is more independent of physical nature, psychological maturation no longer has the natural support of physical biology and therefore is more likely to go wrong. Many of the problems that beset young people of this age – tobacco, alcohol, drugs, youth sects, black masses, and all the nonsense that finds a market exactly at this unstable age – make the time of psychological puberty even more risky than in the past.

Yet, I would not consider the dissociation to be wholly negative, for it is definitely a historical development that approaching youth is no longer tied as much to human physiology in the 20th century as it was, and has become more independent. Psychological maturation thus gains purely soul character. Happening at a time when the growth processes relating to the natural world are already slowing down, the soul quality of today's young people is a bit more independent of the body than it probably was at the beginning of the century. Hence, the great spiritual openness we see today.[8]

It also shows, however, that the third 7-year period brings forth questions which hover between life and death, and therefore brings an increasingly important task for educators. In the last century and the beginning of this century, it was certainly possible for most young people to begin vocational training by going into a trade when they had barely left their childhood behind at the age of 14. Today, the occupations as such have changed, and so have the young people, who have not matured sufficiently even to learn a trade at 14. Community school boards are actually asking that young people should stay in school for another year or two, up to class 10. This reflects something we are all very much aware of – the increasing educational significance of the upper school. The development will no doubt continue in years to come, and we are therefore able to say: The therapeutic skills we need to acquire in working with the third 7-year period will be an important help to us in future education.

Two lectures by Rudolf Steiner are entirely devoted to this change young people go through.[9, 10] In the lecture given on June 16, 1921, he gave a deep analysis of the processes that happen in puberty, going into the marked differentiation in girls' and boys' development concerning the relationship of the different aspects of the human being. A difference does, of course, also exist in childhood, and there is also much boys and girls have in common in high school life. Several times in the lecture we hear that teachers need to develop an eye for the differences. Not only does subjectivity of inner soul space waken earlier in girls, but it also offers much greater potential. In the female gender, the astral body is much more differentiated, rich, talented, gifted from its birth in adolescence and throughout life than it is in the male gender. The male astral body tends to be coarser and more ungainly. We see this in the awkwardness many boys show, especially in class 9. Profound questions and issues still tend to pass them by.

I remember studying Goethe's *The Sorrows of Young Werther* in main lesson in class 9 and how I kept asking myself all the time why we were supposed to read this. I could not make anything of it. And then we were asked to write a summary of the contents. I don't remember my own effort, but one of my classmates was told off by the class teacher for writing just one sentence. This was read out to the class as a deterrent example, and I still know it by heart: "Werther was a young man who fell in love with a married woman and shot himself because she would not be his." My classmate remained unmoved at being told off. When the teacher asked him what he had to say in reply, he said, quite dryly: "Well, nothing else really happened." The highly differentiated emotional responses in Werther – the only one of Goethe's works that was widely known in Europe, with his later works largely unknown – were beyond our comprehension. Even Napoleon had taken Werther with him on his campaigns, but we boys did not know what to do with it in class 9, and I expect it still is the same today. The girls were able to enter into every fiber of the soul at that age and wrote magnificent essays.

Another example is taken from biology lessons. When the eye and the ear were our subject, I would often ask, as a teacher in later life: "Who'd rather be deaf, and who'd rather be blind, if you had the choice?" This question would always affect the girls deeply. A conversation would immediately get going. The boys, however, would shrug their shoulders: Why ask such a question? I am able to see and hear, so why should I imagine anything else?

The mobility which the female astral body has from the beginning enables it to take in the I early, as if "soaking it up", as Rudolf Steiner put it.[10] This gives girls their special mature human outlook and their charm. Even at this age, I-nature comes in strongly. In boys, the generally coarser nature of the astral body means that the I is still further away initially. Because of this, Steiner continued, boys tend to be more "servile" at this period of transition.[10] The girls on the other hand grow "valiant." It is often they who'll represent the class if problems have to be voiced. Just take a look at the ball held at the end of a course of dancing lessons! You'll often get the feeling that the girls are leading the boys rather than the other way round. At an upper school carnival party the girls tend to pick partners from a higher class, because the awkward boys from their own class are apt to tread on their toes.

We also find that the best of the boys at this age are reticent and quiet. And that is good. When they reach their twenties – says Rudolf Steiner – it will be easier for a young man to bring the I to birth and come of age than for a young woman who experiences a certain "counter pressure" at that point.[10] It is harder for them because the I has been taken hold of early by the astral body and may thus be closely bound up with the emotions. It needs some extra pressure to let the I become independent in a female individual. We note, therefore, that girls find it easier to make the transition from childhood to youth with the birth of the astral body but face greater difficulties with the birth of the I. Boys find it harder to bring the astral body to birth, and suffer much more from being awkward, with lack of harmony and an inability to express their inner feelings as these gradually awaken; they have an easier time of it, however, where their coming of age is concerned. This makes it the "golden rule" in upper school education to encourage the boys more at the beginning of the third 7-year period, helping them to overcome their awkwardness, clumsiness, cheekiness, and rough and ready manners in the right way, and co-education is in itself a great help with this. It is much harder in a class that has mostly boys and few girls to achieve refinement of soul for the boys. Girls may, of course, also show one-sided development at this age. Rudolf Steiner spoke of the girls' need to show themselves, present themselves, have the floor, and this may go so far that they become chatty and superficial. Girls face the danger of becoming superficial and extroverted, boys of becoming too introverted, withdrawing into their shells and presenting themselves as brutal, coarse, and rough to the outside. We need to help both, initially more the boys, and towards the end of the upper school period the girls, who then have to find their feet where capacities of soul and spirit are concerned, so that they learn to act more independently and bring their I to birth in the right way.

We might consider the karmic background to this polarization which does not always emerge in the individual case but does so in the majority, for individuals are born with different astral body configurations. Individual boys or girls will, of course, not always fit into this typology, but in overall terms it is noticeable that despite all the changes in this century, the main trend is as presented. What is the karmic background to this? Why is the female astral body so much richer and more differentiated? How does the female astral body learn so quickly, and why do men later have to catch up on this with much effort, cultivating the inner life, and then endeavor all their lives, awkwardly and by trial and error, to achieve out of the "I" – the "baby among the aspects of the human being"[11] – what they see presented to them in almost prophetic form in the female constitution which is often much more harmonious and complete in itself?

The answer to these questions offers insight into the reincarnation process. The one-sidedness of gender can only be balanced out in spirit by being the other kind of human being in the next life. A deep-reaching basic karmic law is that anything the I achieves for itself in a life – irrespective of whether one is a man or a woman – determines the quality of the astral body in the next life, its special gifts and talents. Anything we live out in the astral during one life, destiny makes into the basic nature of our ether body in the next life. And the configuration of one's ether body will later become the basic physical constitution.

You see, we live from the inside to the outside: the pleasure and pain that lives in the astral body appears again in the ether body; the permanent drives and passions that have their roots in the ether body will become the physical disposition; and what we do here, using the physical body, will be our outer destiny in the next incarnation. And so the activities of the astral body become the destiny of the ether body; the ether body becomes the destiny of the physical body, and what the physical body does will come from outside as a physical reality in the next incarnation.[12]

Thus, a man's female ether body will normally be transformed into the basic female constitution of the physical body in our next life on earth. These reincarnative metamorphoses of the aspects reveal something of the basic law of education which Rudolf Steiner formulated in the *Curative Education* course: The nature of the higher aspect influences the one immediately below it.[13] The law of karma thus provides the macrocosmic education for humanity.

Concerning the "I", we may say that the female astral body has its many gifts because the preceding male incarnation made special demands on the I, and that conversely a man has to create the necessary beginnings of the next astral body out of the I, which requires considerable effort. If something is achieved in this life out of the I, it will create the disposition for a future astral body that is also particularly receptive to higher things.

The different gifts people have – irrespective of gender differences – only tend to emerge clearly at onset of puberty. Many boys and girls are themselves surprised how much they are now able to grasp all of a sudden. This creates major changes in the social relationships in a class. Childhood friendships, often going back to kindergarten days, will often break up in puberty. You suddenly find you have quite a different set of friends. A classical situation often seen in puberty is a class suffering the pain of no longer being a natural community. I had one class where this was so bad that I thought it best to take them on a week's walking tour to give them a real experience of community. We went through magnificent mountain woods, visited quarries, and saw glorious views from the mountain tops – but from morning till night all they would talk about was how to be a better class community again. When their teacher told them: "All you have to do is carry the backpacks of the weaker members of the group," they said: "Yes, we'll do that, but first we must solve the problem in principle!" The subject occupied their minds for a long time. The answer finally came from quite a different direction, when the class did their special education practical in special education institutions. This gave them practice in social skills, and true community was restored to the class.

Social issues cannot be solved by establishing social principles. As the German author Erich Känstner said, there's nothing good in the world unless you do it! Two girls who had been close friends all through their childhood years at school, suddenly no longer had much to say to each other in class 9, for one was showing considerable intellectual gifts at this time when the other did not. They did, of course, treat each other kindly after this, but their social contacts changed enormously.

If a young person fails to find the longed-for friends, he/she feels greatly deprived. Loneliness is experienced. Questions as to life's aims come up. Life's dreams are full of idealism. It is difficult for an adult to bring to mind again what moved them at age 15 or 16, because life was so much a dream then that whilst one may later think one still remembers, it has often fallen into oblivion. Later one would be increasingly less confident in one's abilities. When my children were young, they greatly admired a 16-year-old who, when asked what he was going to be, said: "President." This had elements of showing off to it and also some self-irony. He later became a geologist. Images of helping the whole world tend to emerge, often of a kind that can never be fulfilled in a single life. People who are in full adult life are watched with the mythological eyes of Argus, because the young do not know if they will be able to meet their own demands in later life. They discover that their teacher, too, has not been able to achieve what might be necessary in life. The expectations of a newly born astral body are tremendous. Questions as to the whole length of life, until death, arise. The shocking experience is made that one is capable of suicide. This is not usually given expression, but it is part of the soul's puberty, the innermost dialogue the soul has with itself. A child would not think of this, but the soul of a young person asks itself: If I consciously decide to live on, what do I live for? And questions as to meaning will often come up: What purpose shall I give my life? Awakening sexuality, on the other hand, brings up the question as to the beginning of life, with responsibility for reproduction also meaning responsibility for new life. Earth maturity means that the beginning and end of life become a real problem.

Is it possible to talk about it? These are powerful questions. Do the different subjects taught at school offer answers taken from life – in English lessons, for instance, descriptions of great historical figures? Rudolf Steiner's advice to connect everything that is taught with the human being applies particularly also in the high school.[14] But the ideals which arise also hold dangers that previously did not exist. One is that the ideals are put aside, and the "it isn't any good" mood develops not only on the surface: It's too late, anyway; there's no point, considering the ecological disaster that has been created. Chernobyl has done untold harm to the souls of the young, probably more than we adults realize. Maybe I'd better forget it. Does the "no problem" device mean something? I am no longer interested, and I'll just be a consumer. This is one danger.

The other is that a young person wants to bring his ideals to realization, come what may. This creates the revolutionary, and indeed the terrorist – brutal actions while proclaiming the great ideal of total liberation! Rudolf Steiner gave a "study of terrorist man" in a lecture on September 11, 1920, when he spoke of what happens if even the letters of the alphabet are introduced unimaginatively in class 1:

If this is suppressed, and a coldly objective individual teaches and educates like this today, he presents to the young child something that does not at all relate to the child: the letters. For the letters of the alphabet as we have them today no longer have anything to do with the pictograms of old; they are something fundamentally alien to the child and should be developed out of an image, as we attempt to do in the Waldorf school. Something without image is presented to the child; but the child has powers in its body – I am of course speaking of the soul in using the term "body" here, for we also say "astral body" – powers that will tear it apart unless they are developed in pictorial form. And the consequence? These powers are not lost; they spread, gain existence, and enter into thoughts, feelings, and will impulses. And what does this mean for the human being? This leads us to rebels, revolutionaries, discontented people who do not know what they want because they want something that cannot be known, something not compatible with any social organism, something they can only imagine, something that should have entered into their fantasy and did not do so but has entered into their activities in the social sphere.

We may say, therefore, that people who in occult terms are not honest in their intentions towards others are people who simply dare not admit to themselves: If the world is in revolt today, it is heaven which revolts, that is, the heaven which is kept in human hearts and then emerges not in its true form but as its opposite, in fighting and blood rather than in imaginations. It is not surprising, then, that people involved in the destruction of the social order actually feel they are doing good. For they sense the heaven that is in them; yet this only becomes a caricature in their hearts. These are serious truths that we have to face today.[15]

Where does help come so that the inner ideals can get going without the brutality that stops at nothing both in soul and body, and without inhumanity being practiced in the name of all that is good? This is an everlasting problem. In 1971 a journalist, Gerhard Szesny, published a book in which he spoke of "supposed goodness – the impotence of ideologists."[16] The books deals with the persecution of heretics and with slavery – crimes committed in the name of Christianity. History speaks of them. But how can we work with our ideals in a meaningful way and not give way to resignation, saying: Let's forget our ideals; it's enough to satisfy our needs, and we shall have peace! This is the approach psychoanalysts use to deal with ideals that have become an urge to destroy. How can we do full justice to individualized ideals but prevent them from becoming destructive? We know the danger from our own Waldorf school teachers' communities where great ideals cause sides to be taken and social divisions to arise. How is such a thing possible? The answer was given in the lecture: It is essential to be artistic in our approach to teaching not only when introducing the alphabet by means of images in class 1, but always, in all classes. This is the social therapy aspect of art: the world of ideals is properly mediated to the physical world through the art of life. Pleasure in letting fantasy come alive in the fine arts develops the powers which later on in life will be not just social therapy but become social art, the art of finding the right, healing moment for making our ideals part of real life.

Education can mediate this faculty in every class, and especially in the upper school when ideals gain real meaning. As teachers we are never quite up to the demands made on us by astral bodies that dream sublime dreams, and we may therefore use something that goes beyond our own selves: the world. We can offer contents that come from history, history of art, literature, and the world of nature. Art history main lessons can be a tremendous help, with the world speaking through the teacher who becomes transparent like glass, as it were, for something entirely different and sublime. Here the boys and girls can find something that will provide the first answers for their ideals. It means that the world we perceive with the senses, the real world, is always presented as though secretly filled with ideal elements. This is what we may call "Goetheanism." It does not mean to see ideas embodied in the physical world but exactly the reverse: To see a plant, a stone, a cloud formation in such a way that moral qualities arise from this, out of the plant, stone, or cloud formation. Goethe said: You can really only look at the sheer magnificence of a rock wall in silent awe, for it cannot be put in human words.

We should talk less and draw more. I myself would like to get out of the habit of talking and speak in nothing but drawings, as creative nature does. Every fig tree, this small snake, the cocoon calmly awaiting its future over there by the window, all these are signatures that have much to tell; indeed, if we knew how to decipher their meaning, we would soon feel no more need for written or spoken words! The more I reflect on this, I find talking to be so useless, so futile, I'd almost say affected, that you get a shock when faced with the sober starkness of nature and its silence as you face a lonely rock wall or the isolation experienced on an ancient mountain.[17]

It may be possible to have the felicity to express something of it in words, but the words need to be given full meaning, something only poets are able to do. They can help a young person who has become introverted and feels no one can understand him suddenly to experience that the unspoken question or longing that lives in him is something the world shares after all. This going inward into self observation exists of its own accord, though often hidden, especially in boys, and may become part of life. But it only becomes deep necessity when school life is over, in the fourth 7-year period, and can then find nourishment in the most beautiful sense of the word when anthroposophy is discovered, the very gate to the gaining of self knowledge. Before that, Goetheanism as a way of perceiving the world should be a pictorial way of gaining self knowledge from the world, as in prophesy, which will lead to alienation from the world unless the eye is also turned inward.

What do upper school boys and girls expect of us? What lives in them as latent expectations that cannot be put in words but are a dream which is part of all that is best in them? Two things: They would like to feel that their teacher is deeply connected with the innermost secrets of our humanity. New teachers always have to go through three tests in the upper school, and their work, including the ability to keep discipline, will depend on these. The decision does not come on the first day when both sides are amazed at each other. On the second day, the first thing expected of the teacher is leadership quality. Can he reach us to teach us? They are looking for a quality that can educate the young people's newly born astral body, i.e. the teacher's power of egoity, which is the next higher aspect. This does, of course, also have to be used to the full in the second and first 7-year periods, but in the second 7-year period it is mainly the teacher's astral body, worked through by power of I, that educates the child's ether body which has just become free by the inner gesture of soul. In the first 7-year period, the teacher's I-filled ether body is most effective. In the upper school, however, the boys and girls will unconsciously first of all test the teacher's I. Is he in control? This is not determined verbally but experimentally, often very strongly on the second, third, and fourth days. Then the second test will gradually come: the test for competence. They want to know if he is a master in his field. This is not so much of interest in the second 7-year period, when teachers may offer many subjects without having studied them all in full. But in the high school they want to know if the teacher is competent and knows his subject – or has he only read it up last night? These disciplinary questions do not relate to material prepared by the teacher but to issues raised in questions asked by the class. Will he have something to say on this? This is of great interest to the class. It is, however, possible to be a great educator and well versed in a subject and yet it is not enough. The third test takes longer and never ends. It is a third question which a Waldorf school pupil might express as follows: He's a good teacher who knows his subject, but is he also a Waldorf school teacher? The boys and girls have a very good idea if what the teacher presents also reflects deepened insight into our essential human nature. This is a crucial issue: Does the teacher know the essential questions relating to man and world? We may also say: Is he not merely an anthropologist but an anthroposophist in the true sense of the word? Deep human wisdom is needed if real trust is to develop between educated and educator.

One question a pupil will connect with this is whether his teacher knows his way around the world outside. Is there a cosmopolitan air? Is he interested in world affairs? Puberty is a time when young people who have reached earth maturity also want to be very much people of their time. How is it here, what lies ahead for myself and my generation? Great solidarity with one's age group develops. The challenge is to move the innermost heart and bring the great aspects of the world's here and now into the teaching process.

We can really experience this in the face of current events and developments. Hungary has just been made an independent republic (1989). Who'd have thought this possible a year ago? A Waldorf school has started again in Budapest this autumn; they'd had a small one before the war. In Yugoslavia a kindergarten opened this autumn. In Poland and in Moscow people are actively engaged in opening kindergartens. A new beginning everywhere! We are seeing history made in our own time. Young people experience these things deeply.

Permit me to speak of a personal experience. On October 23, 1956, when the uprising started in Hungary, I was a student at Marburg University in Germany. Flyers were distributed that day inviting people to a service in St. Elizabeth's Church. You may know this, the first Gothic church on German soil. A Hungarian priest stood in the pulpit praying that the uprising in Hungary might be successful. He said more or less the following: Here, in this place, for St. Elizabeth was the daughter of a Hungarian king, I call on God and the free world to help Hungary. And exactly 33 years later, on October 23, 1989, Hungary was proclaimed an independent republic. We see history in the making.

What do we know of St. Elizabeth? Francis of Assisi sent her his cloak. The Stauffen emperor Frederick II asked for her hand. Rudolf Steiner is reported to have said that if she had married him, much would have come of this that would have been a great blessing in social relationships in Europe. She wore herself out instead working for the sick and the weak in just three years. She had totally given herself to social needs.

Who was this woman? A secret physician, a secret educator, a secret curative teacher? Was she all three of these? The physician deals with the infirmities of the body, and spiritually their causes lie in a constitution given by earlier incarnations. The curative teacher is, on one hand, working with something that is not so much connected with the previous earth lives of those entrusted to his care, nor with the present life, for much that can be learned on this earth is not taken in by the handicapped. Where does the teacher find the spiritual breath for his work? The greatest help for the whole of curative education comes from the words of Rudolf Steiner that the handicapped individual is, on the whole, already preparing for the next life. The work of curative education is to help development for the next life. Most educators – parents, kindergarten, and school teachers – have to provide direct guidance for the present life, assisting incarnation into the here and now.

We are not only part of our present incarnation, for at any moment in this life the previous life is present in us, constituting our gifts and our negative aspects. And in our aims, which we cannot yet achieve and perhaps will never achieve in this life, we are all handicapped. Like the handicapped, we also work towards our future lives on earth, providing we do not give up. We are thus able to say that in every human being lives a hidden physician, teacher, and curative teacher. Only we cannot be all of these in outward terms during life on earth. Here we have limits, with differentiation into sexes, constitutions, occupations. And each of us can only be truly effective if we do not seek to do it all at once but the three professions – physician, teacher, curative teacher – come together to complement one another, saying ". . . a single individual cannot help, but only someone who united with many others at the right moment."[18] Let us do the inner work that needs to be done, and on the other hand be citizens of this world and work for the future also within it.

BIBLIOGRAPHY AND NOTES

1. Steiner, R., *Erfahrungen des Übersinnlichen. Die Wege der Seele zu Christus* (GA 143).
2. Steiner, R., *The Study of Man* (GA 293), lecture of September 4, 1919. Tr. D. & A.C. Harwood, H. Fox. London: Rudolf Steiner Press, 1981.
3. Matthiolius, H., Schuh, C., *Der Einfluss der Erziehung auf die Akzeleration des Menschen*. Beiträge zu einer Erweiterung der Heilkunst nach geisteswissenschaftlichen Erkenntnissen 1977; 30: 129-40.
4. Steiner, R., *Essentials of Education* (GA 308), lecture of April 8, 1924. Tr. J. Darrell. London: Rudolf Steiner Press, 1968.
5. Steiner, R., *Occult Science – An Outline* (GA 13). Tr. G. & M. Adams. "The Stages of Human Life" appendix. London: Rudolf Steiner Press, 1962.
6. Nold, R., *Grössenzunahme, Wachtumsbeschleunigung und Zivilisation*. Munich, 1964. Portmann A. Biologische Fragmente zu einer Lehre vom Menschen. Kap.: Wandlungen des Reifens in neuerer Zeit, Basel, 1969.

7. Bühler, C., ***Das Seelenleben des Jugendlichen. Versuch einer Analyse und Theorie der psychischen Pubertät***. Stuttgart, 1967.

8. Schad, W., ***Zur Menschenkunde des Jugendalters – vom Wesen des Astralleibes. Zur Menschenkunde der Oberstufe, gesammelte Aufsätze***. Printed for private circulation, Pädgogische Forschungsstelle beim Bund der Freien Waldorfschulen (Libanonstr. 3, D-7000, Stuttgart 1), 1981.

9. Steiner, R., ***Erziehung und Unterricht aus Menschenerkenntnis*** (in GA 302a) Stuttgart, June 21, 1922.

10. Steiner, R., ***Waldorf Education for Adolescence*** (GA 302). June16, 1921. Tr. not known. Sussex: Michael Hall, Kolisko Archive, 1980.

11. Steiner, R., ***Cosmic and Human Metamorphoses*** (in GA 175), lecture of March 6, 1917. Tr. H. Collison. London: Anthroposophical Publishing Co., 1926.

12. Steiner, R., ***Theosophy of the Rosicrucian*** (GA 99), lecture of May 30, 1907. Tr. M. Cotterell, D. Osmond. London: Rudolf Steiner Press, 1981.

13. Steiner, R., ***Curative Education***, lecture of June 26, 1924. Tr. M. Adams. London: Rudolf Steiner Press, 1981.

14. Steiner, R., GA 302, lecture of June 12, 1921.

15. Steiner, R., ***Changes in the Meaning of Speech*** (in GA 199). September 11, 1920. Tr. not known. Anthroposophical News Sheet (UK), 1950,19-22.

16. Szesny, G., ***Das sogenannte Gute. Vom Unvermögen der Ideologen***. Hamburg, 1971.

17. Goethe to Falk, June 14, 1809.

18. Goethe, J. W., ***The Tale of the Green Serpent and the Beautiful Lily***.

CHAPTER 10

OPPORTUNITIES AND RISKS IN THE THIRD SEVEN-YEAR PERIOD[1]

by

Gunhild Baldini
Translated by Christian von Arnim MA, M.Litt, FIL

When we, as educators, doctors, or adults, come to deal with the third stage in life, we encounter a young person who has already been involved in the education process. Education, Rudolf Steiner once said, consists of welcoming the human ego to earth in a fraternal way and attempting to help it, by preparing a suitable instrument for its incarnation, to grasp its destiny or – and this, too, may unfortunately be called education – to thwart it in its destiny. The young person whom we see in puberty or after puberty has completed the process of formation or malformation of the component parts of his being by the time that we come into contact with him or her. It is very important to be aware of this since the moment of puberty, and thus the first years of the third stage of life, are characterized by tremendous crises, chaotic and turbulent states which can be explained in terms of our knowledge of the human being simply as the result of the liberation of the astral body. We know, after all, that this is the distinguishing mark of the third seven-year period in life. We will describe this aspect and then go on to discuss what has happened to make the crisis even more critical, the chaos more chaotic, and the muddle even worse than it is merely through the fact of growing up.

DEVELOPMENTAL INSIGHTS
Discussions Between Doctors and Teachers

Although I have been dealing with the consequences of the inability to overcome this crisis for sixteen years, I do not wish to say much about this particular aspect today, about drugs; rather, I want to attempt to look at the third stage in life from the perspective of our knowledge of the human being as it relates to this period. For I know that we are all very fond of these young people who are waiting for our help, our brotherliness – that is not the problem. But the preconceptions which arise in us when we attempt to apply this love, and find that it is not accepted in the way that we believe it should be accepted, stem from the fact that we know too little of what is really going on in such a situation. Over and again we fail to realize sufficiently that the help which expresses the love which is in all of us must take a specific form, and that form is knowledge of the character of the young person, of human nature in general, and of this particular state when the astral body is born and the birth of the ego is prepared.

What happens with the onset of puberty? In his comments on puberty, Rudolf Steiner says that the just ended second seven-year period brought maturity in the breathing, the concluded first seven-year period brought maturity of the senses, and the third seven-year period which has just begun brings sexual maturity. All of these together produce puberty. It is also very important not to relate the concept of puberty constantly to the birth of the reproductive organs. What, then, happens during the process in which the astral body is born? What does it mean: "The astral body is born?" It means that after a period when the soul of the child has worked on the body in hermit-like fashion, it breaks through into the outside world, after having formed the body down to the level of the bones and the muscles. The young person from his or her perspective has the following feelings: I come from a soul and spiritual world which has worked on men unconsciously. They know it, and now I am being thrown into a world which reveals itself only to my senses; I am thrown into a brutal reality, as people would say today, which hits me hard. That is similar to the way that we might imagine the commonly used bright light of the delivery room striking the child like a blow when it is born. Seeing the light of the world for the first time is not such a peaceful experience! Similarly, seeing the sense world, the etheric, and physical world, which is now perceived in its naked state by the young person through his or her sense organs, is like a blow aimed at the soul activity wanting to enter the world. This is the moment when the spiritual and the physical elements crash into one another. One might also say: the divine element in the human being comes up against the hard sense world.

This produces a tremendous feeling of pain in the subconscious of the young person, which can subsequently come to expression as a powerful feeling of having been wounded by the world and its influences. It represents a vulnerability towards everything which the environment can throw at the young person. He or she is no longer mercifully protected by an astral and etheric shield, which brings back the equilibrium in many cases when the educationalists have made a mistake. Now the protective wrapping has gone. Instead, there is direct access to everything which the world has to offer and to refuse what it presents in destruction, happiness, and false happiness, and what it can give in truly great joy and great suffering. All of that, including their childhood past, turns into direct experience and awareness for young people. "Awareness" is not the right word, for these things represent the subjective experience of young people. Many of the things which we experience as the rudeness, the self-defense, the apparent aggression is connected with the fact that the environment is no longer perceived as something which is part of them but as something utterly foreign. It is a pity sometimes that we forget this as adults, for it is also a tremendous moment when a spiritual being has to come to grips with the world and has to learn to cope with it in the seven years or in the period when we come of age.

If we examine more closely what it is that is born with this soul or astral element, we see that it possesses a dual nature. Being thrown in at the deep end is supplemented by something which can be described as an inner split. This is a split, which young people slowly become aware of and have to come to terms with, in the two faculties which are mediated by the astral body. It is, on the one hand, the opportunity independently to make judgments with the liberated etheric body which provides the vehicle for thinking activity, for ideas. In this way they are no longer dependent on the beloved authority within which they existed beforehand. On the other hand, the astral body is the vehicle of the will forces which can and must come to expression and which now become equally liberated. That is to say that we as adults have to cope with a young person whose intelligence has grown very quickly, so that he is often much more intelligent than we are and can rapidly construct an argument, first from one side, then from the other. On the other hand, desires thrust their unbridled way into the world. These are the two phenomena which we may observe in the soul sphere.

Very peculiar things happen on an organic level as well. The will forces, the forces of desire, which are detached from the human being on a soul level, become linked, on the other hand, very intensively and strongly with the metabolic and limb system, as Rudolf Steiner describes. The element which becomes detached from the soul and visible, on the one hand, is linked profoundly with the metabolic and limb system, on the other hand, with the blood system which pulses through the metabolism and from there surges with explosive pressure towards that part of the human being associated with the head. The limbs lengthen in relation to the rest of the organism: the force becomes directly visible. And during this surge upwards towards the nervous and sense system a second head is created as it were; a blockage occurs with the effect that the larynx becomes bigger, something which is particularly evident in the male. The voice slides down into the depths in a visible sign that the maturity of the breathing process goes as far as a transformation of language. Rudolf Steiner describes how this is not only an organic process, but how language wants to be seized quite differently from the point onwards when the male and female voice evolves from the light, clear, cosmic voice of the child. That in turn affects teachers and the way they handle language. These organic developments also contain the possibility of deviance. Perhaps language is used with more conscious intent, or it turns suddenly into strange jargon, a pseudo language. That has far-reaching consequences for the subsequent development of the human being.

We know from Rudolf Steiner that the things which we speak during the day continue their action during the night and are carried up to the world of the archangels and angels, from whence we receive language, when the astral body and "I" unite with the hierarchies during sleep. But that can only happen if language is vitalized by and interwoven with ideals and spiritual content. Yet consider the way that language is used today between people as the vehicle, at best, of intellectual and materialistic content, and more often as the vehicle for empty phrases which no longer contain any sort of reality. This type of language surrounds young people in all different ways, through others, through radio, newspapers, and television. In other words, at precisely the time when language imbued with soul and spirit is born in the human being, misunderstandings occur which prevent a person, and young people in particular, who have only just left their divine world, from establishing a proper connection with language so that this connection remains ineffective. Rudolf Steiner says: The hierarchies are left with the mineral noises and the noises from the physical world which take the form of rattles, clicks, or hissing. What kind of music is being decanted into our young people today? "Music" has become devoid of everything except a rattling and hollow noise. Thus, young people are surrounded at this important stage by hollow noises and empty phrases which prevent them from establishing a connection with the spiritual world in which they should be at home. Rudolf Steiner describes how something incredible occurs in the heart organization of the human being between the second and third seven-year period; and that is that the etheric body decants into it everything in the way of cosmic beauty which it has brought with it from its progress through the cosmos before birth and then forms a new etheric heart for itself at the end of the second seven-year-period. The birth of a new heart occurs after the old, hereditary-based etheric heart "rots away."

This is a typical time of crisis: What is old has not yet quite disappeared, and what is new is not quite there yet. We know that during this period people often have the feeling of being completely alone in the world and unable to establish any feeling contact to the world, not only because they feel "I have been thrown out of the spiritual world," but also because of this process of transformation in the region of the heart. States of great depression, states of being driven, arise as a result of this moment in which the transformation of the heart takes place. It is a dangerous time, a time of risk!

A second thing which happens during the second seven-year period is that those things which the astral body brings from the world of the stars by way of its own destiny are decanted into the organs down to approximately the limit of the diaphragm, and into the respiratory organs in particular. Hence, they are liberated. The rhythm of the heart and lungs matures at the end of the second seven-year-period to the extent which we can see at that point. And once again something is formed in the region of the heart which is the remnant of those things which the astral body decanted into the other organs. This concentration in the region of the heart is described by Rudolf Steiner as something like an organ which is capable of forming new destiny following on from the previous destiny which was brought by the astral body and distributed in the organs. An organ of destiny, has formed in the region of the heart in which all the deeds are inscribed which that person does on earth, including those deeds which he makes others do. Everything which is done in the world leaves its trace in this newly formed astral organ, soul organ in the region of the heart. That is also why we say that we take something to heart, because we feel that it is something which really does come to expression in the world. This, too, represents a very destabilizing influence, for a person now becomes responsible for the consequences of his deeds, that is, he becomes capable of guilt. Children up to the end of the second seven-year-period are not capable of being guilty; they are innocent whatever they may do. But at the point at which the soul is concentrated into a new organ with the facility to assume the consequences of deeds, to preserve them and carry them over into a new life, the capacity for guilt also arises in the young person and the assumption of responsibility for guilt.

Thirdly, let us look at the limbs. They grow big, long, and heavy. Out of the springy, light-footed gait of the ten year old develops the heavy, sluggish gait of the adolescent. This uniting with the world of desires has an organic counter effect; that is, the blood becomes heavy (i.e. the red blood cells). They contain more iron, and they now pull the human being down and even "into" the earth. We, as humans, have more of a tendency not to want to touch the earth; then we are made heavy, and we experience a different relationship to gravity, the real earth force with which the young person has to become linked. Rudolf Steiner describes as symptomatic that our gait changes again to become more light-footed with the conclusion of the third phase of life, because the relationship with gravity has turned into an experience which human beings can overcome. From that point onwards they can stride over the earth in quite a different way, which also represents a renewed focus on the spiritual world away from the gravity of earth.

The fourth element to be given a new form is the sexual organs, creating a new twofold division. From puberty onwards the person as such no longer exists, but there are two images of the human being which together make the person. At this point untruth enters a person's life, Rudolf Steiner says, for neither woman on her own is a true person nor man, but only both together result in true humanness. And at the same time this creates a lack of understanding of what happens inwardly in the soul of boys and what happens from an outward perspective in girls. It is due to the woman wanting to remain in the cosmic element to a greater extent and the man penetrating too deeply into the earth with his physical body, because the soul of the man first turns inward, while the soul of the woman first turns outward. This creates a great deal of misunderstanding between people, which never ceases throughout life. And it also creates the faculty of lying in human beings, because they no longer find themselves in a position of comprehensive truth as far as their physical bodies are concerned. It is a fact based on our knowledge of the human being that lies came into the world, and also that we have to deal with this throughout our lives. Guilt and lying are facts based on our knowledge of the human being, which accompany young people for the rest of their lives, because they enter the third seven-year period.

Rudolf Steiner says that it is important for young people at this point that they should learn that the deeds which may be inscribed in their souls should be supported by ideals which are always greater than what can be achieved in reality, which are not lesser and narrower than what they do. This is what they subconsciously want. Ideals are very important in the third seven-year period.

If we now look at the division into two human beings, this creates something like an incredible need to create unity once again, which we call human love. Such specific sexual love is an expression of something which ensouls the whole of the young person, namely an incredible love towards the things which come at him from the outside world. On the one hand, young people feel separated from the things with which the world presents them, while on the other, it is precisely such a feeling of separation which men and women feel towards one another. It is quite clear that young people bring with them an incredible need to reunite themselves with the outside world, and that is then called a lively interest in the outside world. It is a challenge demanded of teachers, that this interest, which is also love for the outside world, should be satisfied to the greatest possible extent. This interest in the external world must be taken seriously, for it is the only spiritual access which the young person has to find his way into the physical world. Indeed, Rudolf Steiner says very clearly that if we do not succeed in making use of the interest in the outside world which awakens in young people for their own benefit, then they will not be able to feel love for other people and that then this special love of one person for another cannot awaken. For if young people with their awakening astral nature, their incredible powers of intelligence, and their desires which keep pushing them further are not bound by such an interest; if the intelligence is not concerned with the values contained in high ideals, with an understanding of what the world is, what it has become and not with what one would have liked it to be, then they will turn away from the external world. And then they are left with very little, namely themselves. They will then turn inwards into themselves on the paths of the astral body, which is already concerned with becoming effective and working in the body. And they meet desires and passions and feel tremendous loneliness. They becomes hermits. They are allowed to be hermits in the second seven-year period, but it becomes dangerous if they do so in the third. They will build relationships with their fellow human beings, with young people like themselves, but if lots of hermits have to deal with one another, a clique which is isolated from the rest of the world develops.

Rudolf Steiner points out, on the one hand, that if will forces encounter one another in isolation and want to carry a person away, then this provides the right kind of nourishment for Ahriman, who wants to drag people into the future without the retarding influence of reason. On the other hand, young people will be interested in a detached way in technical and electronic details, which they do not really understand and which drag their thinking down into a one-sided intellectualism. It means that they really want to stay in their state before birth, because that is where the faculty for intelligence comes from, and it means turning towards the Luciferic element, which wants to trap us in the past, which wants to hinder earth development. Both adversaries then clasp hands, and it is no surprise that the things which come from that quarter are of interest to young people. From the moment at which young people are thrown back on their own resources, abandoned by the external world which can no longer arouse their interest, tremendous fear and despair also arise, as they are left alone with these forces of desire. There is nothing beautiful about such a hermit existence, for it is accompanied by fear, despair, and anxiety. These things are always present in young people as a tendency. Such fear and anxiety should not be reinforced by the adult turning away from this life, tired and disappointed. But despite all dangers, despite the threatened final end of which we are all aware, despite Chernobyl, despite everything which has spread on earth through the acts of people, we must continue to believe in those things which allow human beings to progress. And that is a transformation in attitudes. A transformation of attitudes in the adult, which overcomes one-sided intellectualism, one-sided will forces, can exercise a healing influence.

That means that we as adults have to embark on the anthroposophical path of schooling, if want to bring our thinking and willing into harmony once again. That is the only way to bring these things together through schooling ourselves. Of course, Rudolf Steiner was much too non-prescriptive to ever put it in this way, but we are left with no other option, if we take everything which he tells teachers for the third seven-year-period seriously. For what does it mean to have ideals? "Every idea which fails to turn into an ideal exercises a weakening influence."[2] And ideals only come into being when we begin to deal with them with our will. Educators in the third seven-year period have to work seriously on their own schooling, if they are to become aware of what young people want.

We no longer have any real influence from a moral perspective. For everything to do in moral education has to have happened in the first two seven-year periods in an imaginative way. If a young person enters the third seven-year period equipped with moral injunctions and is tied up in moral reproaches, he feels himself crippled in his will . This leads to an extraordinary skepticism in thinking. Rudolf Steiner says that this is still relatively harmless; but the feeling and – very seriously – the will are also affected by such skepticism. Skepticism in the will means that I am no longer interested in what is moral; I reject it, and I am no longer accessible to it. We constantly hear complaints about youth crime today. It is a consequence of an intellectualizing, inappropriate education with a moral overlay in the first few years of a young person's life and cannot be defused by further reproaching young people morally in order to stop them doing what they want. They know all about that already, and it is of no interest to them whatsoever. On the contrary, it merely strengthens the skepticism in their will.

What do I do as an adult in such a situation, for by acting in this way I am merely reinforcing what has happened previously? But if the moral element was buried deeply in the sheaths of a young person, then love for one's own deeds can develop. Love for "the doing" is the best moral base, for it allows one to become both a free and an engaged person in the world. Apathy towards the world is programmed through the media, especially through television. This results in a weakness of will followed by a rampant acceleration in the darker realm of our desires.

As an adult one faces a task of a cultural dimension with regard to the third seven-year period. That task is to stimulate in the young person a civilizational principle – guiding reason into the emotions what is a principle of initiation for ourselves, namely bringing together feeling and thinking. In this way a transformation of the thinking can take place, which moves away from a purely materialistic and intellectual attitude to become living thinking. That is what the young people want who come to us today!

Rudolf Steiner points out[3] that for the first time in history things are the opposite way around from normal. This time the Aristotelians are present on earth, and the Platonists are being born. Normally, it was the other way around: Aristotle completed what Plato had begun. But this time the firmly set Aristotelians are being followed by the Platonists who want to keep their ideas flexible, who have an inner need to find living, warm- hearted thinking, but who are too shy and too delicate to express that in any radical way, and who have to be approached with sympathy if one wants to discover the love of the world and the love of the idea which is hidden behind the loudness, behind thick make-up, long or short hair in exotic colors, or some other transformation. Whatever we encounter in the way of such provocative acts means nothing other than: "Please help me. I cannot express it in any other way!" It might sound somewhat challenging if I say that we should see a Platonist behind such a person with a Mohican haircut, who is asking for admittance to the human community. When people come together in such hermit-like cliques, then the danger exists that they have little to talk about with one another – a lot to chat about, but little to talk about – and their interest in the outer world has to be developed slowly.

I recently saw musicians producing an opera in the Waldorf School in Ueberlingen, which was accompanied by a choir of Waldorf pupils, and I observed the tremendous changes which took place in these young people of between sixteen and eighteen in the four weeks of continuous rehearsal and in the time that the performances took place. I saw how the young girls suddenly turned into self-confident young ladies (they formulated it in this way themselves), who were suddenly able to express themselves, quite shy beings who were suddenly able to say what they wanted. And then there was the example of a young man: He had annoyed me at the end of a "study of man" main lesson – you can already see from how he did it that he was quite considerate – by his response to the fact that I had embarrassed him in his inner modesty; it was my fault of course, as is always the case. For I had said to him: "Do you always have to be so phlegmatic? Can't you do that a bit more quickly?" On the last day a cassette recorder was suddenly heard from Philip's corner playing some piece of pop music or other. And then he began to dance as well. It took a little while before he found the off button, and while this was going on, everyone else was standing around giggling and laughing. We could not, of course, continue with the morning verse after that. We sat down and started the lesson, and then it was time for an exercise. I went to him and said: "Philip, why did you do that? Did you intend to annoy me?" "No," he said, "I only wanted to show you that I am not really such a phlegmatic person." He then went on to take part in the musical project, after very great initial difficulties, one might add, and found his way into this very complicated opera, Mozart's *Cossi Fan Tutte*, in a splendid way. At the very end he approached me and said: "I just wanted to apologize. I only intended it to be very short, but I could not find the off button." Thereupon I said: "Well, Philip, that was being just a little bit phlegmatic, wasn't it?" And with that we were the best of friends again.

If something like that is unsuccessful, that is, if an opera production, a proper walking tour or a period working in curative education, is unable to stimulate a real interest; if this whole process takes place in ordinary life with its unfortunately much wider range of influences, then the formation of such cliques becomes like an undertow which pulls the young person under. Then we see all the consequences connected with these influences: music which is not music at all but is designed to engender mechanical movements in the body and decant the soul from it; then there is the violence and losing oneself in sex, with constantly changing relationships in such a clique. And then there are, of course, the drugs, which can make those who have difficulty in expressing themselves speak, which drive away anxieties and which suddenly appear to create a whole new sense of self among young people.

If the point has been reached at which such things have become widespread among young people, then there is still hope that in the preceding seven-year periods everything was well, and that the present critical situation has only been brought about because the young person has failed to meet the right people, has failed to find proper understanding for his searching and questions. In such a situation there is still great hope that destiny, which now begins to work through the development of the new astral heart, will decisively intervene and introduce the prince in the form of the awakening "I" in order to help the young person back on his or her feet – and that does indeed happen quite often. But unfortunately, it is not always the case. In the vast majority of cases what happens in the third seven-year period only represents the tip of the iceberg, and a great deal of destruction and mutilation of the component parts of the human being have already taken place in the preceding periods. One can see that this is happening in epidemic proportions – people drifting into sects, cliquishness, crimes of violence, drug addiction. The underlying distress and destruction are so deep-seated that the way back appears very difficult, when we observe it as helpers, therapists, teachers, doctors.

The thing which we really want, an education which makes people free, an education which creates a free ego which is able to act in the world in a healthy way, is lost if thinking, feeling, and the will do not interact in freedom. What we want to achieve in the first three seven- year periods is to liberate the thinking, feeling, and the will to create a consciousness which the young person can use at twenty-one, when the thinking can freely be given over to the ability for abstraction, the ability for intellectual thought. If, however, the component parts of the human being have been mutilated; if the thinking has not been liberated early enough, or, which happens much more frequently, if it is torn from the body at much too early a stage; if this leads to the birth of the human constituent parts in a premature or malformed way – perhaps from the first day of birth onwards or even before then, during pregnancy, if the mother receives the child with a dark cloud of rejection and fear, perhaps even wants to get rid of it; then everything which can be found in such a biography – what Rudolf Steiner describes as the "higgledy-piggledy interaction" of thinking, feeling, and the will occurs so that they can no longer develop freely alongside one another. This results in the numerous neuroses. Thinking which takes hold of the feeling results in many instances in anorexia. The result of the will and feeling flooding into the thinking produces impulsiveness, restlessness, the wish to cut all links permanently and not just temporarily, the many forms of illness, of obsession. And at the base of all this, we find what we always find when human beings lack self-consciousness in their approach to life, fear. We can see that this is the exact opposite of the real task of our time.

The imperative of our time, the thing which has happened to us whether we like it or not, is that the crossing of the threshold has already occurred. We live in a time of change in which human beings are no longer protected by the strict separation of perception and thinking; the spiritual world has come close to us again and breaks into our daily life whether we like it or not. It is better if we want it, if we do something about it and experience it in a waking state, but in most instances that is not the case. Instead a chaotic element is created. Drugs are able to separate thinking, feeling, and willing for a short moment. Heroin, which very one-sidedly only affects the reason, helps its users to achieve a cool and superior feeling of being rulers over the whole world. One is no longer ruled by caution, but suddenly experiences the feeling of being free! Marijuana and hashish lead one into the world of images where one experiences strong feelings of oneself – one imagines that one feels the surrounding world, but in realty it is only oneself – and loosens one's feelings from the entanglement with the thinking and willing. The danger of drugs is still – next to all the others – the strongest, because it can disrupt what the young people have come on the earth for – to be educated as well as possible for this new form of consciousness, which enables them to cross the threshold to the spiritual world in a waking state, that is, increasingly to experience thinking and perception as one again and to transform their own thinking. Rudolf Steiner described what happens when we set out on the schooling path, how these three capacities, which are beneficially united in the soul, begin to separate and have to be guided by a very strong and self-conscious "I" so that they do not become one-sided. Our young people have been partially weakened in their ego through education and are not strong. That is how thinking and the will have become mixed up. For the will, which we have brought with us from before birth, exists in order that we want to do what we have to do at any given moment, namely to broaden our outlook, not narrow it, and to cross the threshold with the rest of mankind. That is why drugs represent such a great danger, because for short periods they create a state which enables this kind of liberation to take place, the separation of thinking, feeling, and the will. The starting point for any sort of progress has to be the separation of these three soul capacities under the self-conscious guidance of the "I". Drugs represent the absolute antithesis of what should really happen. But to young people they act at that moment like a cure. They have to pay for it in the sense that when the poison stops working, they feel all the worse. But initially drugs appear like a cure for the component parts of the human being which have been destroyed, for their thwarted mission on earth. And it takes a very long time until they begin to notice that drugs do not represent a cure, and that this has to be sought in quite a different direction. If there is to be any possibility of reversing such a situation, the ego has to possess sufficient strength for self-conscious action, for a transformation of outlook; this can only happen if anthroposophy is understood not in this case as a philosophy but as the power to transform one's own personality. Only the ego can be educated. And to what end? To begin to train oneself. And what is the real method of self-training, apart from the natural education provided by the world in school and in life? It is that a person should start to transform his outlook and personality on the basis of his will, so that the thinking is filled once again with heart, and the will is interwoven with illuminated thoughts, that they are brought together as shown on the schooling path. That is a real cure for drug addiction. I know that there are people who succeeded after all in finding the connection to their own destiny by this means and in moving forward from the point where at a certain period sustained obstacles were placed in their path by education.

The underlying principle of Waldorf education is that young people should be educated to be free, which is particularly difficult today, because the opportunities to stray into dependencies are so great. We have to strain our will to the utmost to help young people to find the paths which lead to freedom, even if such paths might sometimes be unusual.

Let me remind you of one of Grimm's fairy tales, namely his most charming one, "Hans in Luck." Let us think of the path which Hans follows with his large lump of gold on his shoulder. This large lump of gold, which is part of his past, is a wonderful present, but it is a heavy burden for him to bear. And tremendous wants live within him which seem to reach much further than the moment is able to satisfy. He always wants much more than he actually has. He is thus rather burdened by the gold of the past, and his wishes fly all over the place. This lays him open to temptation. What happens then? He is on his way home to his mother, from his father to his mother. The path to the mother means: Hans is on his way to mother earth. And thus he gives away his possessions one by one. At the end everything sinks into the deep well of his subconscious, deeply hidden; the stones plop into the well. And then something quite wonderful happens: Hans falls on his knees and thanks

God that He has freed him from his burden. Then he jumps up with hands, which are free, a happy heart and light feet, and skips home to his mother to be of service to her, to help her – this is my interpretation now – to transform her. There is such a great necessity that the young people whom we encounter as partners should become free human beings who walk over the earth with a light foot, not destroying it, transforming it, taking possession of it in order to prepare the future and make the present worth living. That is what we depend on.

BIBLIOGRAPHY AND NOTES

1. These remarks are based essentially on the following lectures by Rudolf Steiner: *The Human Soul in Relation to World Evolution*, Anthroposophic Press, New York, 1984, lecture of May 26, 1922, and "Erziehungsfragen im Reifealter", in *Erziehung und Unterricht aus Menschenerkenntnis*, GA 302a, 1983, lecture of June 21, 1922.

2. Rudolf Steiner, *Knowledge of the Higher Worlds and Its Attainment*, Anthroposophic Press, Spring Valley, 1986, "The Conditions for Esoteric Training."
3. Rudolf Steiner, *Karmic Relationships, Vol. IV*, Rudolf Steiner Press, London, 1983, lecture of September 16, 1924 in Dornach.

CHAPTER 11

THERAPEUTIC POSSIBILITIES IN THE HIGH SCHOOL LESSONS[1]

by

Dr. Hergart Asamoah/Wolfgang Schad
Translated by A. R. Meuss, FIL, MTA

Maturation of Young People

Crisis situations are needed before new steps are taken in human development. One such crisis is the achievement of "earth maturity" in puberty. The process has, however, changed with time. In the present century, physical development has accelerated, psychological development slowed down. Girls will be young women in class 7 or 8 today, but puberty of soul, with its critical attitudes towards adults and (outward) reserve will only come in class 8 or 9. This creates an inner space that may be hidden from the outside. Apparent lack of interest should not make the teacher think the young person is not following the lesson with inner interest. Physical changes are today largely gone through before the soul matures, and soul development is more independent of physical maturation, which is not entirely negative. It means that the maturing of the soul is experienced more strongly in an inward way, compared to biological maturing, and the young people are inwardly freer to prepare for their coming of age; an opportunity arises to be much more autonomous in soul and spirit.

Other aspects of childhood maturation were also considered in our conversation: In class 6, the handshake feels more bony, and the world of objects is approached in a more direct and objective way; volcanic eruptions are frequent but soon over. In class 7, the whole class becomes restless, with dynamics that are difficult to control, but the process does not yet have individual character. It is only in class 8 that inner responses become highly individual. In class 9 the individual still feels relatively secure in the group context. In class 10 he is very much on his own and experiences the dark depths of soul, even thoughts of suicide, and the depression of the young. Trust in one's own inner powers and new contact with spiritual realities can only be gained slowly in class 11. In class 12, the new certainty provides a basis for addressing oneself comprehensively to the world of nature, to history, and the social sphere.

Puberty of soul involves becoming inwardly concerned over the beginning and end of life. Where does my own inner nature come from? Where am I going? I could put an end to my life – but what if I decide to live on, nevertheless? Young people feel disappointed if they sense, or think they sense, that an adult is no longer living with these questions. At school we have a good opportunity to enter into such latent questions by reading literary works with the pupils that touch on such existential issues.

It is to be expected that young people will distance themselves from the adult world earlier and earlier. Primarily this probably means distancing themselves not from the human being but from the whole world, an element that today is often even brought into class 1. If teachers find the right approach, a child who has already become too much of an adult may actually grow young again.

Childhood Problems Persisting in the High School

On the second day Dr. Asamoah referred to some of the problems boys and girls bring with them in the high school. Consider how much is involved in climbing stairs for a young child, and which of the senses have to be active in this. Think of the different ways in which it may be done. And all this happens before the child knows that these are the stairs. The world had to be approached, although it only gradually resolved into defined forms. Many children who join class 1 today have never had many of those experiences (circle games, for example). Even learning to walk means to go out into the world, to approach things. In many schools today, up to 25% of children show restlessness with memory disorders, problems of concentration, movement disorders, aggressive behavior, disruptive shouting, and lack of mobility in the psyche. All this calls for therapy to be given in the classroom, though not all of it will have been overcome when the young people reach high school. How far do they still experience the world of nature today, the stars, plants, and animals? When new schools are established, and whole classes only start Waldorf school education in class 3, 4, or 5, it will be necessary to reflect which therapeutic elements must be given extra space, so that at least some of the deficiencies may be corrected. If things are out of balance in the second 7-year period, or, which is worse, in the first, it is not always possible to make up for this in the high school. Fortunately, other children prove to have a good thick skin. We can no longer merely ask where we want to go with the young person. We have to see the situation clearly as it is. Here the school doctor can be a real help to the teachers, for he is in the habit of asking about things as they are.

Example of Pathological Factors: Abnormal Thyroid Function

Dr. Asamoah gave two syndromes as an example.

1. Hypothyroidism (from birth). We hardly see such children in the West today, for treatment is given early. The skin is dry, doughy, and tough, the heart beats slowly, growth is stunted, the tongue is enlarged and coarse, facial features coarse, the whole face broad, with the bridge of the nose depressed. They show little inner response to the world, with facial expression, gesture, and speech inhibited.

2. Hyperthyroidism. The skin is warm, with good capillary blood supply, the eyes wide open; they almost suck in the world, are wide awake in their senses, and very responsive inwardly. In extreme cases these children are restless and edgy, with a tendency not to see the world as it is.

The thyroid is influenced by the way we live with the world. We may ask: Does proper development of this organ have something to do with being "able to breathe" properly in the second 7-year period? And if children in their second 7-year period resist entering into the world's rhythms, how does this affect their relationship to the world when they are in high school? How does it affect the birth of the astral body even before this?

The thyroid plays a special role in puberty, with hyperactivity of the gland common in girls. When this manifests in a goiter, a physician soon realizes what is going on. More subtle changes are not always recognized, however, and go untreated. A girl at the school in Kassel was regularly playing the fool, running after all kinds of high school boys. Lessons would pass her by almost entirely. She also suffered continually from a blocked nose and blocked sinuses. This took her to the school doctor, who told her that air had to be brought into her head, and this could be done by singing and speech formation. It was then possible to treat the situation. In a similar way, lack of drive may point to a depression that has not yet become overt. Missed classes and being late merit careful observation in the high school, for they may indicate lack of drive. If that is the case, and the doctor explains to the boy or girl that this is connected with liver function, the young person gains distance from the condition and may perhaps learn to handle it in a free, I-determined way.

Eurythmy therapy is a central element in helping with many conditions that touch on the pathological. It should not simply be "prescribed", however, but the school doctor might encourage the young person to ask the eurythmy therapist if there is a place available. It is not always necessary to mention all the reasons, and we may speak more of the physical aspects.

Different Rates of Development or Learning Disorders?

Developmental differences also need special attention. Some youngsters rush ahead; others are slower, with the delay not necessarily a bad thing. There are some who are definitely "late developers." It seems as if they oversleep, but the truth may be that they are protecting themselves from elements that would still demand too much of them. Sometimes they will "catch up" quite suddenly later on in the high school, and catch up on mental development in no time at all. It has always been one of the strong points in Waldorf schools to accept such delays with equanimity and love. The increasing pressures imposed by official examinations (matriculation) should not make individual rates of development unacceptable.

The situation tends to get particularly acute at the transition from having a class teacher to being in the high school. The class teacher has intensely followed the children's development for 8 years, also maintaining close contact with the parents. Extreme differences in development are usually much more apparent in the early years at school, and class teachers are used to living with such inequalities – which does not, of course, mean that they do not make efforts to balance and harmonize the situation. High school teachers often know too little of what has gone before in the young people's development, and so a boy or girl may feel quite lost in class 9. The impulses high school teachers want to give are not based on the natural relationship which the class teacher had and are addressed directly to the life of feeling and will. Some boys and girls will, therefore, have difficulties getting to grips with a main lesson, and it may be necessary for the individual who is caring for the class or for the main lesson teacher to give a bit more personal guidance than will be required later on. Classmates may also help on occasion. On one hand, poor "performance" in the early stages of high school should not be automatically equated with inadequate development. On the other hand, we need to be aware of what is happening and observe carefully, so that we do not miss the early stages of pathological development if they exist.

There are young people who'll always "fall ill" towards the end of a main lesson period, when a test is impending. This need not necessarily be a (morally judged) case of escapism. It may well be a weakness or disorder of liver function. Wolfgang Schad thinks about 50% of learning disorders at school have physiological causes. Inability to manage a whole morning's lessons may be due to a pupil having come to school without breakfast. This is often the case. A class 10 boy fainted on one occasion, because he had had no breakfast. Mr. Schad then asked the rest of the class, who showed concern, which of them had had a proper breakfast. Only a fraction of them had.

Being able to attend fully in a lesson also needs a good rhythmic part to it. Some high school teachers think they can cut it short or even leave it out, so that they can cover more of the subject matter. Experience has shown that this is the wrong notion. The high school teacher does not have to be perfect in speech formation, though training in this does help. What matters is that the teacher fully recognizes the importance of the rhythmic part and recites poems or prose pieces with the class that are also dear to his own heart. Without thus bringing powers of will together with those of heart and mind – this can be done extremely well in a "full blooded" rhythmic part – the study part of the lesson which follows is in danger of becoming rigid, abstract intellectual thinking, and of being too much for the class, also, where time is concerned. It then creates an inner emptiness in them, and they have to look elsewhere for the inner satisfaction they need (youth sects, drugs). Bloodless intellectual thinking also causes problems right down to the physical level, something that needs no special mention among Waldorf teachers.

Dr. Asamoah also said the following with regard to lack of drive. All hormonal glands – points where soul and physical body connect – are reformed in puberty. The astral does not come in sufficiently strongly at this time, which results in lack of muscle tone and hypertension. It is, therefore, important to give iron (going from high to low potencies). If there is no real interest in the world, or in this earth, digestion, metabolism, and appetite will also present problems, and the consequences of this are apparent in the upper human being. Medicinal bitters may be given in this case, for they bring in the "I." If we are unable to activate the astral body in its relationship to the world, the "I" does not come in strongly enough, resulting in lack of drive.

Differentiation of the Sexes

Up to class 5 the difference between girls and boys is not very marked. This changes with puberty. So you'll note in pottery, for example, that the boys make a simple, cylindrical vase while the girls give the vessel a curvaceous form, with feeling. Girls are "constitutionally" more mature at this stage of life and often take the lead. If you ask the class in an anthropology lesson if they'd rather be blind than deaf or vice versa, the subject will often touch the girls deeply. Many boys do not really know what to do with the question; it seems unrealistic to them, since they are able to see and hear. In a lecture given on June 16, 1921 (in *Waldorf Education for Adolescence*), Rudolf Steiner said that the astral body is born more easily in girls, but young men usually do better with the birth of the "I" (at age 21) than girls whose "I" has been more strongly "absorbed" into the astral body earlier on. Girls may therefore find it easier to give a talk in class 9, and that is normal. Boys are "servile" at this age, as Rudolf Steiner put it; they withdraw into their shells. It would not be right for them to go too much into presenting themselves, though this is quite normal for girls. Rudolf Steiner said that during this time we need to feel concern if girls are introverted for an extended period, and boys become extroverted too soon. Infantilism sometimes occurs as a pathological phenomenon and may have a physiological basis. Thus, you may occasionally have a "sweet child" in class 9 who is incapable of offering opposition.

Here we have to be in touch with the class teacher and ask ourselves what developmental element lies behind it, e.g. very domineering parents (mother or father), with the child always trying to please them. The "fault" does not necessarily always lie with the parents; a child with a different nature might well go against exactly the same kind of parent, developing greater powers of "I." A good way of bringing out suppressed powers of "I" is to do drama exercises at all ages.

We now have to ask ourselves how the differentiation of the sexes can be taken into account in our teaching. Apart from the passage just referred to, Rudolf Steiner had important things to say on this in the education courses he gave in England in 1922 and 1923. He said he had found that girls are more active in needle work (handwork), with the boys more liable to look on; and the boys were more active in metal work, when the girls would look on.

To understand this we have to understand that girls, with their rich astral bodies, tend to incarnate only loosely; boys tend to incarnate deeply and become introverted. Girls should be helped to experience morality through beauty, boys through inner experience of power. Yet are we not fixing gender roles in this respect? We have to ask ourselves what effect individual activities really have. When girls deal with questions of nutrition, or with fabrics when they make dresses or sew, the loosened state we have mentioned guides them to their own bodies. This creates a balance and makes it possible for incarnation to gain a certain depth. We have to ask ourselves if such "female" activities were not actually therapy for a female incarnation in past centuries. Today we have different tasks as adults, but in puberty these things are a major help to the girls. Boys, who would rather hide in their shells at this age must go out into the world – "drawing locations" (surveying). And we may ask ourselves if the role formerly given to men: "Go out and face life and its difficulties" was a kind of civilized long-term therapy, to make them open to the world and prevent their crouching inside forever.

In a lecture he gave in Ilkley, Rudolf Steiner said that they let boys and girls do everything together at the Stuttgart school, but when they did woodwork or metal work, the girls would of their own accord tend to fetch and carry for the boys rather than do the work themselves. And this is something we can see to this day. Boys really like to make the most of the instruments they use in surveying, while the girls (in a mixed group) prefer to keep careful records, work things out, and do the drawings.

A German language teacher reported that in poetry periods the boys were more interested in establishing and investigating poetic forms, while the girls took more pleasure in reshaping those forms. It is important that they become aware of these differences, with the teacher gently bringing them to mind. It is also helpful to offer choices in a lesson, e.g. letting individual students choose their own poem to interpret. They would, of course, have their own poetry book. One might then ask who has chosen which poem, read some of the interpretations out aloud, and thus enable the students to perceive each other.

Conscious, and indeed conceptual, work on the gender issue may be done in social studies in class 10, when "equality in the eyes of the law" is discussed.

The following is an example for the school doctor's first aid lessons. Girls are good at bandaging. But sometimes one likes to do something that may not "come naturally" really well. Thus, some girls are enthusiastic workers in the smithy.

Wolfgang Schad said Rudolf Steiner insisted on equal numbers of male and female teachers at a school; this is particularly important for the high school. Otherwise something is out of balance. The young people need to see that it is possible to be a full human being whether male or female.

An important element in the upper class is to work with infants and young children. In Kassel they had a kindergarten unit in the high school, though later this had to be replaced with "rural domestic science." Another way was the following: in a main lesson period when every pupil was able to choose a project in classes 9 - 12 and develop it together with the teachers, infant and child care proved a very popular choice among both boys and girls. Indirect parenting skills are also developed during curative education practicals, when a pupil tells the child a bedtime story.

We have heard of a biology teacher in the United States who did six months basic theoretical studies on early childhood with a class 12, after which the boys and girls went to the kindergarten. It was also important to the teacher that the young people should be able to meet the child within themselves. These lessons were voluntary, by the way. When Dr. Glöckler was still a school doctor in Witten, she also gave lessons on infant care. Class 12 students today are certainly capable of conscious awareness and understanding in this field. At the end of a zoology period Wolfgang Schad devoted a week to a study of the human being, with the last days given to the young child. This helps to develop powers of maturity and prepare for the birth of the "I", for the child's state is surely the image of the true "I", the "baby among the different aspects in the human being", as Rudolf Steiner said on various occasions.

Typical Diseases of Adolescence

Skeletal instability frequently develops during growth phases in adolescent boys (Scheuermann's disease, etc.). Tendovaginitis is also common, showing itself when boys play the cello or do stonemason's work. They are not simulating. Weakness of tendons and ligaments is not infrequent, and sudden gains in height will often result in cardiovascular weakness. Psychiatric conditions are on the increase in this century. About 20% of adults in the German Federal Republic require psychiatric care at least once in their lives. Hebephrenia is a juvenile form of schizophrenia. A girl who had already been fairly reticent in the lower school never said a word in class 9. In class 11 she went through an acute mental phase: "I have to save the world through prayer." She spent a long time in the juvenile ward of a government psychiatric unit, was then re-admitted to the school one class lower down, and had weekly talks with the school doctor. She passed her final examinations. In another case, brief medical treatment dealt with a psychotic cum schizophrenic episode; the condition did not recur. We have to be specially watchful if we are aware of hallucinogens being taken; they open the way for psychoses.

Brief reference has already been made to juvenile depression. This is particularly common in class 10. It is not easy for a lay person to tell if one is dealing with a depressive mood change that is still in normal range or a case of incipient psychosis. If specific anxieties, self-reproaches, and thoughts of suicide keep recurring, in spite of helpful talks, it is advisable to consult a psychiatrist specializing in adolescence. Medical treatment will often deal within days with a psychotic episode which otherwise might have meant months of being off course, requiring admission to a hospital (taking powerful drugs for a long period). The problems that may have led to the psychosis cannot be tackled during the acute episode; any attempt to do so will only increase the anxiety and self-reproaches. But when it is over, it will be necessary to talk, and then a physician's objective approach is a great help in clarifying problems in which everyone else (parents, teachers) is more or less personally involved.

With reference to medical treatment, Rudolf Steiner's view that psychiatric conditions have an organic basis and organic diseases a psychological basis is of real importance. This is also the reason why a healthy diet is important, something we must also make clear to the parents who may otherwise think we approach nutritional issues on a purely physical basis. Fortunately, dependence on the organs is not total, and the teaching given in high school is as important therapeutically as medical treatment. Individual talks can also help. Thus, a boy lacking in drive may be helped by a half hour talk every week in which he is asked to consider what he has done in the week in question and what his plans are for the following week. It is not enough for an adult to observe from the outside.

With quiet children, whom one does not dare to challenge, it is often difficult to tell what goes on inside and if there are pathological tendencies. It often proves helpful for a teacher to attend other lessons such as eurythmy, gym, wood, and metal work. The teachers who give these lessons often have special skills in "reading" the posture and movements of a boy or girl, and a talk with them may provide important clues.

Anorexia has a major psychological element, with the classical form actually thought to be psychogenic. The domestic environment plays an important role; experts speak of the "overprotective mother." She rules the roost, does everything that needs to be done herself, "sacrifices herself", still calling her 16-year-old daughter "baby", and in a talk between three people answers all questions addressed to her daughter herself. If the child then also "leaves the nest" (in puberty), the mother's life has lost all meaning. Mothers who have strong astral bodies create such a powerful protective environment that the child's (especially a girl's) astral cannot free itself. The situation would begin to resolve itself if the daughter was also able to sass her mother or be a bit aggressive towards her; but she is incapable of doing this. As teachers, we should not, however, encourage her to go against her parents. It often needs a physician to help in this situation. There are also excessively powerful fathers. Their children will often be highly adapted, "an example" in everything. Only children who are very strong in themselves can resist such a father. Anorexia may also be an extreme form of "defiance" of which the adolescent is not conscious – the child gains a firm hold on her mother who now worries night and day.

A participant asked if stopping to eat in anorexia was a loosening process designed to release the astral body. Dr. Asamoah felt it might even mean releasing the etheric from the physical. In his book *Die stille Sehnsucht nach Heimkehr* (Silent Longing to Return Home), Henning Köhler shows that anorexics seek to release themselves from the earthly sphere altogether. Earth maturity demands that the young person come wholly to earth, and this is something they shy away from. The crisis often befalls very special young people. An example from literature is the figure of Mignon in Goethe's *Wilhelm Meister* (see Husemann, F., chapter on Mignon in *Goethe und die Heilkunst*). It will often be impossible to avoid admission to a hospital, or indeed tube feeds for anorexics. What matters, however, is what happens in school after this. Hospital physicians or parents will often ask Waldorf schools if they are prepared to accept a boy or girl who has not been at a Waldorf school before, and this is where we have an important role to play.

For prevention it would be important to look out early for girls who are very much "adapted." We cannot really incite them to disobedience, but if there has been no change in class 7, 8, or 9, it will be necessary to consider the young person in a teacher's conference and have a talk with the parents. Drama work in class is a help, as already stated, also in high school, and so is practical work in agriculture, curative education, and so on.

Taking a fundamental look at pathological episodes at high school level, it is important to realize that these are not simply negative; illness also offers opportunities. But the young people need our help if strokes of destiny are to prove fruitful in their lives, whatever their nature. Indirect help is given in lessons through the biographies which are told, initially by the teacher and later also by students, for these show destinies where illness was made into something positive. We also need tutors who care for individual students and offer regular tutoring, and we need far more child conferences than we usually have for our high school students.

Apart from anorexia, there is also obesity due to psychological causes. If a young person is distinctly adipose, we also need to consult with the school doctor and the parents, and seek to establish if there are organic causes or if it is inner development (often unconscious) taking a pathological course. Overeating when one is worried is something we also know as adults.

Therapeutic Effect of a Curriculum in Tune with Developmental Needs and of Work Set at the Right Level for the Age

Let us consider the beginning of high school. Much that has been taught in class 8 is presented again in class 9, but from different points of view. Thus, in history lessons the great revolutions will have been taught in a more descriptive and biographical way, whereas in class 9 the ideas are considered. An American participant once asked a class 9 at the beginning of a history period: What kind of world do you want your children to live in? A lively discussion followed in which the aspects of the threefold social organism arose as though of their own accord. The whole history period was then presented from this point of view. Up to class 8 children will, with luck, absorb the subject matter at the level of entering into the experience. In the high school they essentially want to shape the world – however imperfect their own powers may as yet be. Our approach to history then needs to be not merely "Epimethean" but "Promethean", looking to the future.

Another participant said he asked his class 9 to choose a significant figure from modern times and each had to present that person's biography and inner goals to the class. Many chose their "hero" from a list that gave names, dates, and key points on the person's life work, but some wanted to go beyond the list. And it was fascinating to see the eagerness and skill with which these young people found the inmost key themes in a person's life from studying diaries, letters, and speeches, but also in anecdotes from that person's childhood and youth. The class would often listen breathlessly, having never seen their classmate so involved and so much "individual" as when they gave their presentation. Some gained impulses from this independent work with a significant personality, even ideas as to their own choice of profession. (Not only politicians and statesmen were listed, but also artists, scientists, important medical people, social reformers, and so on; and it is important to include women.)

Here we can also see how students can be inwardly activated by giving them individual work. It has a deadening effect if throughout high school only prepared texts are copied into their books. Some students will not be sufficiently developed, of course, to formulate more complex issues (e.g. in the sciences) on their own in class 9. But it is sometimes enough to join forces at the end of the work part and collect key words which may then be made up into sentences. Or the first sentences are thought out together and written up in class, to overcome the common problem of "getting started", after which suggestions are made orally as to how to go on.

It has a stimulating effect if different tasks are offered for young people with different gifts and levels of maturity to work on the same subject. In history lessons it is also possible for students to add to the subject matter discussed in class by consulting books at home, thus creating their own "history book." Experience has shown that most students will do this with enthusiasm. This prevents the resistance and boredom that so easily lead to letting oneself go or perhaps even resorting to drugs. Homework can be "therapy" in this sense, and should be such more and more.

Technical classes have more emphasis on construction in class 8; in class 9 it is exact fit which matters. Art history is an important new element in class 9. The transition from Greek antiquity (the faces of the statues still show more than an individual smile, as if mirroring the glory of divine light) to the classical period (statues of young men whose faces often show mild melancholia) reflects the inner step young people take at this stage, from the protection of a divine and spiritual world into the earthly sphere with all its darkness, but with the opportunity to become wholly individual in soul. It is not a matter of going through the whole history of art but of putting the emphasis where the subject matter relates specifically to the inner questions of adolescents.

For the therapeutic element in the high school it is, thus, highly important how the themes that occupy adolescents are taken up in literature studies (see Christoph Göpfert's series on German literature in German high schools, *Erziehungskunst,* 1989).

The Main Lesson Principle, the Planning of Main Lessons and Practical Training

Why do we have main lessons? To make concentrated work possible. This cannot be done continually but has to be done once and then left to rest.

Wolfgang Schad said that it would be good to have four-week main lesson periods in the high school, too, above all in subjects that come up only once in the year. The 4-week rhythm is the rhythm of the ether body, which is the memory body. With language and literature, history and mathematics, which have two main lesson periods a year, it is easier to manage with 3-week periods. There is no formal solution to the problem of fitting all the main lessons in the year. The high school teachers' faculty will have to arrive at a compromise that makes educational sense. It might be, perhaps, that the language and literature and the history teacher agree to forgo one period and then have 4 weeks next time (see Wolfgang Schad's paper in *Erziehungskunst* Heft 6, 1979).

Unfortunately, practical training often gets short shrift in planning the main lesson program, which suggests doubt as to its value. According to Wolfgang Schad, however, practical social work should only be for a fortnight, as students may otherwise bond too strongly with the people they care for, even feeling committed to them more or less for life. Industrial training, on the other hand, should not be limited to a fortnight; even 3 weeks may not be enough. It can be of great benefit to students to enter into a completely new environment in their industrial training. Students from Freiburg, on the western borders of Germany, therefore, do their training in Berlin-Kreuzberg.

Agricultural training is often found to be truly therapeutic. If it is in class 9, it can be an invaluable aid to students, helping them to find their will. Hard physical work is extraordinarily useful in achieving earth maturity, and the connection with the natural world also influences the sphere of the ether forces. Agricultural work can also bring a thoughtful, serious mood to a class 9 that can hardly be achieved in any other way.

A class once wanted to have a class trip rather than do practical training in agriculture, which was a new thing at the school in question. A compromise was reached, agreeing to add a few days of "fun" after the practical training period. Yet when the students had come to the end of their time on the farm, they absolutely insisted on staying there for the remaining days.

Moving agricultural work to class 11 or 12 will no doubt result in deeper and more comprehensive understanding of ecological issues. The faculty will always have to consider which is the more important aspect. Agricultural work can, or course, also be replaced with forestry or other ecological work.

To come back to main lessons. It has already been said that an intensive rhythmic part is important in the high school. It is also important how main lessons conclude, which should not consist in summing up the lesson in one's main lesson book. If it is, the students are not relaxed during break and in the lesson that follows, and experience has shown that the specialist teachers have to bear the brunt of it. It is possible to have a period of telling or reading out stories also in high school, and this need have nothing to do with the subject matter of the work part. A mathematics teacher was in the habit of presenting and discussing current events, political and otherwise, at the end of his main lesson. This was greatly appreciated by his students.

A high school teacher cannot make it his excuse that there is no time for a separate beginning and end to the lesson. He should rather ask himself if he has made a sufficiently concentrated selection of subject matter from the vast amount that is available. If the head has been given too much to hold – as a school doctor noted when sitting in on main lessons – this creates problems for the rest of the school day. It also happens that one item of information kills another, and nothing of all the material presented will then work on unconsciously to benefit the student. It is altogether an illusion to think that students will have knowledge taken up in classes 9, 10, and 11 available for their exams. Apart from the practice element in mathematics and foreign languages, we are well advised to abandon any idea of preparing the students for their final exams. Rudolf Steiner spoke frequently to teachers of the hygienic way of making demands on memory. A mass of intellectual detail that does not combine to create an image will weigh the powers of memory down rather than strengthen them. We have to work on a subject when preparing lessons until the details have either become part of the picture or have shown themselves to be unimportant, so that they may be omitted. It can be helpful to be consistent in asking oneself key questions arising from the study of man when preparing history lessons, for instance. This helps to bring out the essence.

For hygiene of soul and spirit in our lessons, it is also important to consider the methodological steps taken on consecutive days. This involves not only the step from presenting the material to digesting it mentally; some experienced teachers have arrived at three steps that may be followed twice in a week: On day 1, describe the subject matter in such a way that it may enter heart and soul; on day 2, do not simply go through it again, asking questions, but let the students tell and retell it, out of personal involvement; on day 3, one goes into the will and cognitive aspect. Another approach: day 1, present the subject; day 2, bring out the problems, go into depth; day 3, consolidate. One participant had found that if he asked for an outline to be developed at the end of the second main lesson, the students would of their own accord ask questions on the third day that led to consideration of the ideal aspect. Here it becomes increasingly more important for the teacher to be able to hold back as the class progresses through high school, and take pleasure in questions and answers (!) from his students which he himself might never have thought of.

Crisis of Soul in Class 10

The soul development of students and classes is not linear in the high school, either. Many enter into a profound crisis in class 10, perhaps the most profound in their time at school. It is as if they face an inner abyss. Many will for a short time be beset with thoughts of suicide – with adults usually having no idea of this. Weinheber expressed this in a poem:

> Doubt in the meaning of the world –
> Creature thus put in torment,
> Who'll help you bear it?

When a language and literature teacher had recited this, a student came to him after the lesson to ask for a copy of it. This was the only sign he gave in the everyday life of the school, but on a class trip he had a long night-time conversation with someone who was later to become a physician, a woman who was one of the adults accompanying the class on the trip.

Dr. Asamoah spoke of another opportunity when many things could be dealt with indirectly. In Kassel, a talk takes place between student, parents, and four teachers to consider which stream the student should enter in the high school. This is an objective way of tackling the urgent inner question as to how to go on into the future.

It happens again and again that students (especially girls) absolutely insist they want to leave school at the end of class 10. If the teachers manage to persuade them to stay on, they will often come to express their heartfelt thanks six months later, saying that this had been when school got really interesting. This critical period, therefore, also offers a chance to take hold of life in a new way, for the first time independently, letting go of social structures that have so far given support, and finding oneself. New social impulses will only be possible once this individual step has been taken, as will a new connection with the world of the spirit. The Parsifal period in class 11 marks this breakthrough, which then becomes possible, though not as a matter of course.

Beyond this threshold, the encounter with the spiritual becomes as vital to the students as their daily bread. It should be a central element in class 12 and not be stifled by preparations for the examinations. An idea begins to stir as to the true home of the astral body. The passions, emotions, and desires we see in the juvenile psyche are not the true astral body. This does not as such enter into life on earth, remaining at the heights of the world of spirit; it is merely reflected in human beings on earth. The fatal attraction to black magic experienced in young years is due to the fact that only the lower astral body is perceived. The true sphere of the astral body, on the other hand, gives rise to ideals. The power of ideals that emerges at high school age lets the young person experience himself as a new human being. Genuine ideals coming to living experience are the most important medicine for the demonic principles that present a threat in adolescence.

BIBLIOGRAPHY AND NOTES

1. This article was from discussions in a working group led by Klaus Schickert.

CHAPTER 12

YOUTH AND OCCULTISM

by

Felicitas Vogt
Translated by Johanna Collis

According to Rudolf Steiner, far-reaching changes occurred at the beginning of the twentieth century in the relationship of humans to the spiritual world and its beings. This has made humans develop capacities that can lead to perceptions of spiritual processes. These capacities are developing naturally as part of the overall evolution of humanity. As a result of certain changes taking place in their spiritual and psychological as well as their bodily constitution, and initially without doing anything about it themselves, people will develop capacities that enable them to have new perceptions of a spiritual kind. This is paralleled by a noticeable increase in the number of people resorting to dubious methods in their search for answers to questions concerning their own spiritual nature and the spiritual background of external conditions in the world. More and more highly questionable esoteric schooling methods have been developing. All kinds of "masters" and groups are endeavoring to tempt people on to their particular path, and in many cases it is easy to discern what is really going on. A pseudo-religious world view is being put about among us, and many individuals are being plunged into psychological confusion and distress as a result. The "opposing powers" of the twentieth century are at work, and will spare no effort to prevent the development of the consciousness soul.

What happens when today's youth get caught up in the spell of these powers? Children and young people are often involved for years in magical practices and satanic cults without teachers or parents noticing anything, simply because they are insufficiently informed. Pupils in Waldorf schools are no exception when it comes to falling under the influence of youth occultisms or drug addictions that promise supersensible experiences and a sense of security in the arms of a conspiratorial community.

It is the writer's intention to describe as concretely as possible what young people are up against. It is also her intention to investigate what it is about occult practices that fascinates them and what the influences are that take hold of their thinking, feeling, and will. The author finds it important to describe the phenomena without passing judgment. The effects, however, must be closely scrutinized. A question that needs asking is: What possibilities remain for the psychological and social rehabilitation of youngsters once they have gotten caught up in these things?

Youth Today

Young people who are spiritually open-minded in their search for meaningful experiences and forms of community are often most prone to get involved with the prospects that youth sects, occultisms, and drugs have to offer. What are they looking for? Where have we, perhaps, fallen short as teachers and as a society at large? What groundwork should we be doing in education in order to enable children to be strong enough ultimately to follow their own individual path to independence? Young people have been changing since 1968. They are rebelling against the constricting materialistic attitudes that have led to the pursuit of "bigger and better", or to the satisfaction of egoistic desires but not to the fulfilment of idealistic yearnings.

Amid all the paralyzing decadence of the present time, this rebellion is actually an impulse of considerable hope. But when young people remain unaware of the yearnings churning in their soul, yearnings they perhaps satisfy by surrogate means, the effect becomes destructive. Youngsters need our help in bringing into consciousness the yearnings for which they are seeking fulfilment. To be able to help them, we must first recognize and understand the phase of development through which young people go between the ages of 12 and 16 or 17. The nature of puberty has changed. In a ground-breaking essay Wolfgang Schad has pointed out that the two aspects of the birth of the astral body are growing apart. The physical side of this birth often begins in the eleventh or twelfth year, without being complemented by the more psychological and spiritual side until the sixteenth or seventeenth year. In this interim youngsters experience a lot of darkness, loneliness, and gloom as well as a complete transformation of their relationship with those around them.[1] They are alone, cut off, and full of desolation, and above all, they have a most profound but deeply unconscious longing for "religio" – a re-uniting with the spiritual world. At the same time this is the point in a young person's biography when independence and destiny begin to assert themselves, so that tremendous demands are made on him or her as regards strength of will and self-control. Before reaching this time of puberty, children have been through fundamental experiences: in the first seven years "the world is good" in the second seven years "the world is beautiful." Now the time has come for them to test the world as to its truthfulness. But these fundamental experiences get turned into the opposite, so that the world is experienced as being wicked, ugly, and untruthful.

Puberty has always been a time of crisis, and youngsters have always had to get through it somehow or other. But there is an important difference between puberty in the past and puberty today. In times gone by young people underwent initiation rites to help them make the step from childhood to adulthood. There are descriptions of ancient tribal rites in which a boy was regarded as being dead during the period of his novitiate. He was removed from his accustomed surroundings and shut up alone or with a group of other boys of the same age. He may even have been weakened physically or mentally in order to eradicate any memory of his childhood. In some cases he was beaten or physically tortured in other ways. Drugged with spirits, tobacco, or mescaline, he temporarily lost consciousness and memory. His earlier personality was extinguished. The trial ended with rites that were intended to ease his passage into the adult world.

These past initiation rites helped young people in two ways. Firstly, experiences designed to extinguish consciousness helped them take leave of their childhood, and secondly, they underwent a preparation for adulthood by means of trials designed to strengthen their self-control.

None of these aids exist nowadays, and furthermore, there has never been an age so poor in genuine ideals or so burdened with pessimistic presentiments about the future. In his book *Der werdende Mensch,* Jørgen Smit wrote:

"In recent years there have been a number of surveys (published in the Scandinavian press) involving several thousand young people who were asked: 'What do you think about the future? What are your expectations in life? What do you imagine life will be like after the year 2000?' The astonishing outcome was that 75 % of youngsters expressed no hope for the future. They said things like: 'I don't believe in the future; it's like looking into a black hole; I think everything's going to perish and life won't be possible in the next millennium.' This was the view of 75% of those covered in the surveys." [2]

An addict from the Berlin drug scene expressed this despair as follows: "At least in the Third Reich you adults had ideals. They may have been the wrong ones, but at least you had them."

Young people undergoing puberty today often feel entirely alone in a world in which they have to experience political and commercial corruption and immorality. Yet, they need to kick over the traces – and they need boundaries in order to have something to kick against. But in our civilized world, devoted to consumerism and passivity, there are hardly any boundaries to be found. Many young people find adults boring and unapproachable, and so they feel let down. So what are the boundaries that young people today experience? They look for perverted boundary experiences such as bulimia, anorexia, drug addiction, alcohol abuse, audio-visual intoxication, black magic practices, sects. But these are boundary experiences that cannot lead to independence and self-reliance. Instances that have happened recently in German Waldorf schools are described in the following.

Table Turning and the Cult of Satan in School Classes

A girl in class 4 began to be noticed by her teachers. Having been a happy, jolly, alert child, she had been growing increasingly pale, lethargic, and withdrawn during lessons. The change led to her class teacher having a long talk with the parents, and it turned out that this class 4 child had become so fascinated by her elder sister's preoccupation with table turning that she could not stop taking part. Table turning is when a group sits around a table with their palms above the table, and their consciousness is intent on calling dead spirits. These spirits come and move the table or spin a bottle toward a card to relay an answer to a question. The elder sister was in class 9.

In another school in southern Germany the following occurred in a class 9. A teacher fell ill, and the substitute teacher did not arrive in the classroom on time. In no time at all a number of pupils decided to have an impromptu table-turning session. They had everything they needed: a glass and the cards. They all gathered in a circle that included pupils who had not participated in such things before. The most experienced boy was chosen to put the questions, such as: "Spirit, are you there? Spirit, answer! When did my grandmother die? Who is going to be my boy/girlfriend?" and so on. The answers ensued by means of the glass sliding toward particular cards. Finally this boy in class 9 asked: "Spirit, what is your name?" The answer was: "Satan." At this moment the door opened, and the replacement teacher came into the classroom. Two of the pupils were so shocked by this sudden recall to reality combined with the preceding answer that they became psychologically unbalanced and needed medical treatment. They were unable to attend school for some time.

Another example: A boy in class 10 was being discussed during a teachers' meeting. His appearance and behavior had been giving cause for concern for some time, and it had become obvious that he had fallen under the influence of a satanic group. During the meeting the teachers examined photographs showing the boy and his fellow pupils when they were in class 7. In these class photos the boy was clearly seen to be making provocative satanic gestures, for instance the sign for Satan which involves holding up the first and little fingers while folding thumb, middle and ring finger into the palm. If these gestures had been noticed on the photos at the time, there might have been other possibilities of helping the boy.

A final example: A boy in Munich, the brightest pupil in a class studying for their school leaving certificate, happened to meet up with a circle who practiced table-turning. It was three months before the examinations were due to begin, and an obvious question for him to ask was, "Shall I pass my exams?" The glass slid toward the "no" card. The boy was completely devastated, began to doubt his abilities, grew nervous, and failed the examination. Instead of passing, this young man ended up in a mental hospital.

There are plenty of examples like these. The latest surveys show that in Germany over 60% of schoolchildren aged between 11 and 16 have had some experience with spiritualism and black occultism. The use of table-turning, ouija boards, pendulum, and other occult practices by schoolchildren for the purpose of questioning spirits is increasing at an alarming rate. Of course, surveys like those carried out by the Institute for Research into Parapsychology do not always provide information about the quality and frequency of contact with occult practices. No doubt they include youngsters who happened to take part in something during a birthday party or some such occasion, so that a good number can probably be included in the categories of "curious" or "willing to try anything once" without adding dramatically to a general trend. Nevertheless, there have been sufficient cases to show that psychologically unstable young people have become alarmingly dependent on such practices. These youngsters deserve our utmost interest because of these phenomena, despite the fact that the media often exaggerate wildly.

Popular youth magazines are filled with crash courses in all kinds of occult practices. Bookshops in larger towns display notices such as "Open Invitation to Attend a Black Mass." Black magic is increasingly being hyped up as a youth fashion. What does the word "magic" mean? It simply means the use of supersensible powers. It means the working of invisible and spiritual powers in the visible, material world. To influence earthly events by means of supersensible powers is to use magic. Black magic is, of course, the opposite of white magic. In white magic supersensible powers are used in a selfless and neutral way to help the progress of humanity. A basic prerequisite for this is a strict schooling and purification of thoughts, feelings, and intentions. The schooling path for white magic can only be followed in the utmost personal freedom. In his book *How to Know the Higher Worlds,* Rudolf Steiner has described in detail the path to be followed for the purification of the soul.[3]

In direct contrast to white magic, the intention of black magic is to aim for the prevention of independent development. It is based on the manipulation of lower instincts for the satisfaction of egotistic aims. A path of schooling has to be followed for this, too. But the capacities to be learned are the direct opposite of those required for white magic. All human feelings such as compassion and love are systematically destroyed, partly by what amounts to a brutal training. Black magic means to call on evil for the purpose of gaining dominion over others.

How do so many young people come under the spell of black magic? We can distinguish between the following stages in the way contact is made:

1. You've heard of it and are curious; you regard it as a kind of game with an added sensation of excitement.

2. Youngsters often try out occult practices; then they have their first success, it works, and they are fascinated.

3. They begin to question former habits of thought. It seems to them that these occult practices provide them with much better, quicker, and more effective solutions to their personal problems. In situations of extreme psychological stress, questions are asked about the future and about personal prospects.

4. Now the youngsters consciously submit to satanic powers. The moment of decision has arrived. They obey orders often under threat of misfortune or illness if they disobey.

People frequently ask whether occult or parapsychological phenomena can be proved. Critics maintain that so far there has been no plausible proof of genuine paranormal phenomena. The scale of objections ranges from accusations of trickery and obvious deception by the practitioner to accusations of manipulating the evidence.

We shall not here discuss whether the occult phenomena described are anything more than tricks or a wave of sensationalism without any foundation or reality.

What is important, it seems to me, is that young people are increasingly letting themselves be guided by "spirits", whether through table-turning or by any other means, thereby relinquishing responsibility for their own future and getting into questionable situations of psychopathic dependency. The governments of a number of Germany's federal states have by now received applications for protective and preventive legislation against occult practices, because of the increasing number of young people who are getting sucked into these things.

Satanic and black magic practices have a history. The satanism of the 1960s might be termed "fashion satanism" if we think of the early vampire films, or the film *Rosemary's Baby* that received widespread acclaim and was awarded several Oscars. Or think of the rock music of the 1960s in which stars like the Beatles, The Who, or the Rolling Stones, who now appear comparatively harmless and nice, used backward masking to include satanic texts in their recordings. These were not heard consciously when played in the normal way but had a more profound effect in the unconscious.

During 30 intervening years all this has developed into what we might call "brutal satanism." Let's stay with the rock music scene. What was still hidden thirty years ago is now offered openly and unconcealed and meets with a shattering degree of acceptance by fans. There is a hit song that millions, mostly young people, have listened to countless times over the months or even years. This is the song *Highway to Hell* by the group AC/DC:

> *I'm on a highway to Hell*
> *Highway to Hell*
> *I'm on a highway to Hell ...*
> *Hey, Satan, paid my dues*
> *Playin' in a rockin' band.*
> *Hey, Mama, look at me*
> *I'm on the way to the promised land.*

The group *"The Dead Kennedys"* dedicated one of their songs to the pleasure to be gained from gruesomely murdering young children. One of the practices of black magic is to gain strength from the agony and slow death of other living creatures.

I have paid visits to the largest record shops in Cologne and Würzburg in order to study the record sleeves. First I had to stand in line for a good while because there were such crowds of youngsters round the records I wanted to look at. On the front of the sleeve of *Highway to Hell*, for example, there is a man having the neck of a guitar rammed into his stomach; blood is pouring out. On the back of the same sleeve, you see the man lying on his stomach with the neck of the guitar protruding from his bleeding back. Nearly all black magic and satanic symbols can be found on the sleeves of records by the bands that are involved in these things.

A close look at the texts makes it clear that, despite varying degrees of codification, many of them have a highly emotional effect and endanger unconscious taboos. Innocent consumers persist in maintaining that they have freely chosen to buy a product, but really it is the way the subliminal message has been "packaged" that has influenced their decision. A good many psychological expert opinions confirm the far-reaching influence of unconscious stimuli. These even reach into our memories and dreams. Our ability to judge what is right or wrong, beautiful or ugly, is becoming unbalanced; emotional over-reactions are being awakened. Basically, it is possible to bring about any kind of change in the relationship between the conscious and the subconscious by means of subliminal stimuli if the intensity and length of the recording and the intellectual capacity of the individual are sufficient. So commercial music provides an effective method of achieving altered states of consciousness. Constant repetition of the same message and the wide distribution of the medium provide an opportunity for mass brain-washing. Thus, Mick Jagger, leader of the Rolling Stones, formulated one of the aims of pop music: "We always work towards directing people's thinking and will." Another famous rock star, Graham Nash, added: "Pop music is a means of communication that determines the way the listeners think. We musicians can rule the world. We have the necessary standing and power."

What could be set against the power of these extreme satanic demagogues of rock? One essential requirement is that adults must take an interest in this music and in the way evil is manifesting today. It is becoming increasingly important for us to begin by studying the phenomena without prejudging them, thus documenting our interest in what is evil as well as what is good. This is the only way we can help young people reach their own independent judgments.

Here is a brief description of another method of counteracting the power of satanic orientated rock musicians. In a large town in Germany, a group of parents joined forces to collect signatures on a submission to the civic youth authority to make 16 the lower age limit for unaccompanied attendance at a forthcoming rock festival that was to include obvious satanic elements. Younger fans would only be allowed in if accompanied by an adult. The youth authority agreed and also undertook responsibility for the implementation. In this way the adults in that town not only became aware of what went on but also in some cases attended the festival themselves, thus gaining information for the first time about the powers that can be released during an event of this kind.

According to a press report, an Alice Cooper show due to take place in Frankfurt in 1989 was canceled. A representative of the concert agency had watched the videos due to be shown during the show and judged them to be so dangerous that the agency refused to take responsibility. The cancellation amounted to a huge financial deficit!

It should be pointed out that despite the dangers presented by satanic rock music, we have no wish to condemn all rock music. This is not the point. Rock music has many positive aspects as well as its own history and mission. But our description of extreme manifestations is intended to show how necessary it is to enter into discussion with young people about all the various kinds of music and help them exercise their critical faculties while encouraging them not to accept without question everything the rock music market has to offer. If we do not discuss differences in our conversations, but merely condemn everything, we put youngsters in the position of having to defend the lot, including the destructive, satanic aspect of rock music.

The Attraction and Fascination of Youth Sects

As recently as 10 years ago youth sects were very much in the public eye. The fact that the media no longer carry such dramatic or frequent reports is most probably due to the reality of the drug scene and perhaps also the brutality of the satanic scene coming more strongly to the fore.

The fact is that millions of young people the world over are still falling for the attraction of youth sects. The main ones are the following even though they have widely differing ideologies and apply very different methods:

> Transcendental Meditation
> Hare-Krishna sects (International Society for Krishna-
>   Consciousness)
> Scientology
> Divine Light Mission
> Children of God
> Bhaghwan sects
> Sai Baba sects
> The Moonies

Why do young people find these sects so fascinating? I shall try to select the main points from many reports from former sect members:

Youngsters meet people who understand their problems, and they feel they are welcomed with warmth, friendship, attention, community. They have hopes of a brighter, better world. They gain confidence by being told: "You, in particular, are needed. Your collaboration in saving the world is the most important of all."

Young people submit to re-education in their thinking, feeling, and will. Interminable lectures, dogmatic infiltration, constant repetition, impose the ideas and aims of the sect on young people down to subconscious levels. Their life of thought and ideas is entirely remodeled.

The youngsters' feeling life receives the stamp of an intense community life; they are constantly surrounded by other friends belonging to the sect, never alone, and thus also never given a moment in which to come to their senses. Every activity is communal: singing, dancing, praying, eating, working.

As for their life of will, this is strongly schooled by means of an iron discipline, a rigidly structured daily program in which extreme commitment, including hard physical work, is demanded of them. Within quite a short time the youngsters are transformed and subordinate their will unconditionally to that of the sect leader.

Their longing for a higher world and for a happy life draws susceptible youngsters into such sects as though bewitched. There they discover a community life that rescues them from their loneliness, a life that is strictly organized and guided and relieves them of their restless search.

However, what the young people experience as a relief and a deliverance is actually something that draws them away from the tasks they should be accomplishing at this age: fighting for their own comprehension of reality, their own capacity to form judgments, and the realization of their own deepest ideals. The capacity to think independently is not something they can practice where absolute obedience, group behavior rather than responsibility for oneself, and meek submission rather than insight into how one is being manipulated, are fundamental conditions in the life of the sect.

The young person's individual ego, which should be unfolding at this age, is prevented from doing so by being swallowed up in the group-ego of the sect.

Young people who have been swallowed up in this way lose the ability to realize their own wishes and ideas, to face up to conflict situations, and re-integrate themselves in the world outside the sect. Without the communal life of the sect, they are egoless. This is the real crux of the problem encountered when trying to re-socialize former sect members.

Parents and teachers should not think they are doing enough by warning youngsters about the dangers of getting involved in a sect. What we should be doing is trying to discover from the fascination exercised over their minds where we ourselves are falling short and giving young people insufficient support. We ought to accept the methods of the various sects as a challenge to work harder at developing the quality of our own ego.

The New Age Movement

Most branches of this movement are directed to adults between the ages of 25 and 40. Since there is only a rather blurred borderline between New Age and other alternative streams including, in some instances, anthroposophically sponsored efforts, it is particularly important to clarify the aims and lines of demarcation of anthroposophical paths of knowledge. It is not possible here to give an exhaustive description of the many facets of the New Age phenomenon.

Even ancient peoples used to divide time into golden, silver, and bronze ages. The ancient Indians gave the name Kali Yuga to a time they saw approaching in which human beings would turn away from the spirit. In a similar way many people have sensed that a new age has been emerging since about the beginning of the twentieth century. Taking the well-known unhealthy aspects of our culture as his starting point, Fritzoff Kapra thus quite rightly says that we require a new kind of living thinking. He rails against the impotence of the intellect. Concepts such as "setting out on a new path" or "having the will to change" are typical of a New Age Movement. Its forerunners are vehement longings and intense searchings, the search for one's own identity, or for an expanded consciousness, whether by means of meditation or of drugs. So it is not surprising to find a movement calling itself New Age making its appearance during the course of this century. It is appearing in so many forms, in so many institutions, magazines, and therapy centers, that it is scarcely possible to make any kind of a complete list. In the following I shall therefore try to present some typical examples.

The tendencies of the New Age movement can be typified by two short examples:

A schoolgirl returned to Germany from a visit to America full of enthusiasm and obviously deeply involved in a New Age organization. She had become acquainted with the "I Am Activity" movement and been taught how it is possible to meditate to the point where you begin to see auras, the super-sensible emanations coming from all living beings. One of the aids towards achieving this was to imagine the "Violet Flame." By meditating on this "Violet Flame," you could resolve any kind of conflict or hopeless situation without anyone else's participation.

Another example: A young woman student attended a lecture in a large town in Germany. More precisely this was a meditation evening with Chris Griscom, one of America's leading New Age seminar leaders and writers. There was to be a communal meditation. First of all the participants were lectured to and given ideas that would prepare them for the meditation, which was to take them to the moon. They were told to turn to the guardian angels on the moon. The young woman had joined in up to this point, but she felt she could not go on when the journey to the moon was about to begin. Afterwards she went to Chris Griscom and asked her why she had got frightened at the moment of decision and had not wanted to continue.

Chris Griscom was unable to reply immediately. She said she would first have to channel, i.e. make contact with her own spirit guide who would tell her what had been the matter with the young woman. So she channeled and received the information that the young woman had achieved a high degree of initiation in her former incarnation but had not yet reached a comparable stage in this life. That was why she had been afraid to meditate to such heights. Griscom advised the student to write some words on a piece of paper and read them every morning: "I want to know." The young woman followed this advice for several weeks but then fell ill and began to suffer from insomnia. She became psychologically unbalanced, but fortunately found a physician who was able to treat her and help her get back "on to her feet."

Very many people in a desperate biographical crisis seek help and advice at one of the New Age therapy centers and choose therapies deriving from I-Ching, sophism, yoga, Tai-Chi, shamanism, or other methods.

Our present time is so swamped with technology that only specialization and computerized thinking can possibly find a way through the thicket. But human beings with a soul and spirit have lost their way among all this high-tech development. A desperate search for one's own ego is a sign of the times, and people are asking more and more urgently: "What is the human being?" "What is it in me that makes me a creature with a soul and a spirit?" So over the last 30 years or so, countless groups have formed where attempts are made to answer these questions. Spirits are called upon, the dead are questioned, spirits are raised, Reiki sessions are held in order to concentrate cosmic energy.

There were already streams running along beside one another at the beginning of the twentieth century. On February 1, 1904, Rudolf Steiner said:

"There is no need for the two streams to be in conflict; their methods of research are radically different, as I have shown. They ought to balance one another. Let the followers of the one bring whatever they

244

have to offer. Let the followers of the other place what they have to offer on the altar of humanity for the good of all. In this way humanity will be genuinely helped by both streams, whereas combat between the two would only make people lose sight of the overall aim. What is needed between the two movements is not combat but concord that should above all lead to their common goal of lifting humanity out of the present stream of materialism." [4]

This may not apply to all the streams in existence today. But we must not stop reminding ourselves that our concern is not to combat other streams but to endeavor to school our faculties for judgment by recognizing them. In this sense it can be said that many of the frequently used methods stemming from the Far East generate a kind of clairvoyance that is based on the functioning of the body. The anthroposophical path of knowledge that follows on from Western spiritual development is entirely different: Here it is a matter of training one's ordinary powers of day-time consciousness to become independent of the body. In 1918 in a post-script to a new edition of *A Road to Self-Knowledge,* Rudolf Steiner put it like this:

"Of the soul processes present in ordinary consciousness, it is only thinking which can disengage itself from sense perception and lead to independent activity not bound to abnormal bodily manifestations. What is here meant by clairvoyant vision does not descend below this soul condition into deeper organic processes, but rather it ascends to regions which start with the power of thought when it is inwardly illumined by the soul and controlled by man's will." [5]

So it is up to us to ask where thinking will end up if it fails to recognize the path leading from the modern intellect to the Michaelic way, not following the Christian path of transformation but bypassing the center in order to attach itself to old forms of spirituality.

Furthermore, in *How to Know the Higher Worlds,* Rudolf Steiner pointed out that in the past some parts of the chakras developed without any effort on the part of human beings, and that our task now is to develop the other half by our own practice and effort.[3] If the wrong kind of schooling were to be undertaken, the parts of the chakra developed in the past might appear alone if activated, whereas those parts to be developed by our own effort would remain stunted. The consequence of this, said Rudolf Steiner, would be distortions in the overall psychological make-up of an individual. We must, therefore, not cease to remind ourselves that any intentional use of meditation techniques must be accompanied by finely tuned thinking capable of assessing the effects of any resulting spiritual experiences.

The phenomena described above, very sketchily in some cases, show us as teachers and adults quite clearly what our task is at the end of this twentieth century. Initially we have to recognize and understand the signs of the times. Although their aim is to attack independent judgment and the powers of the ego, it is not so much our job to do battle with these movements and streams as to work at developing and strengthening the individual ego. The need for this is growing fast, since these phenomena are increasingly also aiming at children and young people, who have not yet reached the point of developing their own ego.

Against this background it becomes obvious that we must help to bring about a systematic development of the ego during the first three seven-year periods by founding our efforts on the Waldorf education given to us at the beginning of this century. If we can come to see the opposing powers of the twentieth century as polarities between which a mature adult can strive to achieve an independent development of the ego, and as a challenge to protect the souls of children and young people by means of Waldorf education, then we shall have found a way of working against the threats posed by these modern phenomena.

BIBLIOGRAPHY AND NOTES

1. Schad, W., 'Zur Menschenkunde des dritten Jahrsiebts' in: *Zur Menschenkunde des Jugendalters – Vom Wesen des Astralleibes* ('Knowledge of the human being in the third seven-year period' in Understanding youth – the nature of the astral body), Bund der Freien Waldorfschulen, Stuttgart.
2. Smit, J., *Der werdende Mensch – zur meditativen Vertiefung des Erziehens* (The growing human being – meditative work in education), Stuttgart, 1990.
3. Steiner, R., *How to Know the Higher Worlds. A Modern Path of Initiation* (GA 10). Tr. C. Bamford, Spring Valley, New York: Anthroposophic Press ,1994.
4. Steiner, R., *Spirituelle Seelenlehre und Weltbetrachtung* (GA 52), Dornach, 1986. Lecture of February 1, 1904.
5. Steiner, R., *A Road to Self Knowledge and The Threshold of the Spiritual World* (GA 16/17). Tr. H. Collison & M. Cotterell, London: Rudolf Steiner Press, 1975.

DEVELOPMENTAL INSIGHTS
Discussions Between Doctors and Teachers

CHAPTER 13

THE QUESTION OF THE MEDIA TODAY[1]

by

Marina Kayser-Springorum
Translated by Johanna Collis

The electronic media began to develop in the nineteenth century at the onset of the Michaelic Age. Human beings became deeply interested in physical facts about the earth. Natural links with the spiritual world had long ceased, and the ego was becoming exceedingly isolated and cut off. Inner loneliness and the cheerless situation of having to search for the meaning of life are the price human beings have had to pay for freedom and the chance to shape their own destiny. The longing for a widening of inner experience gradually emerged, a longing to fill an anonymous world once again with the warmth of human understanding. A profound need for a "religio", a re-uniting with higher worlds began to grow.

The new media appear to meet this need. Creating an ever denser network of global communication, they overcome the close confines of personal space (conquering space) and by conserving speech, sound, and images, they also overcome the transitory nature of all earthly events (conquering time). We now have an unbelievable degree of freedom and are in a position to discover an infinite amount about the external world. However, the expansion of our awareness via the media is restricted to two senses, sight and hearing. Does this curtail or broaden us as human beings?

Environmental and citizens' initiatives attain world-wide recognition by means of the media. News of natural disasters requiring immediate aid reaches everyone within seconds. The media inform us – but what then? One possible reaction is: "Everything's so terrible; there's nothing I can do!" Another is: "I can join in everywhere, helping to put things to rights!" A great deal that is important and significant has indeed been achieved by such means. But there are also many dangers that take effect particularly when the media are used for entertainment instead of information. Earthly space and time are overcome by the media, but not by human beings. Our senses reach out further and further, but our actual activity tends to grow weaker as our perceptions are swamped by a deafening, numbing profusion. In consequence we only perceive what is peripheral and superficial without really connecting our humanity with any of it. The ego is paralyzed instead of growing in dynamic spiritual presence of mind. We gain an ersatz sense of having crossed a threshold, and boredom and aggression set in. The opposing powers can force their way into empty souls.

What stance can teachers take in view of this? They must be well-informed without becoming hooked themselves (e.g. on TV or computers). How do recordings of sound and pictures affect the viewer? They delude us into thinking that we are experiencing the real thing. Some people even prefer the recording to the real event, because its technical quality is better. High school pupils were asked to listen alternately to live and recorded music and state which was which. They got it right in 80% of cases. Asked what differences they had noticed, some said that in one case they got a feeling of being bounced off a wall and in the other of being met by something alive. Others used expressions like cold and warm, boring and stimulating. From the anthroposophical point of view:

Live music

+ refreshes the life forces,
+ the ether body is stimulated,
+ ego encounters ego.

Recorded music

- exhausts the life forces and lets you experience only yourself,
- concentration is lost,
- there is no commitment,
- it causes lack of respect for music,
- one's ego meets no partner-ego,
- the ether body is not stimulated by another ether body.

The conductor Celibidache, for example, persists in refusing to have his concerts recorded, saying: "Every concert is an unrepeatable human experience, or you could say: an encounter between human beings."

Recorded music is used in all kinds of ways nowadays to influence people subliminally (this began in the 1950s). People worked better to music. For example, fewer workers reported sick in the United States weapons industry during the Second World War, and production rose by 25%, because of "functional music."[2]

Recorded and live music both cause strong reactions in the autonomic nervous system that show up in ECGs, EEGs, and secretory and respiratory parameters. Powerful drugs are the only other way of bringing about such strong reactions. Some kinds of music affect the nerves and senses more strongly, while others affect the rhythmic system, and others chiefly the limbs and metabolism (rock). The music of one composer has been found to affect all three systems evenly, i.e. the human being as a whole, and that is the music of Johann Sebastian Bach. Gerhart Harrer (Salzburg) made this discovery while engaged in music therapy research.[3] The firm of "**Muzak**" broadcasts music to suit every requirement 24 hours a day: sedative music for dentists; music that promotes secretory functions for the gastronomic industry; music for calming airline passengers in case of emergencies; music to ensure an ideal shopping spree for customers in department stores.

Many children are incapable of doing their homework without music to put them in the "mood" (background music to which you don't listen). Such music works on the sense of life at the level of a damped down unconscious soul life, while the conscious life of the soul and the ego remain detached. Functional music works on the ether and astral bodies via the physical body.

Why are young people particularly vulnerable with regard to this music? They want a communal experience of music; they want to vibrate with the rhythm of the world from which they feel so dreadfully isolated. When you play an instrument yourself, the path goes in the opposite direction, beginning from the ego. Youngsters often realize quite clearly that the music does not in fact satisfy them and simply makes them more lonely in their search for companionship and expanded awareness. It is the tragedy of the twentieth century that they fall short of realizing that only one's own strong activity can lead to genuinely satisfying experiences. They keep on trying to satisfy their perfectly justified and deeply human longing by starting from the wrong end. Increasingly powerful stimuli and stimulants are expected to bring about from the outside what they cannot achieve from within: drugs (perceptions of the spiritual world), loud volume (the body joins in the vibration), inaudible frequencies (all the soft parts of the body vibrate with this truly "shattering" music). What are the consequences as far as the physical body is concerned? A Walkman can reach 93-120 dB and is usually used at full blast. Listening at this volume for two hours is the equivalent of eight hours at 90 dB. The resulting damage to the ears leads to hearing loss and deafness (as health insurance companies report). Surveys have shown that every tenth German is hard of hearing, and every fifteenth needs a hearing aid. Young people are under the illusion that the stronger an external impression is, the stronger will be the inner experience it generates. In actual fact what they need to strengthen is their own approach to the world; they need to begin asking questions and showing a genuine interest. Rehearsing and performing a play with a class, for example, provides an opportunity to generate powerful soul experiences that can lead to profound inner satisfaction.

Backward Masking and Subliminal Techniques

What is backward masking? Texts in English are recorded backward onto rock music tapes. These cannot be heard consciously, and the content is usually satanic. Meanwhile, it has become unnecessary to do this, since Satan worship is openly included in rock music lyrics. Over 40 rock groups admit to this. Are such lyrics still effective? Many people do not take them seriously and regard the devil as a metaphor.

The Beatles are said to have started using backward masking about 30 years ago, presumably at the suggestion of Alistair Crowley, a black magician in England who said: If you want to gain power over people, learn to read, speak, and think backwards; that's the gateway to the unconscious. Since then the evidence is that adding satanic lyrics to releases by rock groups has always led to a surge in sales.

The opposite side of the coin is that cassettes with subliminal messages are available for therapeutic purposes. These are music cassettes that lull consciousness. The suggestive texts are not consciously taken in. Subjects include "Be a success in life"; "Let go of your fears"; "Harmony and inner peace"; "The school of self-confidence"; "Improving inter-personal relationships" and so on. Without exerting yourself in the slightest – in fact to do so would be counterproductive – you are supposed to bring out the best in yourself if you listen to these tapes regularly.

What sort of people put out this kind of thing, and why? Are these a question of spiritual inspirations achieved by means of drugs? There is a connection between the New Age movement and subliminal technology. But surely such things were also done in the past, by means of military music, or suggestive political speeches and slogans. What is being prepared this time? Is there going to be another world dictatorship? Do taped subliminal messages always work and with every individual? They only work if you are nicely relaxed. If you do not want them to work, they will not, or at least not so strongly. The power of one's own thoughts should not be underestimated. To direct one's awareness at something specific prevents the opposing powers from taking possession of one's conscious mind.

Occult symbols that have a negative effect if they remain undetected are used in films such as E.T. or Indiana Jones. Advertising graphics use optical subliminal texts such as "Buy it!" that cannot be seen consciously.

These phenomena raise all kinds of questions. What ought we to think of "super-learning", the use of subliminal techniques for learning foreign languages, for example? How can you talk to parents, children, and young people about these things? Do backward masking and subliminal techniques affect the organs through the senses? How can I protect myself from something I am not consciously aware of? How can we help young people who do not help themselves? How can we counteract these technological developments? What can we do? We shall have to develop a high degree of awareness and train our powers of judgment with regard to what the aims and the various means of getting there might be. It is all too easy for any efforts to achieve supersensible perceptions, schooling paths, New Age phenomena, and for Anthroposophy itself to end up in the same melting pot, and this can lead to dreadful misunderstandings and errors, not the least in our own circles.

BIBLIOGRAPHY AND NOTES

1. The group worked with Marina Kayser-Springorum and Rainer Patzlaff.
2. Liedke, R., *Die Vertreibung der Stille. Wie uns das Leben unter der akustischen Glocke um unsere Sinne bringt* (The Expulsion of Silence; How Background Noise Is Depriving Us of Our Senses), Munich, 1985.
3. Patzlaff, R., *Medienmagie und die Herrschaft über die Sinne* (Media Magic and Its Power over the Senses), Stuttgart, 1992.

CHAPTER 14

NOTES ON PREVENTION OF MENTAL ILLNESS AT SCHOOL AGE

by

Johannes Bockemühl
Translated by A. R. Meuss, FIL, MTA

What can teachers do to prevent such illness?

A class teacher can first of all practice taking note of individual children and learn to ask questions such as the following.

♦ Has the child reached the level of development for his/her age? How old would I think s/he was if I had to guess? Why do I get the feeling s/he is older/younger than his/her age? Are there discrepancies between body and soul, in the social sphere, in the child's performance at school? These aspects need special attention when a child is presented, for instance for admittance to the school. Trial periods should be strictly limited and not too long, otherwise the human bonds that have formed can hardly be severed.

♦ What is the child's constitution? What kind of build is he or she–slender, compact? How do the hands relate to the body? What does s/he eat and how? Does s/he perspire easily? How are the vital functions?

♦ How does s/he express her/himself in the soul sphere? What is individual, original in this child? What does s/he not have in common with the others? Depending on age, changes in constitution must, of course, be taken into account. Am I able to establish the child's temperament? It is not a question of making a diagnosis but of posing the question (a fidgety boy need not necessarily be sanguine).

♦ How are the child's perceptive skills? Does s/he pick things up quickly? Is s/he able to go deeply into a perception? Does s/he show interest (intentionality of sensory process)? How does s/he perceive a shape or a line, for instance, and reproduce it (early assessment of writing and reading skills)?

♦ How does the child move? How does s/he walk on level ground, how on irregular ground? Does s/he perform a movement strongly, with concentration? How about dexterity, freedom of movement? Are there inhibitions of movement?

♦ How can a child gain orientation, make connections, choices, decisions ("I" functions)? Is s/he tidy (trained or of her/his own accord)? Does s/he show initiative? Can the child do "what is necessary?" What about attentiveness?

Some Aspects of the Anorexia Problem – Potential Early Signs

Such children are "an example" in all ways, often reticent and quiet. They are so much engaged in the matter at hand that the teacher always finds himself acknowledged (magnificent main lesson books, with every sentence the teacher said reproduced). Essays will always exactly reflect the preliminary discussion of the subject, but the child does not express any thoughts of her/his own (extreme precision of memory, but no individual powers of imagination).

Inner mobility (moving between joy and sadness) is increasingly lost, and the child may also be showing marked "pigheadedness", almost flaunting aggressiveness that reflects fear. S/he does not identify properly in her/his relationships, objects included. These children often feel the inner emptiness that lies hidden behind the facade.

What do these "symptoms" show?

Fear must be seen as a sign that the I has not yet "become flesh" in accord with the child's age. We know that Steiner spoke of increasing numbers of "I-less" people in our time. Anorexics are not "I-less" but suffer stress in their development, because the I has not been fully "invited" into the body. The history often shows that potential obstacles were always removed in childhood, with parents feeling that the child should not know deprivation, pain, or suffering. (Such apparent difficulties actually help the "I" to incarnate.) These young people are often much attached to their mothers, while their fathers, who are more in the background, will often make great demands on performance.

The whole situation of our times must be seen as the background to this disease – little opportunity for imitation in the sphere of human actions, relatively subtle deprivations (e.g. the ecological crisis), loss of sensory functions as educators have lost inner orientation, a civilization with a one-sided male ideal given up to externals. Inadequate realization of the "I" in the body takes effect when the "I" is increasingly determining life – physiologically – as the second 7-year period comes to a close, and the authority of those who train and educate the child is increasingly replaced by the young person's own ability to decide. The powers of will that should develop from inside are not there. (The anorexic will then be active in the sphere of the will, often indefatigably so, but with no activity arising out of himself or herself.) Apart from the absence of activity based on the individual's own inner will, one increasingly sees deficits in two other areas: lack of breathing in the soul and the inability to form one's own judgment.

The sufferer will complain: "I want to show my feelings, but I can't." (They will often only be able to put this into words in the course of treatment.) Anxiety (cornered feeling) develops when the inner life loses its breadth; there are signs of generally "freezing up" (become "manly"). Worry and anxiety determine behavior. The rational mind avoids feelings, and a one-sided, extremely acute intellect increasingly determines the outlook. (Anorexic individuals do not feel themselves to be sick; they have no insight into their condition). Gradually the notion "I am big and fat" grows stronger than the feeling "I am small and thin." Inner standards of comparison are lost, and the young person no longer has the inner ability to measure and weigh things. Doubt develops as well as anxiety, with a painful search for the middle position. Vomiting is a symptom of seeking artificial satisfaction, giving the beginnings of a feeling for the body. Left untreated the condition becomes increasingly more life-threatening. Even if treatment is later given, 10 - 15% of patients still die of the disease.

Where does the teacher's influence lie?

Apart from the parents, teachers have the earliest opportunity to note such serious developments. They may become aware of early signs, above all increasing loss of, or inability to develop, an independent approach. The ether body grows rigid (functionally this may relate to constipation as an early symptom). Teachers find themselves more and more echoed – they have to be critical of themselves; they need to sense the painful emptiness that lies behind the child's blandishments.

"Rebelliousness" needs to be seen in the right light: Does it reflect fear of the emptiness being discovered? (Generally speaking, get a fine feeling for the phenomena the child displays. Do not look for the phenomena as such but the individual nature they reflect.) We should not merely see the outer phenomena but ask ourselves why the child is like that, increasingly overcoming sympathy and antipathy in our approach to the child and in inner calm, experiencing compassion.

Rudolf Steiner said: "For as long as we feel sympathy or antipathy [towards obvious aspects presented by a child], for as long as we are apt to be moved by them, we cannot really be effective educators. But when we have reached the point where such a phenomenon becomes an objective image, and are able to take it as an image, neutrally, and feel nothing but compassion, we have the right inner attitude that puts the educator on the child's side in the right way."[1]

Pointers to a Therapeutic Approach

A teacher should bear with a child's resistance in a positive sense, perhaps even encourage it. Thus, one may well praise neatly produced work, but remind the child to find his own examples; support the child's efforts to form his own opinions; help a child to sustain a risk, e.g. coming to school without a copy book or with a flower in her hair (or even "done up" more provocatively); try to strengthen the child's inner self (also in eurythmy, which may be "wonderful", perfectly correct formally, but not individual, not entered into with feeling, with the child not really identifying with it).

A teacher can help a child to develop initiative; taking initiative always has an "I"-element to it. He can awaken the child's powers of imagination. Memory should not be overtaxed. It is important to look for opportunities to learn from experience and consciously accompany the child in this. Sensory faculties and will power are in inverse relationship and should become equal in weight. A teacher may even encourage a child to get something wrong! Courage needs to develop as a basic attitude; imagination has never yet flourished if there is anxiety, only fearfulness.

Therapeutic education means that art is not something separate, no "compensating sport." To combine our perceptions with insight, that is, proceed phenomenologically, is a first step towards working in an artistic way. Seek to make everything you do, everything you say, artistic, acting out of the phenomenon at any given moment. All approaches to art therapy can be seen in their beginnings in Waldorf education.

Early and Open Involvement of Parents (as well as a Physician)

Parents are almost always afraid their own lives may be affected. "Incarnation difficulties" may often be seen in parents: strict rules, apparently to give security; subtle anxieties, and so on. Start with small steps, therefore, and do not immediately threaten the structure. Shocking the parents would merely cause them to withdraw, with the child becoming more and more difficult to reach, while vital time is lost. The parents should be given the feeling that they can help the child: "You are in a position to do so, for the child has after all sought you out!" Parents need to be increasingly included in therapeutic aims and the approach to education which results from them. They need to be helped to accept and put up with possible mishaps; for these will often bring about a change. We have to show them that obstacles and difficulties are an essential part of developing our humanity. The teacher should gradually develop a close relationship with the family, which will enable him to relax habitual elements, rituals, and life stereotypes in the home. Every change, even the smallest, is a major effort. Parents need to be shown that they are needed, for instance by getting them to help with school affairs. Let them get to know and do eurythmy and join study groups. We have to use both imagination and trust in getting the parents involved: there is no other way. Courage is something parents must first develop themselves before they can convey it to their children. Admission to a hospital will often be unavoidable, especially at an advanced stage.

Guidelines for Treatment – Onset – Starting Treatment – Healing the "Scars"

It takes about as long for the not uncommon "scars" to heal as it took from onset of the disease until the child was admitted to a hospital (often for a whole year). Behavioral therapy (e.g. focusing on weight) is not appropriate, as it does not touch the individual personality which is the essential principle.

Inpatient treatment at the Therapeutic Community for Pediatric and Juvenile Psychiatry at Neuenweg: The children have no visitors for about 3 months. Because of the absence of a middle principle, the therapeutic approach offers firm guidance "to mediate the middle principle." The therapist (teacher, physician, care-giver) must inwardly hold the patient (and parents) close (offering security); and give the patient's day a strongly rhythmic structure, with marked alternation between activity and rest. Initially the youngsters are not able to make meaningful use of rest periods. Gradually it becomes possible to encourage individual initiative. The work they do (on a farm) speaks for itself; small groups make it possible to relate properly to one another. Afterwards the young people often need a transition period in a foster family. One needs to sense carefully when a return to school becomes possible. There follows an extended period keeping them on a "long lead." Complete recovery is rare; scars tend to remain (meaning that inner development potential is ultimately limited). It is, however, definitely possible to achieve self-determination in later life, putting the capacity for memory to positive use.

The Problem of the Over-protected Child

A child in class 8 was admitted to a pediatric psychiatric unit because of severe stress taking the form of a hysterical twilight state. The child was burdened with the mother's concern (previous miscarriages). Will all be well? He was less gifted than his brother and seemed to have problems with reading and spelling. He was aware of his lack of skill but was kept away from all problems in life.

It is generally the mother's task to introduce the child to the world through the lower senses. The mother, or father, later also the teacher, is the one who "breathes" between world and child. The "mother as a sense organ" brings the child to himself again when something has been learned from experience, helping him to make this his own. The child gradually enters more and more into dialogue with the world, which helps to strengthen the "I"-function at a very early stage.

The child needs to be helped gradually to leave age-determined limits behind and find confidence outside those boundaries; we take him out into the environment and provide for encounters, through touch, for instance. One extreme would be "release into the world of nature", inadequate protection, letting the child go wild, as it were. Another would be the anxious avoidance of anything that might cloud the child's protected life; keeping off all "evil." Such children often retain a glory, a "protected aura", something cosmic, unclouded and pure that is normal only in the newborn.

People's approach to bringing up a child is often governed by removing all potential challenges. Life becomes increasingly smoother and problem-free for the child and later the young person, but "the smoother life is, the more dangerous do the curves get." Experience of the world is thus prevented in many areas. Modern technology, media, etc. contribute a great deal to this. As the child does not have the encounters with the world that would correct this, a "kingdom" removed from reality slowly develops around him, finally reaching a size where it can no longer be controlled. (The problem presented by the media is that the relationship is one-sided and not one of give-and-take. The eye cannot differentiate between external and internal determination, a will activity, and it grows shallow and loses its "I"-function which is so important.) The child says to himself: "What do I need the world for?" To develop self-esteem?

A potential danger for educators is that they do no wish to hurt the child, by showing up deficits; they will gloss over problems, which does not help the child to experience the impact of the world in a beneficial way that will help him to come awake (become "I"-orientated).

261

DEVELOPMENTAL INSIGHTS
Discussions Between Doctors and Teachers

Later the young person tends to be a troublemaker (defense against his own inability, which he senses), and violence develops because domination has become a habit. Things go well only as long as there is no challenge. The young person is not able to judge himself in a sound way. His search is for pleasure (what do I like? what's fun?), and not for what he needs.

This in a way describes the trend for children growing up neglected in affluence, materially overprotected, and forced to grow up in an atmosphere of subtle anxiety. It is further complicated by an upbringing that, on one hand, explains everything, and on the other is based mainly on sympathy and antipathy, i.e. centered on feelings. The child is lost to his parents, because attention has not been focused on the "I" which stands behind it all.

Suggestions for Treating Children who have Slipped from their Parents' Grasp

The adult must first of all learn to get a feeling for his own boundaries again and catch up on a process which should have started very early (e.g. set limits when breast-feeding) – slowly, bit by bit, distance oneself a little. The child will revolt at first, being used to a different attitude. (Parents will need help with this; we must help them to translate the child's language, often provocative, and understand it.) The excessive care and attention previously given will increasingly be in danger of changing to hate. It is therefore important not to use a frontal approach in cutting the cord, saying: you must! but to do it indirectly, addressing their reason (usually well developed), resorting to humor, and above all always maintaining the child's dignity.

Exercises for Teachers and Parents, and All Who Are Involved in Bringing Up Children

1. Get to understand how we ourselves react to confrontation. Become aware and then behave differently, controlling ourselves, i.e. work on ourselves. Address the child's life of inner responses, which has gone awry, via our own "I." In the evenings, look back calmly on situations that arose.

2. In the evenings, consider the child in your mind, calling to mind his body (e.g. his ear – for three whole weeks, until it emerges clearly). Build a new bridge based on interest, quite scientifically; this stimulates and activates the sense of "I". A bond is created from "I" to "I". The child feels secure and fully understood. Then "ideas" will come concerning upbringing.

3. Ask ourselves: Can the child take me as a model? Am I consistent? The child must be able to rely on me (overcoming our own unreliability is "I"-activity and a precondition for further capabilities of the I).

4. Increasingly make life rhythmical in all spheres, including alternation between concern for others and reflection on oneself.

Early Symptoms of Impending Psychosis in Young Children

These children tend to look older than their age when starting school. Some show early melancholic traits (children are not naturally melancholics). Behind this one often finds stresses at home or a broken home, forcing the child to take responsibility too early. This will wake him up too early, with the "I" called to perform other activities when it is still needed to develop the sheaths that envelop the body. Precocity will be seen in children who are mainly among adults, and bright awareness of everything that is going on. The trend is towards excessive, focused awareness.

A typical physiognomy may be a strongly formed-out profile, a knowing, focused look that will only rarely embrace people or things with love; fine, straight hair, on the thin side and not shining in the light but dusty-looking. The skin is thin, slightly wrinkled, looking old, with a touch of blueness. The whole head looks as if held in a frame by the hair, which is often dark, and not open to the world.

Behavior at school involves a tendency to detail and perfection in his work – focused! Over-eager, conscientious, with a growing tendency to be compulsive. Lack of contact may develop into isolation. There is a tendency to create thought edifices that seem scurrilous and complicated. Later, sleeplessness may develop, along with intrigue, growing existential anxieties, delusions, and so on.

To sum up, we see gestures of increasing one-sidedness, a striking, strongly formed-out constitution, movement and language not very childlike, motor skills poorly developed, dominance of abstract thought elements, narrowing of the view (scotomization = refusal to accept certain facts), and progressive withdrawal.

Suggested Educational Approach to Those in Danger of Becoming Psychotic

Create compensatory elements early on; generally endeavor to prevent one-sidedness developing; balance out extremes with humor. Thus, the comment in an over-conscientious and excessively accurate child's report might read: "God has his eye on me when I work, but he also loves me when I sing." Take note of signs that a child is unable to relate to objects, people, and the world of nature. Really sit up and take notice when a 9-year-old says: "When I sit down, I always have the feeling of a cushion in between."

Observe the handwriting as well – is it getting tall and wobbly and increasingly more spidery and chiseled? Pictures – do they end up as scribbles? Do they reflect less and less of the world and become "constructs?" Above all, if the constitution is weak and lacks strength, avoid excessive intellectual strain, as this will not infrequently prove the trigger for a psychotic crisis.

Later, if admission to a psychiatric unit has been necessary, offer trust, a nest, inner warmth. Give help in small steps, forbearing, so that rigid habits (strong habituation body) may change slowly.

Always meet the child where he or she is. Enter into bizarre notions with humor; do a lot of eurythmy. Music is important, and the choice of instrument. The child will almost always make the choice out of the pathologic situation and pick an instrument that is apt to emphasize the pathologic trend (clarinet, C flute, or similar).

The range of therapies one offers needs to be extended quite considerably. The basic aim is to guide towards interest in the world physically (supporting the incarnation process), psychologically (creating emotional mobility, breathing between self and world), and in mind and spirit (creating ideals that warm right through, "fully individualizing" the child).

The evolution shown above, leading to paranoid (hallucinatory) psychosis, involves extreme development of the melancholic temperament. Hebephrenia, a juvenile form of schizophrenia, is a "caricature" of the phlegmatic temperament. Drives increase and become increasingly uncontrolled, limiting the other spheres of the soul; potential inner development seems increasingly leveled down, "mud-clogged." The facial expression gets weaker, the skin yellow, dull and pasty; hair grows greasy and matted. Hygiene is also neglected. All earlier abilities vanish. The "I" and astral body will often separate from the body at 16 or 17. Treatment of hebephrenia is extremely difficult, and a genuine cure is only rarely achieved. Generally it may be said of psychotic conditions that the more dynamic and "flourishing" the symptoms, the better the prognosis.

Cooperation between Teacher and Physician

Both professions know too little of their respective work situations. The physician should sit in on classes whenever possible (warmly received by the teacher, one hopes), but should be "silent", that is, give advice only if asked. On the other hand, the physician should ask the teacher to sit in on consultations (with children). The physician should endeavor to contribute knowledge and experience that is as comprehensive as possible to the common education work; knowledge gained in curative education establishments (it is most important to have a background knowledge of these situations of human life, "distorted images" which are potential extremes); knowledge obtained in medical practice (everyday situations); and above all, also from psychiatric and psychological experience, plus insights gained in nurseries, and the examination of infants and school children.

The key element of one's knowledge is rich experience, and the ability to ask questions. Physicians must be freed from the pressure of unrealistic expectations; they must first of all be able to perceive (which may take a long time). They must endeavor not to use perceptions to confirm knowledge (probably losing sight of the child, who is an individual). A quick diagnosis is often mere prejudice; it does not help the child.

BIBLIOGRAPHY AND NOTES

1. Steiner, R., *Curative Education*. Lecture given in Dornach on June 26, 1924. Tr. M. Adams., London: Rudolf Steiner Press, 1981.
2. See also the author's following essays in Soziale Hygiene– Nr. 129: Magersucht und Freusucht; Nr. 140: *Die Pubertät und ihre Krisen*; Nr. 143: Das unruhige Kind.

CHAPTER 15

SOME EXPERIENCES IN
SPECIAL NEEDS EDUCATION[1]

by

Armgart Trendelenburg
Translated by Christian von Arnim MA, M.Litt, FIL

Increasing numbers of disruptive children or children with learning disorders cause problems in classes or disrupt them to such an extent that they become impossible to hold, so that many schools are endeavoring to introduce a special needs provision. How can therapeutic methods be found when no doctor is available? How can the structuring of the lessons, and artistic therapies help?

Using the example of the Hibernia School in Wanne-Eickel, Christiane Wendt gave a presentation of special needs work to accompany class lessons for children who may be helped by means of slower, more intensive learning processes or through other measures, such as for reading and writing difficulties or hyper-motor symptoms. Care of and special needs action for children with learning disorders or disruptive children are not possible. During main lesson, some four to eight children from a grade are sent to the special needs teacher during the work part of the class, such as arithmetic, grammar, or form drawing. Putting children from parallel grades together turned out to be less beneficial. Special needs lessons begin during the second year. First grade should initially be devoted to establishing the community between children and grade teacher;

moreover, many difficulties only become apparent in the second year. The children should participate in the rhythmical part of the class; only in exceptional circumstances should a particularly disruptive child be removed. In subject lessons the children are looked after singly or in pairs, for example, children with reading and writing difficulties or with motor unrest. The children who are to be given special needs lessons are examined by the school doctor and the special needs teacher, and the measures to be taken are discussed on the basis of the situation of the child, the grade, and the teacher. Coordination with the parents is essential; it has to be made quite clear that this is not coaching! The child has to be well prepared for work in the special needs group which, after all, represents special separation from the grade. "You may . . . ." is a phrase which works wonders! The special needs accompaniment of arithmetic in the fourth, fifth, and sixth years is of particular help. Curative eurythmy and artistic therapies are coordinated with the special needs lessons so that there is no bunching at any time of the measures for a child.

Gerhard Föhner described the origins, development, and structure of the Michael Bauer School in Stuttgart. It was founded with small classes for children with learning difficulties; the "normal" size classes were only built up later. Four years ago, it became possible for pupils from the special needs stream to transfer to the Michael Bauer workshop, where they can train to become joiners, mechanics, or students in domestic science, starting in the eleventh year. They finish with the exams of the chamber of industry and trade at the end of the thirteenth grade. Grade ten is organized as a preparatory year for vocational training. The workshop is financed by the labor office; classes (as a vocational school) are supported by the education authority. The work is based on the whole school forming one organism in which an intensive effort is made to include the parents. As far as possible, teachers take both the large and small classes. Little is possible in the way of therapies. The school has three curative eurythmists. The three speech therapists work intensively above all with the teachers. The doctor is available only on one afternoon per week! Teaching in the small classes is determined completely by the abilities and possibilities of the children. Every child is given the time which he or she needs for his or her development; the children work hard and thoroughly. At the monthly gatherings the small classes – particularly grades seven, eight, and nine – display a more distinctive character, even better performance, than the "normal" children. One can feel the greater effort which these children have to make. The personality of the teacher is a key element (special needs teacher or master in the workshop). The children should feel at home in the classes.

From Holland, Mr. Moens reported on a special needs establishment in which the staff as owners work fully independently. The financial basis is provided by the parents, sometimes with great sacrifice and inventiveness in organizing events. A good social situation is created by having children with various difficulties – learning disorders, disruptive behavior – together and helping one another. The children are carefully observed, particularly the way in which they move, and are then jointly discussed in order to find the appropriate therapy. The key thing at the beginning is to dismantle barriers through other activities, such as going for walks or through play, and thus to kindle a willingness to learn. In the discussion it became clear that many children in the first and second grades found difficulty in changing from the grade teacher to the various subject teachers. Some children cannot cope with the number of subject lessons. It was reported that when demands were reduced in the early school years, the children were able to catch up with everything in grades three and four. Cornelia Hahn (Oberlingen) spoke about various therapeutic possibilities. During massage, which is directed at the physical body, the child remains passive. In curative eurythmy he or she becomes active through his or her own movements. In language the "I" combines with the physical body. Painting therapy addresses the soul element. It should only be used from about the age of twelve; indeed, age in general should be taken into account. It may sometimes be possible to provide a balance for premature development. The artistic therapies should help to guide the soul into the body. The treatments to be applied at any particular point are worked out in joint discussion between teachers, doctor, and therapists.

A teacher from Heidenheim recounted how there were considerable sense-disorders in a series of very difficult children of a grade four: one boy had difficulties with his balance when asked to walk along the top of a row of chairs; another was unable to distinguish between smells; a third was unable to follow a form with his eyes. It was noted in general that there had been a reduction in perceptual ability, but this was due only in part to organic functional disorders and was partly caused by the absence of proper interaction between the soul element and the sense-process. Disorders of perception and of movement should be examined more closely.

Starting with embryological development, during which time the developing human being is formed from out of the cosmos, Cornelia Hahn spoke about the significance of the senses as the vehicle by which the environment affects the child after birth, assisted by the human community which lovingly surrounds and nurtures the child.

Example were given of ways in which the senses of the child could be addressed in a living way, so that his or her soul experience is combined with perceptual activity. Every kind of mechanical practicing is harmful! Some things from the first seven-year period have to be made up when school starts: things to do with sense experiences; movement games – it is important that children can hop and balance; activities in the house and kitchen or on the farm; natural experiences on walks – whereby it is good if the teacher can prepare the children for such soul experiences by means of an inner picture. Age, too, must always be taken into account.

Experience in special needs education with difficult children shows clearly that good, sympathetic cooperation with the parents is essential. Parents may be involved actively in giving assistance. Thus, some parents in the Michael Bauer school accompany the third grade when it spends one day per week on the children's farm. Parents also participate in a rural retreat – over a long weekend – in which they take part in some of the lessons. In the evening the teacher is able to involve them in conversation about the temperaments, for example. It can be an important experience for parents to see that other children may have problems greater than their own! The important thing is to establish a relationship of trust with the parents, including confidence in their own abilities. Parents should be set tasks at parents' evenings, for example in making observations or speaking about certain questions and issues. It should be parents who think about pocket money, not the teacher in the first instance! It is important that the teacher should strive for openness. Mr. Föhner reported that the objectives of the school, as well as what it cannot offer and do, are clearly stated before a child is admitted. With difficult parents the teacher has to struggle for a positive attitude – as with the children – and seek the good in everyone. Agreement with the parents must be found if it should be necessary for the child to move on to another establishment – from the normal class to a special needs class, from the special needs class to a home. All opportunities should be properly exhausted beforehand, while a necessary change should not be delayed for too long on the other hand.

Every special needs action requires:

* the understanding cooperation among everyone involved both in observing and treating the child;

* the loving recognition of the situation of the child in that his or her will to learn is spurred on by making appropriate demands and by recognizing and affirming the achievements of the child;

* the courage to be innovative with new ideas for lessons and therapy, so that it may perhaps be an unconventional solution which reaches and helps the child.

BIBLIOGRAPHY AND NOTES

1. Report from a working group led by Cornelia Hahn and Armgart Trendelenburg.

CHAPTER 16

ASPECTS OF LEFT-HANDEDNESS

by

Michaela Glöckler, MD
Translated by A. R. Meuss, FIL, MTA

The lectures which follow were given at a specialist conference for curative education held at the Karl Schubert School in Stuttgart on 16 and 18 October, 1987. They were recorded on tape and then revised. They are reproduced here, because the issues and arguments they deal with tend to come up again and again, and the group working with the subject at the Kolisko Conference has not produced a report.

Basic Principles Based on the Study of the Human Being

Every Waldorf teacher is familiar with the words Rudolf Steiner said at a conference with Waldorf teachers: "Left-handedness should always be corrected."[1] It is, however, getting increasingly difficult to understand the reasons for this, reasons that come from the anthroposophic and the conventional medical points of view, in such a way that we are able to stand up to the demand to "give the children a free hand," which psychologists say is in their interest. The aspects given below may help the reader to maintain the essential dialogue with parents, who are often interested and also informed where psychology is concerned, and not let it end too soon.

The mission of Waldorf education is to guide children so that they may freely use their capacities. As teachers, curative teachers, and physicians, we therefore endeavor to educate out of freedom, both in self education and in our work with the children. Out of freedom – this has special significance in the present time. The anthroposophic movement has many enemies who maintain that we often do not leave or make people free but rather present ourselves as forceful, dogmatic, and indeed compulsive. If we have this effect, it does not arise from our method of education but rather from our own bound state, our present inner lack of freedom, and this is something every individual has to solve for himself by seeking to achieve the "moral intuition" postulated by Rudolf Steiner.[2] It means that we should not base ourselves on principles, and we should not have a preconceived idea as to what is right and wrong. We consider everything we know to be open to potential realization or not, and in relation to a child, and the parents, we take the given situations which destiny shapes from the impulses for freedom in life on earth. In *The Riddle of Man*, Rudolf Steiner wrote: "At moments when the soul finds itself to be free, its eternal life shines directly into the here and now and is present within it."[3] In this experience of freedom, it is possible for moral fantasy and moral intuition to be active, and this is the source from which Waldorf education has sprung – education for freedom and independence, education out of freedom.

I wanted to say this first because left-handedness is a subject on which people tend to be dogmatic, creating tensions and misunderstanding. Some parents have actually become opposed to Waldorf education, because pressure was brought to bear on their children, who were compelled to write with their right hand, which was against the parents' will. I am, therefore, not making a plea to "re-train" left-handed children, but intend to present material that will help to broaden and deepen our understanding a little and provide a basis for acting out of freedom. The decision made in the individual case may be helped by this, but it is not laid down in advance.

In 1987, a booklet on the subject appeared as part of a series for training in curative eurythmy.[4] The preface was written by the late Dr. Braumiller, school doctor at the Krähewald Waldorf School, a much esteemed colleague. The booklet presents an excellent compilation of Rudolf Steiner's most important statements on the subject and refers to a number of lectures where more can be found on the subject of laterality. It is, therefore, very useful if one wishes to study the issue. At the end of his preface, under point 2, a summary of pieces of advice given by Rudolf Steiner, Braumiller wrote, however: "It [the change-over] can only be done up to the 9th or 10th year; after that it is risky." Stated thus categorically, I feel this sentence can only lead to prejudice in our assessment of given situations. Rudolf Steiner's own formulation leaves us more free. He was asked at the conference if children should be broken of their left-handedness. His answer, in his own words: "As a rule, yes! It is possible to get left-handed children to use their right hand when they are young, more or less up to their ninth year, in everything they do at school. It would only be right not to do so if it might prove harmful, which will only be the case in a few instances."[5] The way I read this statement is that changing to the right hand in everything done at school is still quite easy before children reach their ninth year, and that it will no longer be so easy after this. This does not say anything, however, as to whether it creates problems to change to the right hand when writing – which is, after all, the main aspect relating to school work. In the recently published new edition of the booklet, the introduction was revised by Wolfgang Goebel and brought in line with current medical findings.[6]

My own experience has been with people of all ages, from children starting school to old people who have had a stroke and are no longer able to use one hand, but can, of course, still learn to write with the other hand without this being necessarily a problem. A boy of sixteen, who had lost his right arm in an accident, soon started to do everything with the left arm and hand, forcefully, with all his will behind it, and no mental problems, such as a stammer or flight of ideas, developed. Clearly if someone resolves on such a thing, he does it with full inner participation, out of his own inner will, and with full sympathy and support from those around him, and is also free to stop at any time if he gets the feeling that it is becoming too much. The same applies to a right-handed person who takes up the violin or cello and has to develop extraordinarily fine motor skills on the finger-board with his left hand, but practices with dedication and interest, often for hours, in order to gain the necessary skill. This shows why problems may arise when people read something into Rudolf Steiner's words which he did not intend, and this leads to maxims as to what people should do or not do, without considering the real situation and testing one's maxim against it.

Another problem arises because statements made by Rudolf Steiner, which have their basis in the state of scientific knowledge in his day and are no longer in accord with present-day knowledge, are accepted and spread abroad uncritically. Rudolf Steiner paid careful attention to scientific research in his time, and some of his statements are based on the then state of knowledge in physiology and neurology. In the 1920s, scientists thought the speech center to be connected with the dominant handedness. The idea was that children initially developed both hemispheres of the brain symmetrically and were able to evolve certain abilities in central representation. If they wrote with the right hand, it was believed the speech center would develop on the left, and if they wrote with the left hand, on the right. This has been considered out-of-date for decades, as studies have shown that only 2-5% of all people have their speech center on the right, irrespective of whether they are left or right-handed.[7] Some publications continue to state what was the accepted view in Rudolf Steiner's day.

If we consider the social history of using the left hand or the right, we find that Chinese paintings and also cave paintings were largely created with the left hand. Writing was also initially done with the left hand, only gradually changing to the right; and there is the famous stone from the 5th century BC where the Greek letters meander, going from left to right and right to left, changing all the time.[8] We thus see an evolution from left to right. When writing became of prime importance in civilization, right-handedness came increasingly to the fore. Parallel to this, civilization became more and more materialistic.

Another aspect is the child's development for its age. Every normal child goes through a bilateral state in infancy. When babies kick and wave their arms, they show pretty much the same motor skills on both sides. It is interesting that, according to the statistics, the left gains a slight dominance after this in the majority of cases, up to the second year. Parents often come to see the doctor and ask if their child is going to be left-handed, seeing it is doing more on the left than on the right at that time. This usually happens during the time when a child learns to speak. It disappears again during the second year of life, with children more likely to be bilateral between the ages of two and four.

If brain surgery becomes necessary at this time, it is still possible to remove large parts of the left or right hemisphere without the child losing much of its capacities. It is quite remarkable that pediatric neurologists find again and again that a child's brain is still unbelievably capable of change. Also, it is easily stimulated to perceive activities from the periphery centrally, developing the appropriate central nervous representations.

It is also interesting that the brains of left-handed individuals retain somewhat more of the childhood flexibility later in life than those of right-handed people. They find it less difficult to compensate for functional losses after injuries. Some years after the Vietnam war, reports appeared in the papers that left-handed soldiers with severe brain damage were almost completely restored after some years, compared to another group, providing the loss of substance had not been too great. This was not in any way connected with the right or the left brain being the affected part. Right-handed soldiers, on the other hand, had more severe problems and handicaps of varying degree later on, again irrespective of which side of the brain had been injured.

As already stated, every young child, be it left or right-handed, is more or less ambidextrous between two and four years of age, with laterality developing later. Right or left-sidedness only shows clearly when children reach their fifth to seventh year. Some do not yet show definite laterality in their first year at school. If the school doctor established this at the examination made on admission, curative eurythmy can help a clear dominance to develop. The interesting fact is thus that the individual development of today's children goes through the process of evolution shown by the human race, being initially more oriented to the left, then going through an ambidextrous phase, with most of them ultimately becoming right-handed.

There is a theory that about 30 - 40% of human beings have a basic inclination to be left-handed, and the rest are right-handed. The number of left-handed pupils in a school is in fact much lower, but this is said to be due to social influences. The customs in our civilization and our institutions, including military service, count on people being right-handed, which results in a degree of adaptation. It has been said that far more people would be left-handed if the social environment favored use of the left hand more than it does.

Be this as it may, we can accept that left-handed individuals are in the minority, their numbers fluctuating between 10 and 40%, depending on which side those with weak laterality are counted. The question is, do we call a left-handed person someone with left laterality, or do we limit the term "left-handed" to those who use their left hand almost exclusively, or include people who are equally good with both hands. These differences in interpretation are responsible for the range of variation in the proportion of left-handed individuals.

Much has recently been published on the subject of left-handedness, especially in the United States. All kinds of investigations, family studies, and comparison of sexuality in left and right-handed people have yielded numerous data. One interesting thing that emerges is that as a result of these investigations people are no longer inclined to think in terms of left or right-handedness, nor indeed of a clear dominance. It has been found that human capacities are distributed in very different ways between left and right. Looking for the dominant laterality, one has to ask: dominant in which respect? In our work as pediatricians and school doctors, this has led us to consider dominance in terms of intentionality and conscious awareness. My dominant side would thus be the one where I take action spontaneously and feel more awake. The other side is the one where I am more governed by my feelings, am less intentional, more willing to wait to see how things go, so that the quality of the unconscious sphere prevails. We may, of course, ask ourselves why the latter should be considered less dominant? Is it less important? Insights and questions like these have led to the concept of functional lateralization. This means we have to establish where the faculties are functionally located. It usually is the case that all active tasks are done better with one hand than the other. Yet, it usually requires both hands to perform the task. When a right-handed person watches a left-handed one putting a nail in a wall, he finds it peculiar, being used to wielding the hammer with his right hand, and considers, wielding the hammer to be the essential part of the job. But we might just as well consider it most important to hold the nail steady with our left hand. Why should wielding the hammer be thought dominant compared to holding the nail steady?

Dominance and lateralization are widely used concepts today. The term "functional lateralization" had the advantage that it encouraged teachers and physicians to investigate the laterality of different activities (motor, sensory) and ask which side of the body would be better suited for the activity, and why this child had a different tendency. To consider the child's intentionality, we can stick with established methods of investigation, e.g. is the child picking up the kaleidoscope spontaneously with the right or left hand? Is he or she holding the watch to the left or the right ear? Or if you give him a sheet of paper with a small hole in it, will he look through it with his left or his right eye? Using the conventional method this is all we need to know. But if we consider what the child sees, the depth, shape, or color he perceives, visual preference relates to laterality in a different way. It is indeed not the case that the intentionally dominant eye is also dominant for all visual qualities. Functional lateralization of qualities shows itself to be a fact the more we go into such details.

When it is a matter, however, of assessing a child's incarnation status, and to help it to incarnate, the concept of "incarnation dominance" proves helpful. We have to ask on which side of the body the child experiences itself more strongly to be itself, present, awake, active. It is a question of the side where the child's own will is experienced more strongly as a force. Spontaneous intentional dominance is the indicator in this case, which is not to say that the other side is less important.

It is the involuntary, scarcely conscious moral value we put on the left and right sides which does so often become a problem when a change of side is discussed. The devaluation of the left is apparent even in our language: gauche and two left feet. On all paintings showing the *Last Judgment*, the devil and the damned are on the left, the angels and saints are on the right. Much the same applies to the right side, except that the signs are reversed: "one's right hand, the hand for taking an oath, the one to rely on." When men and women are seated apart in a room, the men will naturally sit on the right and the women on the left. The place of honor at table is on the right; the person seated to the left is left out of the conversation, cold-shouldered.

It happens again and again that a child coming to see the doctor puts out his left hand to say hello. If the parents then say: "Give the doctor the proper hand!", this is a real problem. The hand first put out was extended with some hesitation, perhaps, yet often with a half concealed radiance; shyly perhaps, or with purpose, out of immediate spontaneity of the meeting. The other hand, however, offered when told to, will be presented listlessly, eyes averted, somewhat subdued and mechanically. Entering into the feelings of such a left-handed child, you can feel how his self-esteem has suffered repeated small knocks ever since he was small. He feels all the time that he's not really right the way he is. If we consider the left in the light of the right, the left is not right. The question is, what is the left?

When children come to our school who have had such repeated depressing experiences and always had to feel they ought to be different from the way they were, this must not, of course, be allowed to continue. It may happen, however, that the parents have learned something about psychology before their child started school, and suddenly realize that they were doing the wrong thing. Understandably enough, they now want the discrimination to stop and express the view to the teacher that their child should write with the left hand. "She's all right the way she is." Yet when the teachers are firmly convinced that the child can and should learn to write with her right hand, there may be a head-on collision. It is then not always easy to get the parents to see that it is not a matter of discriminating against the left, but of enhancing appreciation of the right when we try and teach the child to write with her right hand. To indicate that the left hand is not devalued, we might give it a beautiful crystal or a seashell to hold as a reward for being able to do so much already, while the right hand practices writing. This avoids discrimination, and ambition arises to develop the right hand so that it will be able to do something it cannot yet do.

Here's a personal experience. Visiting class 2 at a Waldorf school I met a child I knew from a previous visit. At that time he had still been in kindergarten. He was a difficult child, and the teachers had initially been unwilling to accept him into the school, but in the end they did. This boy was considered to be distinctly left-handed, and on my visit I noted that he wrote with his left hand. During the main lesson I went and asked him: "Why don't you write with your right hand, the way the others do? Haven't you learned it yet?" He said, "No, I have not yet learned it." "Did no one tell you that your right hand is also able to write?" "No, no one has told me that." "Would you like to try?" "Oh yes, I'd very much like to try." I sat with him as he wrote for half an hour and found that he was extremely skilled in writing with his right hand. I spoke to the teacher about this afterwards and to his mother, who was also a teacher. Both were horrified, for they had agreed to leave the boy in peace where his left-handedness was concerned, seeing that he was getting enough criticism as it was – a decision one could well understand. Yet, this brief conversation with the boy had the consequence that he really enjoyed writing the way the others in the class did, and it remained like this. In the next lesson the class did some drawing, and it is, of course, well known that genuinely left-handed people simply cannot use colors with their right hand, even if they have learned to write with the right. Yet, in this lesson the boy drew his picture using the right hand. The teacher observed that he picked up the crayon with his left, but as he was about to start he reflected for a moment, took the crayon in his right hand, made the left into a fist, and very slowly drew a number of small mice, black mice, their tails somewhat crooked. Today the boy writes with his right hand. He is praised for this, which has increased his self-esteem.

I know there are also different stories, and the above must be taken as anecdotal.

From the anthroposophic point of view, we must also consider the many potential dangers if writing with the right hand is enforced. The inner conflict this creates leads to the kind of symptoms one sees with other forms of inner uncertainty, or tension due to the parents' divorce, for instance. A child who has the ground taken from under his feet even a little, is in danger of being thrown into uncertainty. He no longer feels warmly welcomed in the world, but rejected. He will withdraw, a little, and this may result in symptoms such as stammering, flight of ideas, nail-biting, sleep disorders, problems with concentration, poor performance, lack of desire to learn, sweats, loss of appetite, morning headaches. These symptoms may develop in response to a number of factors. If they occur when writing with the right hand is taught in an inappropriate way, this is not connected with the act of learning to write or with "restructuring of the brain", for these are classic autonomic and psychological reactions resulting from lack of desire and inner uncertainty. It is important to know this when we meet the worries and concern of parents who have read what can happen with the change-over and resist it, not wanting their child to develop a stammer or become unstable in its autonomic reactions. This only happens, however, if proper care is not taken with

281

children who are learning to write and too much is asked of them, or if parents are not involved in the process in such a way that they are able to be supportive.

The situation is excellently presented in a book published by the Ludwig Boltzmann Institute in Vienna – an institute for the investigation of brain damage in children.[9] It is easy to see why the conclusion arrived at is "Give the children a free hand!"

I, too, would say that it is better to give the children a free hand, if one does not know exactly how to guide the process of learning to write with the right hand, so that it strengthens the individual nature of the child, helps the child to incarnate, and makes him more capable. This should be our aim, and if it is not feasible, it will of course be better to let the child incarnate in accord with its destiny in the present life. We have an education for freedom – it is a freely made decision to give the child something she would not or could not develop out of her own destiny, but can only be given by another human being here on earth who does something with and for the child. If the child is not surrounded with this positive attitude in the endeavor, with this feeling for freedom, which is inseparably bound up with love, we fail to be true to our own educational principles. We must be concerned to give the child a gift of destiny, but need to be very sure that it truly is a gift. It will then be a matter of gaining the parents' consent.

I have known a case where I could not have obtained the parents' consent on my own. The father was a physician, the mother a psychologist, and she wanted her left-handed child to learn to write with the right hand. The father was still in doubt. For as long as the parents were unable to agree, the child showed the classic signs of uncertainty, and the mother was, therefore, on the point of giving up. The father was also interested in acupuncture, however, and consulted a specialist in that field who was to examine the child for the distribution of energy levels. The acupuncturist said it would be good for the child to write with the right hand. From then on the teachers' efforts were also supported by the father. The child now writes with the right hand and is proud of the progress made, which is also praised by the parents.

Let me try now and consider anthroposophic aspects that can help us understand why Rudolf Steiner said that left-handedness should always be corrected.[10] The demand goes totally against the prevailing view, and it is, therefore, important to look deeply into the reasons. We'll begin by considering the physical aspect of the problem and then consider the aspects relating to the science of the spirit.

Physically, it is interesting to use simple observation to see how economically we ourselves or another person are organized as regards left and right. When an arm is put in plaster, the muscles atrophy. Anything left unused in the organism regresses; anything that is exercised develops further. Development is the consequence of a child's incarnation activity, which after birth consists in constantly coming to terms with the environment. To stimulate cerebral activity if abnormalities exist in infants, we give them physiotherapy, for it has been found that repetition of certain well-coordinated movements provides a healthy stimulus for brain development. The other organ systems also continue to develop in accord with their functions. If we consider the body in terms of left and right, the first thing we note is symmetry. All nerve structures and sense organs, all organs of conscious activity are symmetrical, which is immediately evident. Yet the internal organs which function below the level of consciousness, organs of sheer will and activity, are asymmetrical.

The organs where we are half conscious, in our feelings, lie in the middle. Heart and lungs are essentially symmetrical, but the four-chambered heart as an individual organ is positioned more to the left, and the lungs, of which we have a pair, have two lobes on the left and three on the right. With reference to left and right we perceive that physically the right side relates more to the outside world and has to deal with anything we take in through sensory perception (brain) and as physical substance (liver). Infections (e.g. tuberculosis) are also more liable to affect the right lung than the left. The left lung has only two lobes, which is not only because the heart needs space. It also breathes less deeply and actively, so that we have to say: The outer atmosphere with all its pollutants, dust, and glorious scents, with all the oxygen that refreshes, is preferably taken in on the right side. We have more room on the right side, and a little more activity. On the left side, however, we are more connected with the inner world of the soul and the processes of hearing and speaking which are in time. The main speech center is, therefore, generally located in the left brain, and so is the assimilation of music and inner experiences in the realm of feeling. The spleen is also on the left, a small spongy organ located under the left costal arch, opposite to the liver. In the light of this basic disposition, writing, being a process of communicating with the outside world, relates more to the activities of the right side of the body, whereas finding the right note on the finger-board of a violin is quite rightly a function of the left hand.

Using the left and right side of the body in accord with this original design helps us to use our energies economically and avoid one-sided overexertion.

Further aspects will be considered in the next section. At the moment, I merely want to say, in conclusion, that when we teach children to write with their right hand, this does not mean we make them "change." They continue to do other activities freely with one hand or the other. All they do is gain a new skill for the right hand, the skill of writing. We can only speak of "change", if the child has already learned to write with the left. This would always be an exceptional case with older children and needs careful thought, with the child included in the decision-making. There will be no need for this if all children simply learn to write with the "writing hand" in their first year at school, which some will find easier than others. The "painting hand" may be left or right, whereas the "string hand" and the "bow hand" for the violin is not a matter of choice, and so on.

The chapter on left-handedness in *A Guide to Child Health* by Wolfgang Goebel and me[11] offers some further practical advice. Reference is also made to the educational value, considering the karmic background given by Rudolf Steiner, for it is because of this that we make such efforts to teach children to write with their right hand. The chapter may also be given to parents to read before the left-handedness of their child is discussed with the staff at the school.

Anthroposophic Aspects

Left-handed children differ enormously, just like right-handed children. Compared to right-handed children, they show more marked characteristics of behavior and capabilities. The left-handed population includes a greater proportion of sick individuals and those who show genius than the right-handed population. Numerous studies have been done, including the one at the Ludwig Boltzmann Institute,[12] Ullmann's work on laterality,[13] and

Sovák's work.[14] They investigate the health and pathology of typical left- and right-handed individuals and those who are ambidextrous. The latter are often counted among the left-handed, which is open to dispute. Studying the findings made, one gets the impression that health problems show a certain concentration among the left-handed, with the following more common among them than among right-handed people: allergies, short-sightedness, hydrocephalus, microcephalus (head too small), birth traumas, and hereditary conditions such as skeletal anomalies or metabolic diseases. They also show more deviation in sexual behavior, such as homosexuality and lesbianism, and are more often mentally less stable than right-handed individuals. The affective respiratory spasms seen in children between the ages of 1 and 4, where fury lets them reach a state where they stop breathing and develop spasms, are typical for children who later turn out to be left-handed.

Added to this are the above-mentioned problems due to repression when a change is enforced, and the left hand denigrated: sweats, headache, loss of appetite, dermographism (red rather than pale pink or white line appearing if skin is scratched), also stammering, flight of ideas, inadequate inner response, taking the form of excessive eruptions of both rage and pleasure, which is known as affective instability, so that feelings are not properly under control. These symptoms may also result in poor performance at school, and, indeed, depression and blocks in the learning process.

If we perceive the connections which exist here, we can see that left-handed children need our special love and attention. Every child needs this, of course, but left-handers need to be given compensation for the specific extra stress to which they are exposed, and we must be specially sympathetic and give them our moral support. If this is done, we need not worry about a left-handed child developing a life-long negative aspect when he has to make the effort and learn to write with the right hand. Quite the contrary, such a learning process, calling for strength of mind, can genuinely increase self-esteem and self awareness. This is, of course, most important for the child's future life. Activity thus calling for strength of mind can largely compensate for a more susceptible physical constitution and strengthen the child for his whole future life.

In terms of destiny we have, on the one hand, karmic elements from the past: we are made in a particular way, cannot change our spots, have to take things as they are. On the other hand, a rich potential for development comes to us from the future. What kind of person is this going to be? What would be the ideal? What should he learn? What is the meaning of it? How will development continue? Between past and future we have the present. It is like a threshold, for it is only here that freedom, as we know it, is possible. There is no freedom in the elements that determine us from the past. Nor does it lie in the future, for our wishes and goals have, to some extent, fixed it. Space for the experience of freedom and for independent action exists only in the present, when we can decide which course to take. Such a free decision may be to use one's right hand for writing. There are no compelling reasons in favor and few that speak against such a course. Yet, where do we find the motivation and strength to make the decision? This takes us into the sphere initially described in this paper as the possibility to educate out of "freedom." It calls for a particular inner climate, a free atmosphere sustained by love. We can do practical exercises to achieve this. Say someone has insulted us, and we react to this spontaneously. In that case we are unfree. The situation is, however, very different if we meet someone who has insulted us in a way we ourselves decide on – perhaps the direct opposite of that spontaneous inner response. If we look for such opportunities in our personal and professional lives, we find that our attitudes are often greatly influenced by the past; we re-act rather than act entirely out of ourselves and in accord with our inner goals. It is thus necessary to learn from the past and always keep an eye on it.

It is equally important to face the next day openly and freely, being prepared to start afresh. Our ability to do so is connected with the power in us that is referred to in the "Our Father", when we are asked to forgive those who trespass against us. We are capable of inner change and of coming to a free decision, forgiving, for instance, where some wrong has been done to us, and the normal reaction would be to pay back in kind. We have the potential, which at the same time is also the precondition, for acting out of freedom. Everything else we ask for in the "Our Father" is a grace given by the world of the spirit. Forgiveness is something we are able to give to that world, for it can only arise out of freedom and love here on earth. If this inner attitude helps us to break out of the difficult strait-jacket imposed by past and future, a space opens up where moral intuitions can come, and the true human soul and spirit can shine into our awareness of the present.

We really cannot tackle the issue of left-handedness unless we develop this inner mood of true humanity. It is, of course, often far from easy to be thus open, especially if the left-handed child is also a difficult child, perhaps hyperkinetic, aggressive, unstable, or cheeky, calling his teacher an ape, for instance. The teacher is often taken aback by this, and the spontaneous reaction is to send the child home or ask the parents to collect him or her. This will, however, affect the relationship between child and teacher, for in his heart the child loves the teacher and expects him not to react in this Old-Testament fashion, but to have done some work already to gain freedom and love. A child will thus be bitterly disappointed when the situation cannot be resolved with genuine humor or moral fantasy.

A child who feels "I have to" cannot be asked to make the personal effort of will that would have a health-giving effect. It is not healthy to have to live under a constant feeling of compulsion. No one can have a healthy relationship to their work in the long run if they are not doing it voluntarily. Any work that is a burden and cannot be seen to have a real purpose will ultimately make people ill. It depletes the inner life, which is made for doing things of one's own volition, and needs to be quickened by love in its doing. It is important to realize the problems and weaknesses a child may have but also his gifts of genius. We know that there have been individuals of genius, some of them great artists, who were left-handed.

Concerning the spiritual scientific background to left-handedness, Rudolf Steiner said the following at the conference on May 25, 1923:

"Left-handedness is a decidedly karmic phenomenon, and it expresses a karmic weakness. To give an example: Someone who had overworked and overstrained in his previous life, not only physically or intellectually, but in his whole life of soul, will be unable to overcome this weakness, which is now located in the lower part of his being. (The part of the human being which arises from the life between death and rebirth is, in the new life, mainly concentrated in the lower human being, whereas the part coming from his previous life appears more in the head region) Therefore, the principles that normally develop strongly will be weak, and to compensate for this, the left leg and the left hand are called in to help. The preponderance of the left hand leads to the right frontal convolutions of the brain instead of the left being engaged in speech."[15]

Let us imagine a possible scenario from an earlier life, say, in the Middle Ages: monastery, enforced asceticism, hard inner work that is not done in inner freedom, and out of love for the world of the spirit, but by someone with a feeling of despair, using common sense, or under moral pressure. It may be that the individual is not in the monastery of his free will, but was sent there by his family and now seeks to adapt and prove himself, perhaps making special efforts to be successful. It has always been the rule that the inner path can only take us forward if we seek it with the greatest inner honesty. Other motivations coming into it will interfere with the inner work, creating a gulf between the true core of one's being and the spiritual relationship between it and the world of the spirit.

The phenomenon of karmic weakness is difficult to grasp. How does it relate to life on earth, life after death, and return to earth? Let us try and feel our way towards these questions.

First of all, imagine a life on earth in which we overexerted ourselves physically, working harder than the body is really able to. This meant a depletion of physical resources, and we had to rest for an extended period or may even have fallen ill. It may be that we realized the work was too much but had to continue, perhaps being compelled by others, being a slave, or because we forced ourselves.

If people continue with physical effort when exhausted, rowing a boat, for instance, they go on half asleep. Consciousness is increasingly less connected with the work; we are absent in mind and spirit. Seen in this light, overexertion also means that we cannot do our work with love, being only half involved and not fully identifying with it.

When do we overexert ourselves mentally? Nowadays, for instance, when taking final examinations. The material one has to cram into one's head daily in the study of law and medicine presents a particular problem. You find that you are learning more than you are able to really comprehend and meet with real interest. This weakens us. It is interesting to note that students may suddenly develop conditions such as allergies or migraine when under this kind of stress, or also afterwards; these conditions may have been familial, or "hereditary", but did not emerge before. Defects in the constitution that have been held in balance while one followed a relatively healthy lifestyle may drop out of that balance on physical or mental overexertion or any kind of unphysiologic stress. They will then take effect suddenly.

The common factor with any kind of overexertion is that the world makes demands we are not able to meet inwardly, and we then attempt under pressure or of our own accord to make "superhuman" efforts where the conscious mind and the heart can no longer be in it. What we have learned remains mere "head" knowledge, it does not become "heart knowledge", that is, taken into the constitution as a whole. The same is true for physical activities. It is not possible to be inwardly wholly connected and identify with our efforts. The body goes its own way, as it were, responding to demands made by the environment, with the conscious mind unable to follow and therefore withdrawing. Mental overexertion means that the head makes extreme efforts, but the knowledge cannot be mentally digested in a way that also involves the powers of the heart.

In either case, the middle sphere of feeling is also weakened. When we die, we only take with us across the threshold the things we really related to in our hearts. All knowledge that has not been really made our own by recreating it for ourselves, letting our own will and feelings enter into it and making it individual; knowledge that has remained superficial and abstract, has no significance in life after death. Our thinking dissolves into the cosmic ether after death. We "lose our head", as it were, and continue our journey in the world of the spirit as human beings of heart and will, that is, as the moral beings we have become by doing what we did when on earth. In the world of the spirit we are not examined for our intellectual prowess but for our moral qualities of will.

After death we take everything that lives in our limbs and our heart from the previous incarnation towards the spheres of Moon, Mercury, Venus, Sun, Mars, Jupiter, and Saturn. Only the things we have truly done ourselves, being fully engaged, will count. Actions done without involvement of the I, amoral, that is, uninterested actions done without love, drop away, for they are not part of us. The spirits of the higher hierarchies perceive us as we truly are. The words of the New Testament: "He who has shall be given" apply. If even a little is brought, twice as much will be added. Those who have nothing also cannot be given anything – it may even be that something is taken away from them, so that they become really aware of their deficiency and make greater efforts to make up for it in their next life.

The result of our journey through the planetary sphere is the spiritual design of the head we shall have in our next life on earth.[16]

In the *Philosophy of Spiritual Activity* we read that everything our I has consciously related to will be part of its spiritual nature from then on. "The I gains in essence and significance from everything it relates to."[17] We might also say: "We are everything we identify with. If this is little, we have little, if it is much, we have a great deal of energy. We only have real power if we identify with the whole world, realizing that I am the world, and the world is I."

This throws new light on something Rudolf Steiner said in his curative education course.[18] He said an incarnation where the individual was in need of special care could, for example, be due to having been in prison in the previous life, with little opportunity to relate to the world. We can see that in such a case it is not possible to gather much of the energy that is gained from identifying with the world, and understanding it with our hearts. After such a life an individual may go through death as an impoverished soul and then need an incarnation where the world comes to him, so that he does little himself but learns a great deal.

Steiner also referred to another possible reason for wanting to gain energy in an incarnation: The decision, made before birth, to do without a healthy body, because one is convinced that one will need great genius in a later life, so much that it will need one life before that where one will not have the opportunity to overexert oneself mentally or physically. One is then born as someone in need of special care. It needs a broader viewpoint to understand that this is not a sphere where natural laws prevail, with inevitable consequences. We know from *Anthroposophical Leading Thoughts* (Guiding Principles of Anthroposophy)[19] that individual moral laws, laws of destiny, prevail, always filled with the light and breath of freely made decisions and the possibility of human beings helping and supporting one another in their decisions and tasks. We see, therefore, that an incarnation weakness that is a problem may arise either from genuine deficiency or a renunciation made of one's own free will, as it were. Rudolf Steiner told the special teachers that they could not know if it was a case of strength or weakness and that they should treat every child as if it was a matter of strength for the future. For, however much we try, if we are working with a weak individual, we always have to fight a subtle antipathy, because we always do feel antipathy to weakness. It is easier to overcome this antipathy if we seek to help the child in his efforts to prepare in the best possible way for his next life on earth.

In the case of left-handedness, however, Rudolf Steiner spoke only of "karmic weakness." Nothing has been said about a decision made for other reasons before birth. To help in this situation, we have to do everything we can to help the child to identify with everything she learns or does, and we must above all see that no activities are pursued where energy is lost unnecessarily. That, however, is what happens when we write with the left hand, for the left side of the body works close to consciousness, yet writing will in time become a routine activity devoid of feeling. This more unconscious action, serving communication with the outside world, should constitutionally belong to the right side of the body. We have seen that the right half of the body is in all its function more oriented towards perception of and dealing with the outside world. The energies of the left side of the body, on the other hand, serve more to sustain the life of soul and spirit and orientation in time.

Under normal conditions, human beings have an excess of energy on the right side of the body, for modern humanity is much more prepared to come to terms with the outside world than in earlier civilizations, and our main energies go in that direction. If the energies are evenly distributed between the two sides of the body, the individual is ambidextrous. A left-handed person, on the other hand, shows that he has come into this life with a weakness in the right side of the body. This has also been evident from the examination of human brains, which confirmed that the brain is more asymmetrical in someone who is strongly right-handed, whereas the two hemispheres are more alike one another in left-handed individuals. Like the brain of an ambidextrous person, the brain of a left-handed individual is slightly less differentiated and fixed in terms of laterality, which also means it has a greater capacity for regeneration, as stated above.

As teachers and therapists we, therefore, have to consider how we can strengthen the powers on the child's right side. If a real effort is made, we are able to give the child something as a gift that it has not brought into this incarnation because of its previous life on earth and the way this was shaped during life after death. Rudolf Steiner also referred to this on other occasions; details may be found in the above-mentioned booklet.[4] He said words to the effect that we do not normally learn to write with the left hand but with the right. This activity depends more on the ether body, because it becomes habitual in time. The physical body is more developed on the left, where it is heavier; it is slightly less developed on the right. This seems a strange contradiction, for we have seen that the lung develops two lobes on the left, whereas the right side, being more active, brings more life to the lung, so that three lobes develop. It is, nevertheless, the case that the physical predominates on the left and the etheric on the right in every human being. Steiner also said that the astral body was stronger on the right than on the left. So we have to consider how all this fits together.

For the spiritual scientist, the contours of the physical body are less clearly defined on the right than on the left, because it is more strongly interpenetrated by the ether body on the right. This side is, therefore, more suited to habitual actions, which are more strongly supported by physical and etheric. Every habit depends on a close bond between physical body and ether body and something happening without our conscious mind being involved. Physical body and ether body may be said to be autonomous in habitual actions. The connection between the two bodies is better on the right, which is also why the right side is particularly suited to the unconscious physical and etheric functions of the liver.

On the left side, the physical body is more subject to gravity. Floating and downward displaced kidneys significantly are more apt to develop on the left, where the physical body is more subject to gravity. These are pathologic phenomena where one kidney shows downward displacement from the normal position, which sometimes causes problems. Some people will never know, however, that they have a floating kidney. The condition is less frequently seen on the right, because there the etheric lifts the physical more into buoyancy. The physical body is more dominant on the left, because the ether and astral bodies are more closely linked on that side, and the powerful astral body absorbs the etheric more intensely. The physical aspect is more left to itself on this side.

The I has been given the task of creating equilibrium between self and world. It has to have its representation in the structure of the physical body, and because of this, one side embodies more the world, and the other side exists more for the self. Self awareness arises when we experience the difference. Conscious awareness can only arise when an inner meets an outer, where self meets world. Marked distinction between left and right, a powerful asymmetry in the distribution of "self" and "world" energies provides the basis for more powerful "I-activity" in creating the equilibrium, and therefore the foundation for healthy self esteem.

If we consider the left-handed child in the light of the above, we can say to ourselves that adverse, tragic, destiny-determined circumstances may have made him spend and exhaust himself in one earth life. He could not be entirely master of the situation, being unable to encompass everything he did with his I, nor relate to everything he did. This meant that he was impoverished when entering the other world after death, and has now returned with a constitution that may have all kinds of individual weaknesses, or may be completely healthy in its outer aspects, but with a distribution of energies that makes the self predominate over the world, the left over the right. This also means greater self-awareness and greater sensitivity to events in the outside world. These should not be taken away, especially if the child has left-dominance, a genuine incarnation dominance. For this also holds the potential for self-healing, with everything the child experiences related more strongly to the self. The child is more awake in consciousness, sensitive, responding more easily at the soul level. This kind of constitution actually prevents the child from doing anything without being fully aware. The child will, of course, also be more self-willed and self-centered, and likes to withdraw from the world around it at times. His abilities are more in the humanities and the arts, and less so in science and technology.

It is vital that teachers understand the special constitution of a left-handed child and do not seek to "change" it. With self-will and inner sensitivity more to the fore, these children are only too often told: "Don't be such an egotist, don't be so sensitive, think of others . . .", and they then feel misunderstood. Yet if we succeed in directing their inner riches to the subject matter taught and awaken an interest in the beauties and events of the world around them, at the same time strengthening the right side of the body by the

293

effort of writing with the right hand, these children will be able to use the gifts they have brought with them with greater inwardness, and they will also have the strength not to falter when faced with life's situations but to be active in the world in a way that proves a blessing for it.

BIBLIOGRAPHY AND NOTES

1. Rudolf Steiner, *Conferences with Teachers* of the First Waldorf School in Stuttgart. Conference of May 10, 1922.
2. Steiner, R., *The Philosophy of Spiritual Activity. A Philosophy of Freedom* (GA 4). Tr. R. Stebbing. London: Rudolf Steiner Press, 1989.
3. Steiner, R., *The Riddle of Man* (GA 20). Spring Valley: Mercury Press, 1989.
4. *Schriftenreihe der Heileurythmie-Ausbildung Stuttgart*, Heft 5. Zum Problem der Linkshändigkeit, 1, Auflage 1978.
5. Ibid. Conference on May 25, 1923.
6. *Zur Linkshändigkeit*, 1990 edition.
7. See Ullmann, J.F., *Psychologie der Lateralität*, Bern 1974. Also Popper/Eccles, Das Ich und sein Gehirn. Munich 1984. A local anesthetic was used to cut out left brain function and see if this caused inability to speak or not and which speech functions would be affected.
8. See Sovák, M., *Pädagogische Probleme der Lateralität,* Berlin, 1968.
9. Ludwig Boltzmann Institut zur Erforschung kindlicher Hirnschäden. *Linkshändigkeit, Analyse einer Minderheit*. Vienna, 1973.
10. See note 1.
11. Glöckler, M., and Goebel, W. , *A Guide to Child Health*. Translated from German, Edinburgh: Floris Books, 1990.
12. See note 9.
13. Ullmann, J.F., *Psychologie der Lateralität*. Bern, 1974.
14. See note 8.
15. See note 5.
16. Steiner, R., *Between Death and Rebirth* (GA 141). Tr. E. Goddard, D. Osmond, London: Rudolf Steiner Press, 1975.
17. See note 2.

18. Steiner, R., *Curative Education.* Tr. M. Adams. London: Rudolf Steiner Press, 1981.
19. Steiner, R., *Anthroposophical Leading Thoughts* (GA 26) p. 99. Tr. G. & M. Adams, London: Rudolf Steiner Press, 1973.

INDEX

Z

Zodiac 125
Zur Linden, Wilhelm 61

THE LAST GREAT EMPRESS
OF CHINA

BOOKS BY CHARLOTTE HALDANE

Marcel Proust
The Galley Slaves of Love
Alfred
Mozart
Daughter of Paris
Tempest Over Tahiti

M. M. Taylor
June 2014

ML

£6